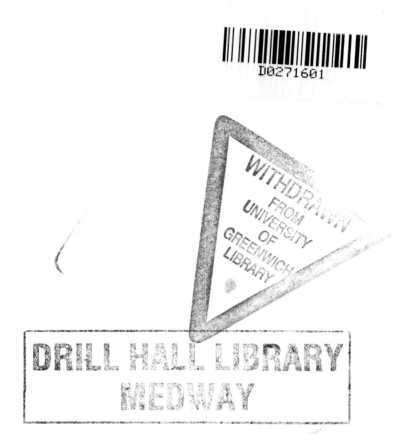

Creating
Market Insight

Creating Market Insight

How firms create value from market understanding

Dr Brian D Smith
Dr Paul G Raspin

John Wiley & Sons, Ltd

Other Wiley Editorial Offices

John Wiley & Sons Inc., 111 River Street, Hoboken, NJ 07030, USA

Jossey-Bass, 989 Market Street, San Francisco, CA 94103-1741, USA

Wiley-VCH Verlag GmbH, Boschstr. 12, D-69469 Weinheim, Germany

John Wiley & Sons Australia Ltd, 42 McDougall Street, Milton, Queensland 4064, Australia

John Wiley & Sons (Asia) Pte Ltd, 2 Clementi Loop #02-01, Jin Xing Distripark, Singapore 129809

John Wiley & Sons Canada Ltd, 6045 Freemont Blvd. Mississauga, Ontario, L5R 4J3 Canada

Wiley also publishes its books in a variety of electronic formats. Some content that appears in print may not be available in electronic books.

Library of Congress Cataloging-in-Publication Data

Smith, Brian D., BSc (Hons)
  Creating market insight : how firms create value from market understanding / Brian D Smith, Paul G. Raspin.
      p. cm.
  Includes bibliographical references and index.
  ISBN 978-0-470-98653-0 (cloth)
  1. Marketing–Management. 2. Marketing–Planning. 3. Problem solving. 4. Organizational effectiveness. I. Raspin, Paul G. II. Title.
  HF5415.13.S594 2008
  658.8′02–dc22

                                                                                    2008001326

British Library Cataloguing in Publication Data

A catalogue record for this book is available from the British Library

ISBN 978-0-470-98653-0

Typeset in 11 on 15 pt Goudy by SNP Best-set Typesetter Ltd., Hong Kong
Printed and bound in Great Britain by TJ International Ltd, Padstow, Cornwall, UK.

Brian
To Lindsay, Eleanor, Catherine and Rosalind

Paul
To Courtney and James

Contents

Preface

This book is written for a specific audience with a definite purpose in mind. It is intended primarily for those whose job includes creating competitive advantage in their marketplace. Its purpose is to help those people create and use the market insight upon which sustainable competitive advantage is usually based.

In writing this book, we have tried to incorporate the lessons we learned as we interviewed dozens of firms and surveyed hundreds of others. These lessons include the centrality of market insight to creating a strong strategy and, subsequently, achieving the organisation's objectives. They also include lessons about the way individuals and teams go about gathering and sorting the vast amount of data they are bombarded with. Importantly, we also learned that insight is a tightly defined concept, quite distinct from data, information and knowledge. Finally, we learned that creating insight is not a matter of gathering huge amounts of data and crunching it with powerful computers. Rather, it is a creative process of synthesis that is more akin to weaving than distillation.

To make the book more accessible to busy managers, we have used every tool we can think of. We have interleaved theory with practical examples. We have broken out key points and inserted questions to challenge the reader, in an effort to contextualise our findings and move them from the page to the mind of the reader. Finally, at the end of every chapter we have pulled out what we hope are the key points of each chapter.

Our hope is that the lessons we have learned and the manner in which we have conveyed them will achieve our goal. We hope that, on completing this book, readers will be better equipped to create insight, apply it in the market and achieve the organisational goals upon which our economy and society rest.

Acknowledgements

This book is the output of years of work by the authors. It is woven together from both their academic research and their work advising many large firms. As such, this work is an artefact of the support and help provided to the authors by their family, colleagues and friends.

Brian would especially like to thank Professors Hugh Wilson and Moira Clarke and Ms Anita Beale, with whom he worked closely at Cranfield School of Management for much of this research. He would also like to thank all his colleagues at the Open University Business School, which has created a supportive environment for his more recent work.

Paul would like to thank Professor Cliff Bowman who supervised much of the initial research into scanning of the business environment. He would also like to thank his colleagues at Stratevolve for sharing their experiences of working with top teams to create value through market insights.

Both Brian and Paul would also like to thank all those responsible for turning this work into a book, especially all of the staff at Wiley and Ms Lindsay Bruce, for her work in editing and improving our manuscript.

1

Success, strategy and understanding

'Furious activity is no substitute for understanding.'
H. H. Williams

In *The Hitchhiker's Guide to the Galaxy*, Douglas Adams describes the output of a planet sized computer which, for billions of years, had cogitated on the answer to life, the universe and everything. The answer was, famously, 42.

The joke of course lay in the contrast between the complexity of the question and the anticipated profundity of its answer with the clear inadequacy of the actual answer. The heroes of the story then realised that they needed to understand the question better. For managers seeking the answers to their questions about how to be more profitable, grow faster or whatever, Adams' work provides a kind of parable. Airport bookshop shelves groan with simple answers that are quick, easy and, when compared to the difficulty of the problems facing managers in real life, hopelessly simplistic. Practising managers, who have to achieve success rather than just write about it, need to understand their questions better.

This chapter therefore aims to help those managers who are the audience for this book by helping them to understand their question better. It starts from the premise that the readers will all have one thing in common; they are all asking something like 'How can I make my business more successful?' Working from that premise, we explore what we mean by success, since it is defined differently by different organisations. In exploring success, we find that it is complex, contextual and about learning. We then go on to explore the management research literature in the hope of finding some

A better understanding of the question 'how can we be successful?' leads us to conclude that we need to understand the market better.

common, generalisable causes of success. That exploration leads us to the conclusion that, notwithstanding luck and inept or weak competitors, success comes from a strong strategy. Exploring further, we find that, for all the loose usage of the word, strategy is best understood as that set of management decisions by which effort and resources are allocated. The conclusion that success has its roots, usually, in strong strategy, leads us to conclude that part of an enquiring manager's question ought to be 'What does a strong strategy look like?' A synthesis of 40 years of management research allows us to answer that question in terms of a series of characteristics that strong strategies exhibit to a much greater degree than weak strategy. In turn, this prompts the question of how those relatively few firms that create such strong strategies manage to do so. The answer to that question is that all firms create strategy by their own particular blend of vision, planning and making it up as they go along. There is, contrary to what most airport books would have us believe, no 'best' way to make strategy. In reality, which blend of these three approaches works best depends on the market conditions. So, success comes from strong strategy, which is the result of an effective strategy making process, which is a function of matching that process to market conditions. So success is underpinned by an understanding of the market.

In short, a better understanding of our question 'How can we be successful?' leads us to the conclusion that we need to understand the market better. But we're getting ahead of ourselves. What is success?

What is success?

To most readers of this book, what constitutes success for their organisation is relatively straightforward. In commercial firms, it is about money and in non-profits it is about achieving whatever goals they have in place of money. Depending where you are in the organisation, the measures you use will range from the simple (e.g. sales of a product line) to the more complex (e.g. overall profitability), to whatever it is the organisation exists for (e.g. creation of shareholder value). However, the nature of business or non profit success is more complex than a simple target might express and since this book is, ultimately, about achieving success it is worth pausing for a minute to reflect on the latest thinking about organisational success.

Research into how organisations measure and manage their performance has, in recent years, moved on a long way from the relatively simplistic view that most practising managers use in their day to day work. Indeed,

Research into performance measurement and management has moved on from the relatively simplistic view used by most practising managers.

these improvements in the way we measure and understand organisational performance have been called the 'performance management revolution'.[1] Before looking at how understanding the business environment contributes to organisational performance, it's useful to understand the key tenets of this new thinking. As elsewhere in this book, the authors have tried to combine depth of content with fluidity of narrative by using text boxes to ring fence important but parallel ideas. In the case of performance measurement, these ideas are captured in Box 1.1.

Box 1.1 New definitions of success

The 'performance management' research is an entire, voluminous domain of academic literature and any attempt to summarise it is necessarily superficial; but for our purposes it is sufficient to understand that effective performance has three characteristics:

1. Performance management is contextual. That is, what constitutes success is highly specific to the organisation. In publicly owned companies for instance, what matters is risk adjusted rate of return[2] so performance objectives depend on where a firm sits in its owners' portfolio of investments. In small firms, it is more about simple profit and especially cash flow. The implication of this complexity is that no one set of metrics is appropriate to all firms. In short, success is the degree to which an organisation achieves its objectives and these are specific to each organisation.

2. Performance management is complex. That is, any simple set of measures tends to mislead. Because sales can usually be bought at the expense of profit and both can be achieved by milking assets, and because assets are both tangible but increasingly intangible, only a complex and balanced set of measures tells the whole story. The most well publicised example of this is Kaplan & Norton's Balanced Score-card,[3] but multidimensionality is the principle behind most modern performance management.[4]

3. Performance is about learning as much as control. That is, traditional performance measures were all about controlling managers, noting exceptions and taking corrective action. By contrast, more modern methods are also about challenging assumptions and gaining new insight into the business environment.[5] The basis of this newer thinking is that the ability to learn is now often considered a 'strategic competence' and a firm's only basis of long-term sustainable competitive advantage.[6]

The rather broader perception of success outlined in Box 1.1 is important because, without it, it is much harder to understand what leads to success. Similarly, it is almost impossible to lead a company, or even a team, if each member of that group interprets success differently. If success is more complex than just sales and profits, then understanding what makes firms successful is more complicated too.

Application point: How do you define success?

Given the points made in Box 1.1, how does your organisation define success? If it is in simple performance terms, how might it be improved to better fit the context of your situation and to enable organisational learning?

Success comes from strong strategy

If it has done its job properly, the above heading will have prompted a small episode of cognitive dissonance in the mind of the reader. That is, the reader will have thought 'No, my experience is that strong strategy and success don't always go together'. We can all think of examples where a strong strategy was not successful or where success came despite a weak strategy. It has been recognised for a long time that luck plays an important part in business success.[7] The link between strategies and success can easily be broken by external events. For example, September 11th when the air travel market collapsed and manufacturers of arms and medical products

The challenge for managers is to understand what it is about strategy that correlates to success. In other words: what makes a strong strategy?

gained hugely as the military geared up for war. Or the impact of BSE on the UK beef industry. Or, more positively, the luck that compression stocking makers had when the newspapers caught onto the risk of deep vein thrombosis ('economy class syndrome') or which condom manufacturers gained from the advent of HIV. Almost every market has its opportunities for good or bad luck.

By definition, luck is out of our sphere of control, as are many of the things, from legislation to technology to competitors and customers, that drive our market. We can't generally control these things, only our response to them. The only thing that is within our control is our own strategy. The challenge for managers is to understand what it is about strategy that correlates to success. In other words: what makes a strong strategy? To understand this, and how it connects with understanding the business environment, we need to digress into the strategy content literature, that body of management research that looks for patterns in the strategies of successful companies.

Strategy is perhaps the most loosely used word in the management lexicon. Because strategy is seen as a synonym for important, it is applied to many aspects of management that don't really merit the term. Worse than this, the abuse of the term leads to confusion and means that any discussion of strategy must begin with defining what we mean by the word. Fortunately, the strategy content literature that studies the components of strategy helps to clarify the resulting confusion. Again, for the sake of narrative flow, this is summarised in Box 1.2.

These two ideas are very useful aids to thinking about strategy. Next time someone uses the word, try to deduce what level of strategy they are talking about – corporate, business unit, functional. Or do they mean a tactic or objective? Try substituting the phrase 'resource allocation pattern' for the

---

Box 1.2 What do we mean by strategy?

Although academics like to quibble about the semantics, there are two fundamental ideas on which they broadly agree and which clarify what we mean by strategy.

- Strategy is about resource allocation. In fact, a good working definition of strategy is that by Henry Mintzberg[8] – 'a sustained pattern of resource allocation'. This is useful because it helps us distinguish strategy from the two ideas that it is often conflated with – objectives and tactics.
- Strategy is multi-tiered. Resource allocation decisions are made between businesses (corporate strategy) and then within businesses (business unit strategy). Within a business unit, resources are allocated between functions and then within functions.

---

word strategy and see if it still makes sense; if it doesn't, they might be talking about objectives or tactics, rather than strategy.

Given this multi-tiered, resource allocation concept of strategy, our question 'What is it about strategy that correlates to success?' has to consider what level of strategy we are talking about. We also need to consider the idea of complementarity, which is addressed in Box 1.3.

In a book about market insight, the area of strategy we're most interested in is marketing strategy. Note that by marketing strategy, we mean that set of resource allocation decisions about which customers to target and what offers to make to them.[9] This is not to be confused with marketing communications strategy, which is about allocating resources between media, messages and audiences. Marketing communications strategy sits below marketing strategy in the decision making hierarchy. This is an important distinction because in many companies (especially smaller and more product-led firms) the marketing function is responsible only for marketing communications whilst the board or leader dictates the marketing strategy proper.

By marketing strategy we mean the set of resource allocation decisions about which customers to target and what offers to make to them.

Box 1.3 The concept of complementarity

As Voltaire said, common sense is not so common. It seems to be common sense that the different components of a business unit strategy work with and against each other and that success depends on getting all the bits right, or at least more right than the competition. This phenomenon is known as 'complementarity'.[10] Roberts describes complementarity as the interactions between variables that affect performance and gives the example that higher quality makes demand less sensitive to price and vice versa. Doing more of one complementary activity makes the other more attractive still. He contrasts complementarity with activities that are substitutes for each other, such as performance-linked pay schemes and close monitoring of employees. Doing more of one substitutable activity makes the other work less well.

In strategy terms, it is not difficult to see that, for instance, a marketing strategy that targets technically discerning customers is complementary to an R&D strategy that focuses on innovation and an HR strategy that focuses on recruiting and retaining technically expert people. This compares with, for instance, a minimum cost, heavily standardised, operational strategy that is most likely to be a substitute for, rather than a complement to, a marketing strategy that offers flexibility and customisation.

If you want to test Voltaire's maxim, look at the business bookshelves next time you are in an airport. Complementarity is a piece of common sense that is largely ignored by all those books that proclaim that doing something to one part of your business (e.g. HR processes or IT systems or leadership style or whatever) will lead to instant, huge success. The reality is that few business initiatives have much impact without considering the complementarity of the initiative with the other parts of the business process.

We are most interested in marketing strategy for two reasons. Firstly, this is because the marketing strategy is the functional strategy most concerned with the external environment. That is not to say other functions are insular but functions such as operations and research tend to focus on those parts of the external environment that affect them directly, such as suppliers or technological developments. Marketing (remember, we mean choice of customers and offers, not promotion) involves understanding the whole external environment. Secondly, in most companies, it is the marketing strategy (i.e. the choice of what to offer to whom) that forms the starting point for the operational, product development and other functional strategies. Again, we do not need to be purist about this. Market-led does not need to mean 'marketing department led', but in most firms the primary responsibility for telling the firm where the market is going lies with the marketers, whatever job title they have and whatever department they work in.

In most firms, primary responsibility for understanding where the market is going lies with marketers, regardless of job title or department.

The basic premise of this book, therefore, is that success (in as much as we can control it in the face of luck) comes from making good resource allocation decisions; and the decisions that depend most on market insight are those about marketing strategy. Hence, it is important that we know what a strong marketing strategy looks like and what that implies for understanding the market.

Application point: What's your marketing strategy?

Given the discussion in this section, how would you define your marketing strategy? Who is really responsible for setting that strategy? To what extent does your marketing strategy complement your other functional strategies?

What does a strong marketing strategy look like?

Given that marketing strategy is that set of management decisions concerning which customers to target and what to offer them, we can get back to the question of 'What is it about strategy that correlates to success?' By that, of course, we are not looking for tactical panaceas, such as CRM, of the type peddled by some consultants. Instead, we are looking for common characteristics about marketing strategies that are associated with success. In other words, if we sorted all the marketing strategies in the world in order of success, would we see a pattern?

The answer is a surprisingly clear yes. The detailed answer is discussed and explained in another of our books,[9] but can be summarised in five points:

1. **Strong marketing strategies define real segments**
   Marketing strategies work best when their targets are 'real' segments. That is, they pass the classic tests that good segments are homogenous, distinct, accessible and viable. In practice, this means that real segments are based on customers' needs and motivational drivers. Contrast this with what passes for segmentation in many marketing strategies, but which is really classification into groups according to available data such as age, gender, income or, in B2B markets, industry, size and usage.[11]

   Real segments work because all of the customers within a real segment respond in much the same way if offered the same compelling value proposition. By contrast, *Poor segmentation often results in a Pareto-type effect (e.g. 80% of business from 20% of customers).* data-driven classifications are often heterogeneous in their needs and motivations and the customers within them show varying responses to any one offer. A good test of your segmentation is to look at the distribution of your sales across the customers in your market. If your marketing strategy is demonstrating a Pareto-type effect (e.g. 80% of business coming from 20% of customers) poor segmentation is often to blame.

2. **Strong marketing strategies tailor the offer**
   Marketing strategies work best when they tailor their offer around the needs and motivations that define the segment. That is, they adapt the 'marketing mix' of product (or service), promotion, price, place (i.e. channel), people, process and physical evidence to meet the needs of the target segment. In practice, companies can rarely afford – and customers are rarely willing to pay for – total customisation, but the best companies do design their offer around the segment, even when that means adding cost.[12] Contrast this with what passes for tailoring in many marketing strategies, which is often limited to the tweaking of the easily malleable parts of the mix such as price or promotion. *A price sensitive market usually indicates that your offer is not sufficiently or acceptably tailored.*

Tailoring works most obviously when, as in many markets, customers have a choice. Given a choice, we will choose that offer which best meets our needs. If no offer meets our needs better than the others (i.e. the offers are commoditised), we choose on price. A good test of your tailoring is the price sensitivity of your product or service. If your market is very price sensitive, it is usually an indication that your offer is not sufficiently or acceptably tailored to the needs of the target segment.

3. **Strong marketing strategies are unique**

Marketing strategies work best when the target and the offer are different from those of the competition. That is, compared to the competitors' strategies, they define their target markets differently, or they prioritise them differently and, because it is tailored, the offer made to them is noticeably different from the competitor. In practice, this means uncovering and satisfying needs-based segments that the competitor has either overlooked or not targeted.[13] Contrast this with what occurs in many markets; marketers from the same industry culture create unsurprisingly similar offers and target them at segments defined using the same classification data bought from the same market research companies.

Uniqueness works because it effectively side steps competition rather than going head on with it. By defying or negating direct comparison, a unique strategy often comes to dominate its target segment, achieving strong loyalty and relative price inelasticity. A good test of your strategy uniqueness is to consider what your customers would do if your firm disappeared tomorrow. If you are unique, your customers would not have an immediate replacement, or would feel significantly saddened by your disappearance. If not, they would replace you quickly and with little thought.

What would happen if your firm disappeared tomorrow? If you are unique, customers would not have an immediate replacement. If not, they would replace you quickly and with little thought.

4. **Strong marketing strategies anticipate the future**

Marketing strategies work best, as we have already said, when they meet customers' driving needs with tailored value propositions in a way that is different from any competitor. All of this, of course, assumes some sort of stasis in customer needs. In fact, the strongest strategies anticipate the way customers' needs are changing and emerging.[14] They then target and design the offer accordingly. Contrast this with the process for bringing new offers to market in many companies. Natural caution and politicised approval systems place a premium on quantified market research and 'proof' that the product or service will sell. Since such data is predominantly retrospective, it rarely anticipates the future of the market.

Anticipating the future works precisely because markets change. This can take the form of changes

If your strategy is anticipative, it will address the changing needs which drive customer behaviour.

in customer needs, competitive forces, channels to market or other factors. When it happens, the match between an offer and the customer needs that had led to competitive advantage is undermined and lessened, a phenomenon known as strategic drift.[15] A good test of your anticipation is to think through the needs which currently drive your customers' behaviour and, especially, how these are changing. If your strategy is anticipative, it will address these changes.

5. **Strong marketing strategies are SWOT aligned**

Marketing strategies work best when, by their choice of target segments and the offers they make to them, they create SWOT (Strengths, Weaknesses, Opportunities and Threats) alignment. That is, they make good use of what the firm is better at than its competition and manage to negate the effects of any relative weaknesses they have. Contrast this with the strategy of many firms, which have a strongly subjective and inaccurate view of their strengths and weaknesses. Hindered by this ignorance, they attack markets they can't win and ignore or under-resource those they could win.[16]

SWOT alignment works because competitors in any market differ, each having a distinctive profile of strengths and weaknesses, both tangible and intangible. By choos-

If your strategy differs markedly in targets and offers from current outcomes, this is an indication that the strategy may lack SWOT alignment.

ing to target customers and make offers based on those, SWOT alignment first helps achieve some degree of strategy uniqueness. It then leads the firm to attack segments in which it is especially well placed to compete. At the same time, SWOT alignment avoids allocating effort to segments where the firm will always be at a competitive disadvantage.

A good test of SWOT alignment is to compare current successes and failures with your current strategy. In the absence of a formal SWOT analysis, current outcomes are strongly indicative of relative strengths and weaknesses. If your strategy differs markedly in targets and offers from current outcomes, this is an indication that the strategy may lack SWOT alignment.

If creating a strong strategy were not difficult, everyone would do it. The result would be competitive parity, not advantage.

These five characteristics of a strong strategy are daunting. Few companies score strongly on all of these tests and perhaps none on the extended list of strategy tests shown in our earlier work. However, three illustrative examples of those that do are given in Box 1.4.

Box 1.4 Examples of strong strategies

Creating a strategy that meets the criteria of a strong strategy is difficult. If it were not, everyone would do it and the resultant strategies would merely achieve competitive parity, not advantage. Even excellent strategies rarely excel at all five criteria, let alone the extended list discussed in our earlier work. And even when they do, it is a constant struggle to maintain such strategy superiority.

However, the task is not hopeless, as a couple of examples have proved.

BMW have a relative weakness of high costs and relative strengths in their engineering and design competencies and their brand heritage. Their marketing strategy, across their range, is to target segments driven by the love of driving and self actualisation needs around discernment and peer respect. To this segment they offer not simply status, but status based on perceptions of intelligence, exclusivity and discernment. Importantly, their offer is not simply promotional ('The Ultimate Driving Machine') but encompasses everything from choice of upholstery materials to after sales service. In doing so, BMW's strategy achieves a high degree of SWOT alignment as well as passing the other four tests.

Waitrose is a 2nd tier player in the extremely competitive UK food retailing sector. It therefore suffers scale disadvantages when it is caught between Tesco, Asda (Wal-Mart), Sainsbury's and Morrisons. Waitrose again target a discerning segment driven by needs for variety, quality and a less anonymous customer experience. That they achieve this at a price premium is the result of a very coherent offer to their target segment, covering everything from what they sell and how they sell it to how they recruit, retain and manage their people. Again, it is summarised in a strap-line – 'Good food honestly priced' – but it is much more than mere promotional positioning.

Xerox provide a B2B example of strong strategy. Again, they eschew the head-on battle with their imitators who will always be cheaper. Their strapline 'The Document Company' reveals the targeting of customer firms who want to manage their knowledge, rather than just buy photo-copiers. In doing so, Xerox leverages its technical superiority and antici-pates future trends in which knowledge management becomes central to their customers' own strategy. As with the previous examples, the Xerox strategy involves not just a promotional positioning but a coherent offer across the whole marketing mix.

All three of these examples involve tailoring offers around needs-based segments in a way that is relatively unique, anticipatory and SWOT aligned.

Application point: How strong is your marketing strategy?

Given the discussion in this section about the five characteristics of a strong marketing strategy, how would you assess the strength of your organisation's marketing strategy? To the extent that your marketing strategy has weaknesses, what do these imply about your understanding of your market?

These characteristics and examples provide an answer to our question about what leads to the complex, contextual and learning oriented success we seek. The more of these tests a strategy passes, the more likely it is to be successful. All of which naturally begs the question 'What do we need to create strong strategy?'

The answer to that question is in two parts. Firstly, a process for making strategy that fits both the market conditions and the culture of the firm. This is discussed at length in our earlier

To create a strong strategy we need a process that fits combined with market understanding and insight.

book[9] and summarised in Box 1.5. The second ingredient is the raw material on which all strategy making processes work – market understanding and insight. This is discussed in the following section.

Box 1.5 How do firms create strong strategies?

The strategy process literature (that is, the study of how firms make strategy) is a huge field of research that overlaps with the strategy content literature (the study of what strategy is) mentioned earlier in this chapter. Again, every academic in the field has his or her personal view but for the managers reading this book three points are important:

Prescription is not description

Most of the textbooks used in MBAs and other courses prescribe similar models of rational, formal planning. These differ in detail from one another but not in principle. The key point to understand is that these are primarily prescriptions of what academics recommend and not very good descriptions of what happens in reality.[17]

Strategy making is firm specific

The descriptive research describes a reality in which strategy is formed by a mixture of processes, from the formal to the ad hoc, from the political to the enforced. Different academics have identified 3, 4, 5, 6 and even 10 approaches to making strategy.[18] In practice, all firms use some of each approach in a hybrid strategy making process that is characteristic of the firm.

What works is what fits

The innumerable possible hybrid ways of making strategy work best when they fit the market. Complex markets tend to need formal planning; fast markets need intuitive vision; and all markets need a little 'make it up as you go along'. Furthermore, the hybrid process has to fit the organisational culture. So what emerges is what academics call a contingency model. Strategy making processes make strong strategies when they fit both the market conditions and the company culture, and the best hybrid is rarely the same as the textbook prescription.[19]

Application point: How do you make strategy?

If firms make strategy by a combination of planning, vision and 'making it up as we go along', what are the proportions of each approach used by your organisation? Do you feel it works well? In what way might it be improved?

What is this 'market' into which we're trying to gain insight?

So far in this chapter, we've argued that success is complex and contextual and, to be sustained, we have to be able to learn from it. Further, we have maintained that, although luck plays a part, success flows from a strong strategy. And we have explicated what we mean by a strong strategy with reference to five characteristics that strong (i.e. successful) strategies share. Those characteristics all share a common feature. In order to consciously craft a strategy that has any of them, as opposed to stumbling across

In order to craft a strong strategy, we have to understand the market.

a strategy which has one or more characteristics by happenstance, we have to understand the market. To understand a market well, we have to be clear about what we mean by 'market' because that term is used almost as loosely as is the term strategy.

The superficial definition of a market, given off-the-cuff by most managers, is something about customers, present and potential. Pressed a little harder, this is extended to include competitors and perhaps channels to market. In other words, managers pay most attention to what they perceive as important and make decisions accordingly. Hambrick and Mason called this an executive's 'constructed reality',[20] an important idea when understanding how managers make sense of their world.

The habit of managers to bias what they look at in the market and create their own 'constructed reality' means that there is a danger that our biases will define the market for us. To counteract this, we need some sort of model, a mnemonic or memory aid, to remind us what is included in 'the market' that we seek to understand. Almost every strategic planning textbook has something of this sort, each often reflecting the author's interest in a specific aspect of the business environment. Each of these different perspectives has something valuable to offer as well as weaknesses. Our own synthesis of the different models yields Figure 1.1, which we will use to structure much of the rest of this book.

All models are an attempt to simplify reality in order to aid understanding.[21] In doing so, they necessarily approximate reality, suggesting sharp division between categories where, in reality, the distinctions are less clear. Our model is no exception to this weakness but attempts to buy as much clarity as possible at the cost of only a little simplification.

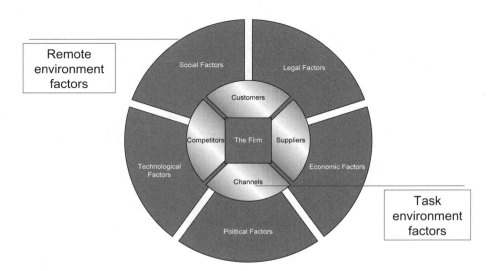

Figure 1.1 *Components of the business environment.*

Remote and task environments

The first distinction to make in understanding the business environment is between the task environment and the remote environment. The distinction between the two lies in the directness of their impact on the firm and the degree of control that the firm has over them. Hence the broad categorisation, in Figure 1.1, of the remote environment as social, legal, economic, political and technological environment. In general, firms can have little or only indirect influence over the remote environmental factors, which tend to act on the market not directly but via their influence on the task environment. The task environment consists of the customer, channel, supplier and competitor environments. These components of the task environment can be influenced, which is not to say managed, by the firm and changes in it are felt directly by the firm. As with any simplification, there are grey areas. Regulatory changes, for instance, are usually classed as legal, but flow from

Firms have little influence over remote environmental factors, which act on the market via their influence on the task environment.

politics driven by social or technical changes. Suppliers making own label products become competitors. This overlap should not overly concern managers because what matters is that everything significant is noticed, not what boxes everything fits into. Omission is a more serious sin than commission in this case.

The implications of the business environment for any firm can be simple or compound. That is, clear changes in any one area can impact more or less directly on the business or multiple changes can combine to impact on the business in a more subtle and complex way. Typically, simple implications are easier to see and manage than the compound variety, as the examples in the next two sections illustrate.

Simple implications of the remote environment

Any of the five components of the remote environment can have simple implications for a firm's marketing strategy.

Social factors encapsulate the structure and values of the society in which

Any component of the remote environment can have simple implications for marketing strategy.

the strategy must operate. So examples of social changes that have simple implications for marketing strategy are:

- The demographic bulge in many developed economies, leading to an increase in demand for everything from retirement cruises, to second homes to incontinence aids.
- The 'feminisation' of values among young men, changing radically the acceptance and positioning of men's cosmetics and toiletries, for instance.
- The 'death of deference' to authority in many developed economies, leading to increased customer expectations in many sectors, especially professional and public services.

Legal factors encapsulate both statutory issues affecting the firm and the regulations to which they lead. So examples of legal changes that have simple implications for marketing strategy are:

- The passage of employment law and regulation that influences the micro-economics of delivering the offer to the target segment, especially in some low margin service businesses, such as catering.
- The passage of environmental legislation that places responsibility for disposal of products or packaging onto the supplier, placing both additional trading requirements onto the firm but also providing opportunities to other firms who might provide this service.
- The passage of increased safety or financial regulations that creates opportunities for the specialist service firms that service this need. Regulations affecting health and safety at work and the Sarbanes-Oxley Act are examples of these.

Economic factors generally refer to macroeconomic factors that impinge on the business. So examples of economic factors that have simple implications for marketing strategy are:

- The growth rate of the national economy, providing an underlying driver of market demand in both consumer and business markets.
- The macroeconomic policies of governments that might provide specific stimulus or restraints on particular sectors of the economy, such as the public sector.

- The health of international or regional economy and the multilateral or bilateral economic agreements between governments that might influence demand either generally or in specific sectors.

Political factors generally refer to political policy factors that impinge on the business in a broader manner than legislative change. So examples of political factors that have simple implications for marketing strategy are:

- Policy towards the public versus private provision of public services such as health, education, transport or defence, which can create or destroy opportunities for commercial organisations.
- Policy towards the environment and development, which can influence strategy choice (e.g. by influencing the attractiveness of a target segment) and implementation through, for instance, local planning regulations.
- Issues of international relations, such as trading agreements, embargoes and, in extremis, war, which can directly and drastically influence strategy, especially in sectors such as arms or sensitive technology.

Technological factors refer to scientific developments that encroach on the business either directly or indirectly. So examples of technological factors that have simple implications for marketing strategies are:

- The development of technologies that impact broadly on the entire business process across all sectors, such as the development of the internet or mobile communications or, less recently, the impact containerisation had on physical transportation costs.
- Technological changes directly and specifically relevant to that sector, such as the effect that PCR (polymerase chain reaction) technology had on the biotechnology sector, or directed drilling technology had on the oil and gas sector.
- Combinations of technological developments and their incorporation into new business processes that significantly change the way that value can be delivered, such as lean manufacturing techniques or offshoring.

Application point: What are the implications of your remote environment?

Considering the discussion in this section, and the examples of remote environment implications, what do you think are the main implications of your remote environment for your organisation?

Simple implications of the task environment

Any of the four components of the task environment can have simple implications for a firm's marketing strategy.

Any component of the task environment can have simple implications for marketing strategy.

Customer factors refer to the needs of actual and potential customers and especially the way unsatisfied needs translate into market segmentation.[22] So examples of customer factors that have simple implications for marketing strategies are:

- Customers' 'hygiene' needs, such as the need to comply with basic quality, safety or compatibility standards. CE marking or software/hardware compatibility issues are examples of these.
- Customers' higher needs, such as the need to satisfy higher performance, relationship or emotional needs. Ease of use, flexibility and self fulfilment are examples of these.
- Segmentation deriving from higher needs. Segments that assume basic performance but are driven by higher needs, such as specialist professional services or luxury goods, are examples of these.

Competitor factors refer to any alternative ways of satisfying the needs of the target customer segment.[23] So examples of competitive factors that have simple implications for marketing strategies are:

- Direct competitive factors. That is, changes in the offering made by direct substitutes, such as price, performance, convenience etc. Supermarket price wars and the technical competition between Intel and AMD are examples of this.

- Substitute competitive factors. That is, changes in the offering made by alternatives to the existing product or service. Rail, low cost airlines and teleconferencing are all substitutes for one another in the business travel market.
- New entrant competitive factors. That is, the entry of new players (and therefore new capital and competencies) into the market. The entry of supermarkets into personal financial services and of Dell into consumer electronics are examples of this.

Channel factors refer to issues regarding the delivery of the offer, or any part of it, to the market. So examples of channel factors that have simple implications for marketing strategies are:

- Promotional channel factors, involving the development of media through which to address the customer. Web, mobile and the advent of digital printing are examples of this.
- Purchasing channel factors, involving development of channels through which the product may be purchased and/or delivered. Online stores, telesales and the extension of ATMs to sell mobile phone time are examples of this.
- Physical distribution factors, involving the changes to channels by which physical products are sold. The concentration of power in the hands of some retailers and the end of restrictive practices in car sales franchises are examples of this.

Supplier factors refer to the influence of suppliers on the business environment. So examples of this include:

- Suppliers creating consumer loyalty for certain components of the offering, such as the 'Intel Inside' campaign.
- Suppliers controlling the supply of vital components, as used to be the case in the supply of diamonds to jewellery manufacturers.
- Suppliers constraining cost structures by near monopolistic control of critical materials, knowledge, or technology, such as in the oil market or in the control of source codes for software.

Application point: What are the implications of your task environment?

Considering the discussion in this section, and the examples of task environment implications, what do you think are the main implications of your task environment for your organisation?

These examples of simple implications, where the connection between the business environment and the firm is relatively straightforward, serve two purposes. Firstly, they illustrate that the list of potential simple implications of the business environment is huge and difficult enough on its own for a manager to understand with any rigour. Secondly, they are reminders, when considered carefully, that many critical forces acting on a market are not simple implications of one factor but, in fact, compound implications of multiple factors in the remote environment, task environment or both.

Combined implications

If, even in our simplified model of the business environment, there are nine directions (five remote and four task) from which important business implications can arise in a simple manner,

The most fundamental forces causing markets to change arise from combinations of business environment factors.

this leaves almost endless possibilities for compound implications. Indeed, it appears that the most fundamental forces causing markets to change and shift arise from combinations of business environment factors. Consider two examples of powerful shifts in markets, the first B2B, the second B2C, and use the idea of combined implications to understand them better.

Pharmaceutical markets have long been dominated by two main types of firm, or strategic sets as they are more correctly called.[24] In simple terms, generic firms make and sell off-patent drugs, competing on price and manufacturing efficiency at relatively low gross margins. By contrast, research led firms spend heavily on research and sell patent-protected drugs at relatively high gross margins. Historically, the market has been dominated, in terms of share of profit and shareholder returns, by the research led firms. More recently, however this sector has struggled to grow and deliver shareholder returns.[25] On the surface, this appears to be due to customers (principally public and private healthcare providers) trying to reduce their costs by shifting from patented to cheaper generic drugs. However, this is not a new customer need. It has always been the intent of customers to reduce costs. So the phenomenon to understand is why this potential problem has arisen *now*. The idea of combined implications provides this understanding.

What is happening is a gradual commoditisation of many parts of the pharmaceutical market. In terms of the microenvironment, this can be seen as:

- The growth of the segment that is driven primarily by cost control rather than excellence of clinical results.
- The complementary development of the generic suppliers into powerful competitors.
- The corresponding growth of channels to market for generic products, especially 'Key Account' sales teams and distributors.

In terms of the remote environment driving the task environment, the important factors can be identified as:

- Socially, a demographic bulge creating higher demand, combined with reduced deference leading to higher expectations of healthcare providers.
- Political goals of 'prudence' manifested as attempts to stabilise healthcare costs, combined with a reluctance to increase tax burdens and easier low cost imports from developing countries.
- Economic trends of steady but modest GDP growth and inflation, hindering inflationary growth.
- Technically, 'flattening' of innovation rates reducing, over time, the clinical differences between patented and generic products.

Although even this analysis is a simplification of reality, it begins to explain the predicament of so many research led firms. Equally, it helps to explain how some firms misread the environment and anticipated a boom market. This is the inevitable result of selective, incomplete reading of the environmental drivers. In this case, the demographic bulge on its own suggested a positive future for the sector.

The second example is a more positive one, the rapid growth of low cost air travel in Europe. On the surface, this looks like a simple example of price elasticity but looking at it from a business environment perspective reveals a more detailed picture.

In terms of the task environment, this dramatic and rapid change can be seen as the result of:

- Customer factors, as several distinct segments either appeared, grew or shifted from domestic only to regional (e.g. European). These included the short break segment, the business travel segment and even very specialist niches such as the 'stag weekend' segment.
- Competitive factors, which included both new entrants and direct competitors growing the market and the premium airlines' lack of ability to adapt, inadvertently emphasising the value of low cost airlines.
- Channel factors, in that the internet enabled the low cost model to a degree that would have been much more difficult in a pre-internet age.
- Supplier factors, in that both regional airports (subsidised by regional development goals) and aircraft manufacturers (involved in a price war) both enabled the model to appear.

In terms of the remote environment, the important factors can be identified as:

- Socially, higher expectations and less xenophobia, resulting partly from many years of package holidays.
- Legally, the EU-led reduction in barriers to travel and encouragement of intra-European business.
- Economically, the increasing affluence at even modest levels, shifting 'mini breaks' from a luxury to a regular purchase.
- Politically, a reluctance to react to the environmental costs of low cost air travel.
- Technologically, both the development of the internet channels but also management processes that allowed much higher utilisation of the main assets, the aircraft.

Again, this example is not meant to be exhaustive but merely illustrative of how combined implications drive markets, usually in a way that is more significant and longer lasting than the outcomes of simple implications.

The importance of market understanding

What the preceding discussion illustrates is both the need to understand the market environment and the difficulty of doing so. Both are illustrated by the travails of companies that failed to do so. The partial failure of Vodafone to understand the implications of convergence in ICT markets, or of General Motors to anticipate changes in the car market, are reminders that even the best, well-resourced firms struggle with making sense of the business environment. But some firms do achieve it. IBM's shift to high added value consultancy and Zurich's impressive management of the potentially commodity insurance market are examples of excellence. The rest of this book is an account of our research into how firms excel at distilling market insight from the complexity of the business environment.

Even the best, well-resourced firms struggle with making sense of the business environment.

Powerpoints

- The success of an organisation is not simply the achievement of a number, but the achievement of a balanced mix of objectives, specific to that organisation, in a manner that allows organisational learning.
- Success is usually associated with strategies that demonstrate the five properties of a strong strategy.
- All effective strategy making is based on understanding the market.
- The market consists of remote and task environments, each of which have multiple subcomponents.
- All of the subcomponent parts of the market can carry important implications for the firm, either in their own right or in combination with other parts of the market.
- Understanding the implications of the market environment is critical to making strong strategy and hence to success.

2

The difficulty of gaining insight

'Change is not made without inconvenience, even from worse to better.'
Richard Hooker

The conclusions of Chapter 1, that success flows from strong strategy and that strong strategy in turn requires an understanding of the business environment, may seem obvious to some readers. In fact, it's unlikely that many executives would say that strategy and market understanding are anything but critically important activities. But executives' actions speak louder than their words. There are many research papers describing how executives actually spend their time (see for instance the classic of its type,[1] and its companion study made 30 years later[2]).These papers consistently report executives spending the bulk of their time politicking, fire fighting and administering the minutiae of business life. Some do this by choice but many are channelled into it by company culture. To that list of reactive tasks listed in 1973, we can now perhaps add the modern evils of answering emails and waiting at airports. The point is that, despite what they say, many executives spend relatively little time thinking in a reflective, non-reactive manner; so little in fact that the late Donald Schön thought it appropriate to name an entire book after the concept of

Executives spend a small proportion of their time and energy gaining real understanding of their market, despite its espoused importance.

that unusual creature, the reflective practitioner.[3] So, unless one believes that understanding can be gained without reflection, perhaps by miraculous flashes of inspiration, we can assume that many executives spend a relatively small proportion of their working time and mental energy trying to gain a real understanding of their market, despite its espoused importance to them.

Taken together, the claimed importance of understanding and the lack of time put into it is a non sequitur, a logical fallacy. It suggests that some, perhaps many, executives think that gaining understanding is relatively easy and can be done by substituting for reflection some other activity, such as simply throwing enough money at the IT department. The primary aim of this chapter is to disabuse readers of the dangerous idea that understanding a market is easy and yields to the application of processing power with relatively little reflection. The secondary aim is to give readers some idea about the difficulties and challenges that must be addressed in order to create, and to continue creating, market understanding. Both of the aims are intended to prepare the reader for the difficult but necessary changes in practice that are required to improve insight creation in most organisations. The illustrative quote about change at the head of this chapter, written by an Anglican theologian at the time of the Reformation, is as true about modern business as it was about 16th century religion.

In summary, this chapter will argue that two inexorable market factors are making the job of understanding markets more difficult: the growing complexity of markets and the increasing turbulence they exhibit. These two phenomena coincide with the advent of more and more IT capability to crunch data and so, unsurprisingly, executives often see IT as the panacea answer to their problems and, almost as often, are disappointed when they get very little 'insight per dollar' for their efforts. The ultimate explanation of this is that data and insight are not the same thing and, whilst data complexity and turbulence may yield to IT, gaining insight requires a lot more than crunching the data. So, instead of insight, IT-obsessed executives get a lot of data and information, so much that it often overloads their cognitive abilities. Hence, despite better IT than ever before, the problem of creating insight remains intractable. Later in this book, we will explore solutions to this intractability, but for now an understanding of how complexity and turbulence make the problem harder is a necessary foundation for solving the problem.

Market complexity is making it harder to create market insight

This section describes, with numerous examples, how the complexity of many – perhaps most – markets is increasing and, in the process, making the job of creating insight harder still. The reader may feel they know this already but as the philosopher David Carr points out,[4] knowing the rules of the game is not the same as being able to play it, so this section spells out what we mean by market complexity and how, by that definition, it is increasing.

What do we mean by complexity?

One of the challenges in researching anything to do with market complexity is the subjectivity of executives. When asked, practising managers very often describe their market as complex. In some cases, their perceptions are borne out by objective analysis, but often they are not. The problem is that most markets seem complex when you are immersed in the tactical detail, just as a slab of marble seems rough at a microscopic level. We need an agreed definition of what we mean by complex, otherwise the term becomes meaningless. Defining and estimating complexity will be covered more fully in Chapter 6, but we need a working definition for now.

Market complexity is a measure of the number of implications the market has for the business. More relevant, significant implications indicate a more complex market.

As a starting point we can say that market complexity is simply a measure of the number of implications that the market has for the business. The more relevant, significant implications the environment holds for a business, the more complex it is. And, using the ideas from the last chapter, that means that market complexity is increasing if:

- the number of significant market factors we have to consider is increasing; and/or
- the implications of each of those market factors are increasing; and/or
- those market factors are combining differently to create more implications for the business.

Since, by market factors we essentially mean those components of the remote and task environments that were detailed in the last chapter, this helps us know where to look for increased market complexity.

Increased complexity arising from the remote environment

When the remote environment of social, legal, economic, political and technological factors becomes more complex, it is not that there are more facets of the remote environment; the SLEPT acronym is merely a mnemonic and one that is meant to capture everything about the remote environment. Rather, complexity arises from any new remote environment factors that emerge within those headings, or from existing factors that have new implications or because existing implications of the remote environment combine differently. Consider the following examples.

Yahoo!, the huge and famous internet company, was by 2007 struggling to combat the onslaught of Google. Part of the reason for this is that, in the late 1990s, it made the strategic decision to be a portal, a gateway to web content. That decision was made, at least partly and perhaps implicitly, on the basis that people would get lost in this new medium and that value could be created by 'packaging' the content of the world wide web in some way that appealed to the poor, terrified customer. Search facilities were deemed by Yahoo! to be only a subsidiary feature of such an offer. At that time, it seemed a good decision and had analogies in other markets, such as travel and insurance, where brokers added value in analogous ways. What seems to have undermined this strategy is a new implication of the social environment. Yes, the web became more used as an information source but, alongside that, users' fear of the web declined. Their reticence to search for themselves diminished and their need for portals shrank as their need for search engines grew. As a result, the appeal of the Yahoo! offer to both users and advertisers shrank, relative to Google's pure play search positioning. So a new social factor that might be called 'web-savvy' created market conditions that, by late 2006, left Yahoo! with only a third of the market value of Google on a very similar revenue base.

The defence industry provides an example of an existing remote environment factor creating a new implication. Many in that industry saw the 'war on terror' as a driver of market growth, especially when the Iraq war led to greater and more sustained activity than predicted. In late 2001, the implications of the military situation for the defence industry seemed both clearly and resoundingly positive; the silver lining to a very black cloud. However, five years after the September 11th attacks, some huge procurement pro-grammes, such as the Boeing C-17 Transport Aircraft and the $165 m Future Combat Systems project to upgrade the US military's communications systems, were in doubt. Although a complex and multifaceted situation, this new pressure on military budgets arises largely from two new implications of the political factors that were already recognised soon after 2001. Firstly, the war on terror is a long-term war, not the sort of short intervention that Bosnia, Kosovo or Grenada were. Secondly, it is a predictably 'asymmetric' war in which 'big ticket' items are less needed than relatively mundane boots, trucks and bullets. So, new implications of known political factors are changing the defence market in unexpected ways.

If Yahoo! is an example of a new factor in the remote environment and the defence industry an example of new implications from known factors, then mobile telephony provides an example of remote environmental factors combining in new ways. In that industry, almost every part of the remote environment is involved:

- Socially, both social and work lifestyles are changing to depend upon the 'always contactable' status inferred by mobile phone ownership.
- Legally, regulation is enabling industry consolidation and has destroyed the idea of 'national champion' telephone companies.
- Economically, the rapid growth of developing economies, which often 'leapfrog' fixed lines and go straight to mobile technology, is changing the distribution of the market potential.
- Politically, trading blocs such as the EU see telephony as a utility and a potential barrier to market harmonisation, thus creating pressure on cross-border 'roaming' price structures.
- Technologically, the convergence of mobile and internet is both chang-ing the possible value propositions and creating new competitors based on Voice Over Internet Protocols, such as Skype.

In the early 2000s, these factors began not only to emerge but to combine differently to change the market. Convergence is now the buzz word in the industry as fixed line and mobile, voice, internet and television all merge into one. In a converging market, the customers have begun to ignore the differences between technologies and, as customers are prone to do, have started to think about how to meet their needs. This myriad of factors and implications seems to have been enough to confuse Vodafone, once the industry leader, and make it stumble. Its mobile-only global strategy now seems inadequate and in 2006 it announced the largest loss in European corporate history.

At certain points in recent years, Yahoo!, Boeing and Vodafone could easily have been held up as paragons of virtue as far as understanding their market went. The way they have fallen victim to complexity of the remote environment is not an illustration of their weakness; they are each packed with bright and educated people and, by the time this book is read, may have overcome their difficulties. However, these examples are lessons to any company that thinks it is obvious that their market is getting more complex, but still devotes little time to dealing with the implications of that complexity.

Application point: How is the remote environment increasing the complexity of your market?

Given the discussion in this section how, if at all, is the remote environment increasing the complexity of your market? How are the implications and combined implications of the remote environment changing your market?

Increased complexity arising from the task environment

In the same way that SLEPT is merely an acronym for the remote environment that is intended to capture all its components, then the task environment is most easily thought of as customers, competitors, channels and suppliers, as previously mentioned. So new complexity in the task environment doesn't mean new facets of that environment, but rather that complexity arises from task environment factors that emerge within those headings, or from existing factors that have new implications or because existing implications of the task environment combine differently. Consider the following examples:

SLEPT is an acronym to capture all components of the remote environment. Similarly, the task environment is easily thought of as customers, competitors, channels and suppliers.

Illycaffe is a 200 million Euro, Italian family firm that roasts and sells gourmet coffee. For most of its 70 year existence, its market has been relatively simple, due to its focus on that quite discerning segment that is interested in premium coffee. For Illycaffe, this niche was well defined as restaurants and diners who were primarily interested in the quality of Illycaffe's single blend of Arabica coffee. However, the coffee market has changed to something more akin to a fashion market. Illycaffe must now consider not only the relatively technical needs for flavour but also those higher, emotional and often ephemeral needs that drive a fashion market. Not only that, but they must consider how those needs vary in multiple countries and not just in restaurants but in the chain of cafés that Illycaffe uses partly to promote their brand. Whereas Illycaffe once had to understand a well-defined, mostly business to business, market with a homogeneous customer base and few competitors who each looked similar to Illycaffe, they must now contend with a business to consumer market, with complex segmentation and competitors, like Nestlé and Starbucks, who have very different business models. For Andrea Illy, head of the family-owned group, the customer task environment of which he must now make sense is much more complicated than it was for his ancestors.

As another example, complexity from a different part of the task environment caused Apple to delay the launch of its iPhone. In selling its desktop and laptop computers and its iconic music players, Apple is used to dealing, in a fairly direct manner, with retailers who pass on their boxes adding physical distribution but often little added value. And customers are used to buying in that manner. But people don't buy phones that way. They are almost always bundled with an airtime package, making the management of the channel a lot more complicated. This is an example of purchasing channel complexity, as referred to in Chapter 1. The risk to Apple was that their phone, no matter how great, may not sell if the mobile providers and their channels did not see it as valuable to them and package it into a compelling value proposition, complete with airtime and payment terms. It was this extra layer of complexity that delayed the launch of the iPhone shortly before its 2007 launch. Apple, in moving from a consumer electronics market to a mobile telephony market, added an entire tier of task environmental complexity that it had to understand or fail to penetrate this competitive market.

A final example of task environmental complexity comes neither from customer complexity nor channel complexity, but from competitor complexity. The market for advertising space is one in which companies and their agencies buy space or contact with their customers from, traditionally, television companies and the press. As a provider of advertising selling in this market, one had to understand the nature of the offerings from those two strategic sets of mass media providers, the press and the broadcasters. As a buyer of advertising, one's options were few and often unsatisfactory. Now, however, this market has been transformed by new competitors and change in the existing competitors. The obvious example is Google and other search engines selling advertising space associated with searches. In theory, this delivers controllable and well targeted access to customers who have, by their search criteria, identified themselves as being in the target market. In addition, however, both the traditional mass media channels have fragmented and become more complex with the help of other new technology. Press, with the possibilities of new digital printing technology, has spurned many new types of publication, especially free papers and tailored print run magazines designed to fit a specific geographic or demographic audience. Television and radio have similarly fragmented, with the advent of internet radio channels and companies like Spot Runner selling predesigned cable TV ads to local firms at very low cost. What was a simple two or three way fight between paper, TV and radio has become a mêlée that is much more complicated to understand. As the providers of traditional media are discovering, failure to gain insight into this complexity is leading to diminishing returns.

As Illy, Apple and the mass media companies are finding, task environmental complexity is increasing and the difficulty of understanding the

Whatever the business and whatever the context, market complexity is making it harder to create market insight.

market is increasing with it. And of course, it is not that remote environmental complexity acts on some markets and task environmental complexity acts on others. Both act on all markets to a greater or lesser extent. Further, remote environmental factors act on task environmental factors and vice versa. In whatever business and whatever context, there can be little doubt that market complexity is making it harder to create market insight.

Application point: How is the task environment increasing the complexity of your market?

Given the discussion in this section, how – if at all – is the task environment increasing the complexity of your market? How are the implications and combined implications of the task environment changing your market?

Market turbulence is making it harder to create market insight

The preceding section looked at how a more complex business environment – or rather its implications – make it harder to find market insight and, by extension, harder to create a strong strategy and a successful organisation. This is true even in a relatively stable market in which the remote and task environmental factors don't change, but merely combine and interact in complicated ways. However, stable markets appear to be the exception rather than the rule. The norm in many, if not most, markets is increasing market turbulence, which amplifies and accelerates the difficulties created by market complexity.

If complexity is defined as the number of different, relevant market factors that impact on the organisation, then turbulence is perhaps best defined as the rate of change of those factors. More accurately, it is not a greater rate of change in remote and task environments that constitutes turbulence, but a greater rate of change in the implications of those environments. As with complexity, increased turbulence can therefore arise from change in any or all of three classes of implications: implications due to new factors, new implications of existing factors or implications that arise from new combinations of factors.

If complexity is the number of market factors impacting on the organisation, turbulence is best defined as the rate of change of those factors.

Are markets becoming more turbulent? The complaints of practising managers about the rate of change in their market often seem like nostalgia, comparable to complaining about teenagers' behaviour or the quality of modern food. From their informed but subjective position, executives seem to fall into two camps regarding market turbulence. The first sees market turbulence as constantly accelerating, such that they perceive themselves to be in a far more dynamic market than their predecessors were even a few years ago. The second group argues that, for all the detailed change in their market, the fundamentals remain the same. Research into market turbulence suggests that the second, more sanguine, group are often right in that many market changes, whilst requiring attention and management, do not have important implications. However, there is evidence that, in many markets, the rate of change is accelerating. To understand this, it is perhaps useful to think in terms of Kurt Lewin's concept of force field analysis, a model that is often applied to organisational decisions but is equally useful at the higher perspective of markets or industries. See Box 2.1.

Box 2.1 Lewin's concept of Force Field Analysis

American social psychologist Kurt Lewin[5] is the person most associated with the idea that change and stasis result from the interplay of two sets of opposing forces, which he named restraining and driving forces. In Lewin's model, markets are never actually static, but may attain a state of 'dynamic equilibrium' in which the two sets of forces balance. Market turbulence results from temporary or sustained imbalance of these forces. The underlying concept of Lewin's work is that the field of forces changes all the time and, although most of his work regarded individuals or group dynamics, the concept also helps our understanding of why and how market turbulence occurs.

Using Lewin's ideas to think about market conditions, therefore, we can see that the rate of change of market conditions (i.e. market turbulence) is a function of how the driving and restraining forces in that market change. Hence market turbulence is likely to vary between markets and to vary within a market over time. We can gain a more specific understanding of the market turbulence in any given market by considering driving factors and constraining factors for that market. Examples of some recent and current factors that drive and constrain markets are shown below:

Market drivers	Market constraints
Developments in information and communication technology, e.g. the internet, mobile telephony and lower cost computing power	Physical restraints on the transmission and processing of information
Developments of new transportation technology, e.g. containerisation, aviation technology	Physical restraints on transportation of goods
Technological improvement of processes or enabling technology, e.g. Computer Assisted Design and Manufacturing	Technical constraints on operational or product performance
Development of new knowledge, e.g. Genomic and proteomic research or development of mathematical knowledge underpinning derivatives	Limitations in underlying knowledge base of the product or service
Freeing of capital markets from regulatory constraints and development of new channels, e.g. venture capital	Lack of investment capital
Increase in direct or indirect competition, e.g. due to market maturation or new entrants	Lack of competitive pressures
Political reduction of trade barriers and supporting institutions, e.g. World Trade Organisation and regional bodies such as the EU	Tariff and non-tariff barriers on international trade
Social change enabled by mass media, e.g. the 'death of deference'	Social conservatism
Economic growth and changes in wealth distribution, e.g. the emergence of a 'mass affluent' segment	Limitations in customer demand

Market drivers	Market constraints
Increased organisational change enabled by managerial competencies, e.g. management education or use of consultants	Organisational inertia
Increase pressure of management teams driven by ownership changes, e.g. institutional shareholding, shareholder activism and analyst pressure	Top management team complacency

This list is clearly generic and high level, but it nevertheless illustrates the sorts of forces acting on markets and how those forces lead to temporary or longer lasting loss of market stability.

Lewin's concepts suggest a mechanism for the origins of increased market turbulence. All it takes is for one or more drivers to become, even temporarily, stronger than the opposing constraints and the market will lose its state of dynamic equilibrium. In reality, turbulence rarely arises from change in one factor, but from a complex set of changes in market drivers and constraints which interact with each other, as shown by the examples in Boxes 2.2, 2.3 and 2.4.

The examples in Boxes 2.2, 2.3 and 2.4 are each from very different markets and are intended to convey that Lewin's force field idea is not simply an academic construct. It is a good explanation of why markets become turbulent. By supporting the model with real examples, we can see not only that some markets have become turbulent, but that many markets can and eventually will become equally turbulent. Even currently stable markets totter in an equilibrium which can be tipped from stability to turmoil by changes in one or more of the forces

Stable markets can be tipped from stability to turmoil by changes in one or more forces acting upon them.

acting upon them. When and if market equilibrium is lost, changes in the implications of the market situation mean that re-evaluation of strategy is often necessary. At the same time, the rapidity and unpredictability of those changes make gaining insight and creating strategy even harder.

Box 2.2 Market maturation and technology drivers vs. switching constraints in the enterprise software market

SAP, the global, German-based, market leader in enterprise resource planning (ERP) software, battles Oracle for control of this $35 billion and rapidly growing market. The market itself has been a surprising example of market stability, given the nature of software markets. Unlike some other parts of the IT sector, a relatively stable dynamic equilibrium has been established, despite important changes such as a wave of industry consolidation.

This equilibrium in the face of continuous technical development and industry players has, to a large degree, been due to the internal costs associated with changing systems. Even upgrading to a new version is very resource intensive, even more so for a complete change of supplier. These 'switching' costs act as a constraining force in the market which has, to date, consisted of a few tens of thousands of large firms, in both manufacturing and service sectors.

However, this equilibrium is now being disturbed by an increase in two driving forces.

- The first is market maturation. As SAP and Oracle begin to saturate the large company niche in which both have traditionally gained most of their revenue, they are now seeking to expand into medium sized companies. This creates many new implications to consider. In this part of the market, orders are smaller; needs differ and are generally only accessible via channels of value added resellers. The competitive environment is also different, with smaller niche players in addition to the traditional large opponents.
- The second is web based technological development. Increasingly, software is being sold more as a service or utility, rather than a product. Based on servers and provided over the internet, 'on demand' supply of software has important implications for providers. It changes how products can be adapted for customers and, therefore, how value can be added and profits made. Software as a service looks likely to change

the segmentation patterns of this industry, with some firms opting for the different benefits offered by the different approaches to supplying the software.

These developing imbalances between, on the one hand, constraining market inertia and, on the other, driving market maturity and technological change are causing this market to be much less stable than it was. As a result, SAP, Oracle and smaller players are now finding it harder to gain the market insight needed to guide their strategy.

Box 2.3 Globalisation and product form life cycle vs. entry barriers and trade constraints in the TV market

For many years, the TV set market has been under pressure from globalisation and the shift to low cost manufacture in Asia, leading to a steady trend in both offshoring and industry consolidation. Even within this trend, however, the market maintained a reasonable equilibrium. In large part, this was the result of the balance between low cost manufacturing on the one hand and, on the other hand, a combination of brand reputations, high barriers to entry (relative to returns) and import constraints, especially in developing markets. Together, these forces created a sort of slowly moving log-jam with the market moving steadily but slowly in the direction of commoditisation.

This equilibrium has now been rudely and rapidly disturbed by the addition of product form lifecycle forces to those of globalisation. In short, the decline of old technology (cathode ray tube based) with a combination of plasma screen, high definition and digital broadcasting has created a technological inflection point. In late 2006, prices were dropping at 10% per month – a difficult problem when it takes 90 days to ship a product.

For TV set makers such as TCL-Thompson, Sony, Panasonic and Sharp, this makes market insight a very fast moving target. Not only is product design evolving rapidly, but commoditisation is changing customer needs and the relative positions of competitors. The relative importance of physical distribution in the value chain has changed and, in these circumstances, it is very hard indeed to make strategic decisions based on sound insight.

Box 2.4 New business models and competitor action vs. trade barriers and culture in the Indian retail market

As in many developing countries, the Indian retail market has been dominated by tiny, family run stores which account for about 97% of retail sales in that country. That this has remained true when in more developed markets the sector is dominated by a few huge companies is an interesting example of dynamic equilibrium. This equilibrium is the result of the restraining forces of Indian government policy and culture. Western firms are required to set up local franchises with Indian companies who must own and run the shops. Although this policy is slowly relaxing, it remains a market constraint. In the same way, Indian shopping habits have also slowed change, despite the huge business opportunity which makes India attractive to firms like Tesco, Woolworths and Carrefour and therefore represents a market driver.

This equilibrium is now beginning to shift, thanks to a combination of new business models and activity by Reliance Industries, India's largest business group. Their plans to invest $5.5 bn in the next five years have disturbed the equilibrium by making overseas companies afraid that Reliance will gain first mover advantage. To get around local laws, they have set up business models in which their wholesale companies, which Indian regulations allow, trade via local retail partners. The result of adding these forces to the latent demand is expected to be rapid growth of both the market and of foreigners' share in that market. Technopak, a Delhi based consultancy, reckons that by 2010 this market will have doubled from 2006 figures causing family store market share to drop to 82–84%.

For both Indian retailers and foreign investors, this market turbulence has implications in the competitive environment, customer segmentation and the design of the value proposition. Most observers expect the market to mature and develop a small number of dominant players, but gaining the insight to be one of those will be very difficult.

Application point: Force fields in your market

Using Lewin's concept and considering the examples given, consider the likely future turbulence of your market. What are the driving forces and will they increase or decrease? What are the restraining forces and will they increase or decrease? What do you anticipate will be the net result for your market?

The frequency of failure

The preceding sections have detailed what we mean by complexity and turbulence. Complexity arises from the ways multiple market factors combine to have important implications for the organisation. Turbulence is the way those implications change as the market's dynamic equilibrium is unsettled. Ironically, complexity and turbulence make achieving insight both more important and more difficult at the same time. This point, that market insight is very hard to create, is the central point of this chapter. Of course, this might simply be the authors' shroud-waving – painting the challenges facing managers as harder than they are in order to make a case for the rest of the book. To test if this is the case, it is worth considering that body of research that concerns firm survival rates.

At any one point in time, executives in any sector can look around and see giant, dominant companies that look invincible and permanent. Today, for example, it is hard to imagine Microsoft, Pfizer, Sony or Toyota succumbing to competitive forces. Yet even a slightly longer historical perspective shows this appearance of permanence to be false. Consider Tables 2.1 and 2.2, which are based on data from the late Peter Doyle and Malcolm McDonald.[6,7]

These tables show clearly that even corporate titans fail with surprising frequency. An even longer perspective provides more evidence. Hannah Marshall[8] looked back to 1912 because that year represented a point in time, following a period of consolidation, at which truly giant firms had first appeared to dominate their sectors. He constructed a list of the world's largest industrial companies, all of which, to executives of the day, must have seemed as enduring as Microsoft does today. However, by the end of his study, in 1995, only 52 of these giants survived. Of the remainder, only 19 were still in the top 100 industrial companies. It is appropriate to be sceptical of any one piece of research, but a similar study was carried out by

Table 2.1 *Britain's top companies (Management Today, 1991).*

Year	Company[a]	Market Value (£m)	ROI[b] %	Subsequent performance
1979	**MFI**	57	50	Collapsed
1980	**Lasmo**	134	97	Still profitable
1981	**Bejam**	79	34	Acquired
1982	**Racal**	940	36	Still profitable
1983	**Polly Peck**	128	79	Collapsed
1984	**Atlantic Computers**	151	36	Collapsed
1985	**BSR**	197	32	Still profitable
1986	**Jaguar**	819	60	Acquired
1987	**Amstrad**	987	89	Still profitable
1988	**Body Shop**	225	89	Still profitable
1989	**Blue Arrow**	653	135	Collapsed

[a] Where a company has been top for more than 1 year, the next best company has been chosen in the subsequent year e.g.. Poly Peck was related top 1983, '84 and '85
[b] Pre-tax profit as a percent of investment capital
Courtesy of the late Professor Peter Doyle

Table 2.2 *Britain's top companies (Management Today, 2002).*

Year	Company[a]	Market Value (£bn)[b]	ROI %	Subsequent performance
1990	**Maxwell Communications Plc**	1.0	5	Collapsed
1991	**Imperial Chemical Industries Plc**	8.6	13	Collapsed
1992	**Wellcome Plc**	8.3	40	Acquired
1993	**ASDA Group**	1.6	7	Acquired
1994	**TSB Group Plc**	3.7	20	Acquired
1995	**British Telecommunications Plc**	22.2	17	Not Profitable
1996	**British Steel Plc**	3.3	19	Collapsed
1997	**British Airways Plc**	6.1	7	Not Profitable
1998	**National Westminster Bank Plc**	19.6	14	Acquired
1999	**Marconi Plc**	29.8	22	Acquired
2000	**Marks & Spencer Plc**	5.3	7	Not Profitable

[a] Each company was a FTSE100 when selected
[b] Market Values as of 31 December of each year
From M. McDonald, *Marketing Due Diligence*, pp 9–10, © Elsevier 2005

Neil Fligstein.[9] In his work, he picked out the 100 largest US firms at the end of every decade between 1919 and 1979, a total of 216 firms altogether. In Fligstein's data, only 34 of the firms in the 1919 list were in the 1979 list. In other words, both studies, using different sampling and different methodology, showed a similar drop out rate of about one firm per year. And this was the rate for established giants with the resources, experience and knowledge to understand the market. The survival rates for less well-resourced, small firms and start-ups are even lower.

The failure of even large firms to adapt to and survive in the market has been put into a fascinating context by Paul Omerod.[10,11] In his book, he uses Hannah's and Fligstein's data sets to compare the survival rates of firms with the extinction rates of species over geological time. Strikingly, he observes similar extinction rates in the two very different contexts. In broad terms, the ability of firms to adapt to and survive in their environment is no better than that of animal species. As Omerod points out, biological survival is driven by random mutations in DNA and firm survival by the thoughtful, deliberate adaptation of strategy by intelligent humans. And yet the two mechanisms produce the same outcomes. To quote Omerod:

> The implication is that it is as if . . . firms acted at random. . . . Firms try all the time to achieve favourable outcomes but they often fail. And they often become extinct.[11] (page 187)

Of course, the fact that intelligent firms are no better at adapting to their environment than randomly-driven biological species does not necessarily mean that firms become extinct due to lack of insight. It is possible that firm extinction is attributable entirely to failure to respond effectively to the market, despite having clear insight into that market. Possible, but unlikely. The failure rate of firms, across all sectors and over long periods, suggests that many firms fail to make sense of their market environments, so make weak strategies, and so fail.

That intelligent management is no more effective at ensuring survival than random mutation is a striking thought. It is even more remarkable under recent conditions, in which business school educated executives have access to huge amounts of computing power with which to make sense of the market. Later in this book, we will explore how firms go about making sense of their business environment and how the lessons of those companies might be applied to your company. However, we must recognise that most companies facing this challenge have a knee-jerk recourse to an IT-led solution. Before going on to our recommendations for creating insight, therefore, we have to understand what it is that makes most IT-led approaches fail.

Application point: Can you see extinction happening around you?

Given the idea of firm extinction, consider what you see in your market. Can you see some firms heading for extinction, by bankruptcy or acquisition? What do you see as the ultimate cause of their demise? How is that related to their market insight capabilities? How do you see the future for your own firm?

The failure of data analytics

Anyone researching how firms attempt to make sense of their business environment cannot fail to observe the pervasiveness of information technology and implicit faith that executives place in it. There can hardly be a firm that has not invested, always significantly and often hugely, in IT systems, the goal of which is to provide a better understanding of the market and control of the company. The labels attached to such IT-based projects vary greatly: enterprise resource planning, customer relationship management, sales force automation, marketing excellence. They all share the fact that they try to combine data, often data that was held in previously distinct functional silos. Industry analysts suggest that the annual spend on such systems is approaching $11 bn.[12]

Despite this huge spend, which does not of course include indirect and opportunity costs, many firms feel that they are not achieving the outcomes they sought. Early research pointed to failure rates of 70%[13] and although more recent work suggests that this situation is improving,[14] researchers still argue that failure is more common than success.[15] More recent work at Cranfield School of Management has uncovered the differences between those firms that manage to turn data into insight and value and those that don't.[16] Smith and his co-researchers[17,18] then developed the Cranfield work into a model which they called 'the data-to-value wheel', in order to emphasise the iterative nature of the process (see Figure 2.1).

Early research points to failure rates of 70% in CRM projects.

Smith's wheel model not only explicates the idea that the process of creating value from data is an iterative process; it also dissembles the

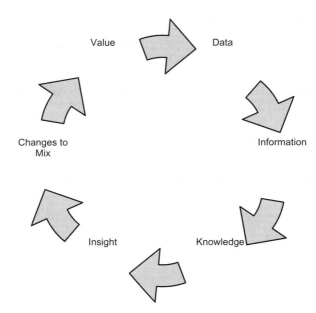

Figure 2.1 *Smith's Data-to-Value Wheel.*

concepts of data, information, knowledge, insight etc. In common executive parlance, these terms are often used interchangeably or at least with overlapping meanings. The Cranfield work helpfully untangled what each of the terms in the wheel model meant:

- Data is the recording of events, such as transactions and other interactions. Data need be neither quantitative nor explicit; it can also be implicit or qualitative.
- Information is data that has been organised into patterns. Usually, the purpose of this ordering is to reduce uncertainties in the subsequent interpretation of the data.
- Knowledge is information which has been placed into the context of the organisational situation. Broadly speaking, there are three types of knowledge:
  - declarative knowledge (knowing what something is);
  - process or procedural knowledge (knowing how something is done);
  - causal knowledge (knowing why something happens).

- Insight is knowledge that meets the criteria of an organisational strength.

  Insight is knowledge that meets the criteria of an organisational strength.

- Changes to the mix are any actions which influence the offering as seen by the customer. Typically, these are considered in terms of the marketing mix of product, pricing, promotion, channels, people, process and physical evidence.

- Value is the increase in customer preference created by the changes to the mix. This value is positive if it exceeds the costs of those changes and negative if it is less than those costs.

When Smith's wheel is used in conjunction with these definitions, we can see that firms translate data into value by a series of sequential transformations. The Cranfield work made two significant and new contributions to our understanding of how these transformations work. Firstly, it untangled the confusion between knowledge and insight. In defining insight as only that knowledge that is an organisational strength, it built on a body of knowledge known as resource-based value (see Box 2.5). Secondly, by seeing value creation as the end point of a chain of transformations, it became clear that failure to create value could be due to a break or weakness at one or more points in that chain. In fact, the Cranfield work identified ten factors that influenced the efficacy of the data-to-value process,[17] as summarised in Box 2.6.

Box 2.5 Defining insight

One of the most influential bodies of work in modern strategy literature is the resource based view of the firm. Based on the work of Barney,[19,20] but with its roots in the much earlier work of Penrose[21] this view sees competitive advantage as flowing from differences in the resources available to a firm. Such resources can be physical assets, access to finance, intellectual property or even aspects of culture. Importantly for our purposes though, knowledge can be a resource too. One of Barney's most useful contributions was the VRIO framework for differentiating resources that are organisational strengths from those that are not. Applied to knowledge, the VRIO framework identifies a piece or body of knowledge as an organisational strength if all four of the following questions could be answered in the affirmative:

- Value: Does this knowledge enable the firm to respond to environmental threats and opportunities?
- Rarity: Is this knowledge currently held only by the organisation and not by its competitors?
- Imitability: Is it costly or difficult for other organisations to obtain or develop this knowledge?
- Organisation: Is the firm organised, or can it be organised, to exploit this knowledge?

The Cranfield work took the VRIO framework and, applying it to knowledge, identified that, of all the knowledge (that is, contextualised information) a firm might have, only that knowledge which met the VRIO criteria of an organisational strength might truly be called insight.

Box 2.6 The Ten Commandments of value creation

- **Use data about *unmet* needs**
  Transactional data, such as sales, tell you about the needs the customer has met. The most valuable data is that which tells you about unmet needs, like complaints, satisfaction and the use of other products and services.

- **Synthesise multiple sources of data**
  Any one source of data, no matter how huge or well analysed, gives only limited understanding of the customer. Since customers are complex beings, real insight comes from the synthesis of quantitative and qualitative, tacit and explicit data.

- **Make and test hypotheses**
  Technology makes it easy to gather and organise lots of data, but the value comes from applying it. In particular, value emerges when firms think about how their market works and use the data to test their beliefs and assumptions about customers.

- **Use deliberate processes**
  Most firms are now process oriented. They have clear, step-wise, methods for doing everything from paying invoices to firing people. By contrast, too many firms see turning data into value as a 'touchy feely' thing. The best firms create amazing value by almost mechanical processes.

- **Start with 'real' segments**
  In some firms, technology driven data analysis is the latest fad, driving out some of the basics. In the best firms, technology enhances rather than replaces traditional, excellent marketing. And excellent marketing always starts with 'real' segments, based not on data but on customers' needs and motivations.

- **Change the mix, don't tweak it**
  Some things, like promotion and packaging, are easier to change than others, like pricing and channels. Some firms delude themselves that value can be created by such easy options. In reality, the difficulty of changing the marketing mix is usually proportional to the value resulting from the change.

- **Target segments that care about tailoring**
  Value comes from customers choosing to give their money to us instead of someone else. This means that value is created only when we target those segments that care enough about how we've tailored our offer to make that choice. Targeting anyone else destroys value.

- **Change it now**
  Value creation is a real-time and relative activity. Using data to change the offer to the customer only creates value when we do it faster than the competition. Changing things more slowly than the competition merely incurs costs for no competitive advantage.

- **Manage the culture**
  Like everything else in a firm, the data-to-value process is either helped or hindered by the company culture. Firms that think business is about products and services fail; those that realise it is about customers and their needs succeed.

- **Break down the silos**
  More than anything else the company does, transforming data into value is a cross functional activity. It fails when it belongs to marketing, sales, IT or R&D. Value has to flow across silos before it flows to and from the customer.

So, although the data analytics approach to drawing insight from the business environment looks an appealing panacea, an impression reinforced by the promotional efforts of the IT vendors, it is far from that in practice. The Cranfield work shows that creating value from this approach is very difficult and involves a lot more than crunching data. The multiple transformations necessary to get from data to insight to value and the multiple preconditions for success help to explain why making sense of the business environment is much too difficult a problem for a data analytics approach to solve.

Powerpoints

- Markets are difficult to understand and this is made more so by increasing market complexity and turbulence.
- Market complexity arises from the implications of remote and task environments and the way those implications combine.
- Market turbulence arises from imbalances between forces in the market place.
- Organisational failure is common and often attributable to failure to understand the market.
- Data, information, knowledge and insight are not interchangeable terms, but distinct entities in the transformation of data into value.

- Insight has the properties of an organisational strength. It is valuable, rare, hard to imitate and the organisation is aligned to use it.
- Insight creation occurs from a series of sequential steps, as summarised in Smith's wheel.
- Creating insight is enabled by certain practices and preconditions, the so called 10 commandments of insight creation.

3

How well do you understand your business environment?

'I therefore claim to show, not how men think in myths, but how myths operate in men's mind without their being aware of the fact.'
Claude Levi-Strauss

So far we have argued that understanding the business environment is a precondition for business success in the vast majority of cases. Of course there are always exceptions to any maxim and sometimes success can be due to luck as much as anything else![1] But on the assumption that you would like an alternative to luck, let's accept for now that a sound understanding of the business environment is needed to gain market insight which is critical for formulating 'strong strategy'.

We have also brought to your attention that gaining market insight is increasingly difficult due to the growing complexity and turbulence of markets. Market complexity is increasing due to increases in the number of significant market factors, the increasing significance of those market factors on business performance, and the intertwining of these factors. This, combined with increased turbulence (i.e. increases in the rate of changes in market factors) in both the remote and task environments, is adding to the difficulty of understanding the business environment.

A sensible starting point for gaining market insight is to begin by assessing how well you currently understand the business environment. If the market is as complex and turbulent as previously discussed then you might expect the answer to be 'not very well'. But which particular aspects of the market are less well understood? Which aspects of the market do you pay most and least attention to and why? How do you learn about the business environment? And what are the implica-

How well do you currently understand the business environment? If your market is complex and turbulent, you might expect the answer to be 'not very well'.

tions of how you learn? These are the sorts of questions that we are concerned with in this chapter. Hence this chapter includes a diagnostic test to help reveal the strengths and weaknesses of your current understanding of the business environment. A further diagnostic test will help you to assess the way that you learn of the business environment and to consider the implications on the scope and depth of your understanding of the business environment. Our intention is that by the end of this chapter, you will have an improved self awareness of how well you understand the business environment.

Armed with an improved self awareness of your understanding of the business environment and related management practices, we will be better positioned to meaningfully assess and influence your management practices to gain a better outcome. Thus, the relevance of the quote at the start of this chapter is to encourage you to improve your self awareness by making explicit what influences affect your ability to understand the business environment.

This chapter aims to provide you with insights into how well you understand the business environment and how you learn about the business environment. The activity of gathering

Scanning behaviour is the activity of gathering data about the business environment, interpreting that data, and learning.

data about the business environment, interpreting that data and learning, is one we term 'scanning behaviour'. In this chapter we will begin by emphasising the importance of self awareness of our depth of understanding of the business environment and our individual scanning behaviour. The argument flows that self awareness of our scanning behaviour is a prerequisite to meaningfully influencing it. We'll then reflect on key learnings from management research that highlight a general lack of self awareness of scanning behaviour by senior management and offer an explanation as to why this is so.

Having highlighted the need for greater self awareness of scanning behaviour, the following section in this chapter will offer a self diagnostic or checklist of items to test your understanding of the remote environment and task environment. For the remote environment, the self diagnostic will refer to social, legal, economic, political and technical environmental factors. For the task environment, the self diagnostic will refer to customer, channel, competitor and supplier factors. Considering the environment in terms of its remote and task components is consistent with our discussion in Chapter 2.

Finally, in this chapter we will present new findings based on our recent research that suggests that scanning is essentially a highly individualised behaviour that is typically 'embedded' or 'routinised' among senior managers. We then offer a further self diagnostic to assess key aspects of your individual scanning behaviour that are likely to differentiate among scanning behaviour which we have labelled 'formality', 'personal', 'completeness' and 'breadth'. The chapter then concludes with comments on the impact of individual scanning behaviours on effective understanding of the business environment.

The importance of self awareness

In general, most managers would agree that a high degree of self awareness of their managerial practices is helpful. With greater self awareness we can appreciate our true strengths upon which we can capitalise, and we can

With greater self-awareness we can appreciate true strengths upon which we can capitalise and acknowledge true weaknesses upon which we can improve.

acknowledge our true weaknesses upon which we can improve. In other words, through self awareness we can better determine what actions to take to be more effective.

It is especially important for managers to be effective with respect to scanning the business environment because the implications on an organisation's performance can be significant. If managers are not aware of significant changes in the environment or fail to notice changes that turn out to be important, then they may not make the required changes to an organisa-

Through self-awareness we can better determine what actions to take to be more effective.

tion's strategy or structure.[2] Effective scanning is a necessary part of identifying valuable resources.[3] Also, if managers misinterpret changes in the environment then sub-optimal decisions may be made that result in performance decline.[4]

Hence, in order to assess the likelihood of sub-optimal decisions resulting from lack of awareness or misinterpretation, we need to understand more about how individual managers assess their environment. We were interested in questions such as: How well do you understand the business environment? Which sectors of the environment do you understand the most? Which sectors do you understand the least? What factors contribute to in-depth understanding? What factors act to prevent or obscure understanding? How do you gain your understanding?

As you might have already ascertained, answering these questions requires a high degree of self awareness and can prove difficult. Some insight into just how difficult was gained through our recent Market Insight Research.[5] For those who are interested in the parameters of the research project that inform this chapter, please refer to the technical note (in Box 3.1) which provides some information on research objective, research assumptions and research methods. Alternatively, feel free to skip over this technical note and read on about key initial insights concerning managers' self awareness and scanning practices.

Box 3.1 Market insight research parameters

Research Topic

Market Insight: an investigation into managerial scanning behaviour.

Research Objective

The overriding objective of our research was to provide an updated and more in-depth understanding of the phenomenon of scanning behaviour and the influences on it, and to consider how to improve the effectiveness of individual scanning behaviour and firm level scanning practices in order to gain genuine market insight.

Research Assumptions

Some key assumptions underlying our research included:

- It is the first, second and third tier managers, or senior managers, who are strategically significant scanners; they can exercise discretion as to how they scan and influence critical decision making and strategy formulation processes.
- Scanning by individual senior managers is not a linear process, but an ongoing pattern of activity that involves simultaneously seeking data and interpreting data about the environment.
- Senior managers differ in their scanning as they develop specific ways to know the environment.
- Scanning is a critically important activity for senior managers because effective organisations are more in tune with their environments.

Research Methods

The research involved two phases:

- Phase 1 comprised in-depth interviews with a selection of senior managers, conducted in their work environments, in order to better understand the phenomenon of scanning and to inform Phase 2.
- Phase 2 involved a broad based survey questionnaire that captured data on a wide range of scanning behaviour and other key individual and organisational variables. Independent variable data captured included hierarchical level, functional roles, age, cross-functional experience, postgraduate education in management, company size, industry group and organisational strategy process types.

All told, 394 valid responses from senior managers were received and analysed. The respondents covered 20 discrete organisational functions, 40 industry categories and companies ranging in size from less than £1m to greater than £1 billion in annual revenue.

Overall, our research showed that managers struggled to clearly and confidently answer questions on how they individually assess their environments. Senior managers' understanding and articulation of scanning behaviour was found to be very limited. We were ini-

Senior managers spend very little time explicitly considering their scanning behaviour, the scanning process, and the related issues associated with market insight and the link to organisational performance.

tially surprised at this result, given the espoused importance of scanning activities. Our results indicated that senior managers spend very little time explicitly considering their scanning behaviour, the scanning process and the related issues associated with market insight and the link to organisational performance!

According to prior research and based on our own study, there are three main reasons for senior managers' general lack of self awareness of scanning behaviour and related activities.

Firstly, scanning is a component within the complex organisational process of strategy formulation.[6] Therefore, it is difficult to isolate scanning from strategy formulation activities. It is also difficult to separately identify and contrast scanning activities among firms and senior managers, as they will differ depending on which strategy making processes are adopted.[7]

Secondly, scanning is intimately involved in the decision making processes of individual managers which makes it a difficult activity to isolate.[8] While scanning and interpretation may be among the most important

While scanning and interpretation may be among the most important functions that senior managers perform, the process is so familiar that it is almost taken for granted.

functions that senior managers perform, the process is so familiar that it is almost taken for granted! Almost all activities in organisations, whether under the heading of structure, decision making, strategy formulation, organisational learning, goal setting, or innovation and change, may be connected to the mode of interpreting the external environment, yet they are done with apparently very limited conscious awareness.

Thirdly, scanning represents a basic behavioural aspect of managers' activity and it not always done with conscious awareness, which makes it a difficult activity to analyse.[9] Many of the senior managers in our study reported that it was 'just the way they did things' without consciously recognising their actions to be scanning actions!

The term 'scanning' is drawn from management literature and is helpful to understand in the context of gaining market insight. We will use the terms 'scanning' and 'scanning behaviour' throughout this book and hence it is helpful to set out a clear working definition. For our purposes, the term scanning refers to 'the activity of acquiring information about events and relationships in a company's outside environment, the knowledge of which would assist top management in the task of charting the company's future course of action'.[10] Further information on the origins of research into scanning behaviour is outlined as a technical note in Box 3.2.

Scanning is an important activity from the view point of practising managers. The respondents in our recent study all confirmed that 'scanning' is a familiar term and a significant activity. This is consistent with the results of a managerial study done by Henry Mintzberg titled *The Nature of*

Box 3.2 Technical note concerning scanning

The term 'scanning', in a business context, was originally coined by Francis Aguilar in his publication, *Scanning the Business Environment*. Aguilar's research was concerned with the way in which top management gains relevant information about events occurring outside the company in order to guide the company's future course of action. A working definition of scanning developed by Aguilar is 'the activity of acquiring information about events and relationships in a company's outside environment, the knowledge of which would assist top management in the task of charting the company's future course of action'. In other words, we are concerned with events and trend information that impact on strategy.

Aguilar's work, published in 1967, primarily described the 'what', 'where' and 'how' of the scanning process and presented an extensive analysis of the types of external information that managers paid attention to, based on interviews and an analysis of critical incidents.

A significant output from Aguilar's study was the proposition of four alternative modes or ways of scanning. In brief, these four modes were:

- *Undirected Viewing* – general exposure to information where the viewer has no specific purpose in mind with the possible exception of exploration.
- *Conditioned Viewing* – directed exposure, not involving active search, to a more or less clearly identified area or type of information.
- *Information Search* – a relatively limited and unstructured effort to obtain specific information or information for a specific purpose.
- *Formal Search* – a deliberate effort, usually following a pre-established plan, procedure or methodology, to secure specific information or information relating to a specific view.

Aguilar did not empirically test the validity of the above modes but, nonetheless, the proposition of four alternative scanning modes was helpful to hint at ways to discern and differentiate among scanning behaviour. In our recent research, we did conduct empirical tests to identify underlying dimensions that usefully discern among scanning behaviour. This is discussed further later in this chapter.

It is also helpful to make one further technical point concerning prior research into scanning versus our recent research exercise. Aguilar's study was limited in scope to report on what is happening when a business organisation scans its

There is a distinction between search and interpretation . . . but we cannot ignore the results of a manager's analysis and interpretation when considering why he searches as he does.

environment for information, i.e. the observable aspects of scanning behaviour versus the interpretative aspects. Hence, Aguilar's focus was on the recognition of, search for and internal communication of external information by individuals in a given organisation, and not on the analysis or interpretation of their information. However, this limitation may be significant and non-representative of practice, as Aguilar goes on to acknowledge that the distinction between the search and the interpretation cannot always be maintained and that we cannot ignore the results of a manager's analysis and interpretation when considering why he searches as he does. At a theoretical level, there is considerable overlap between the tasks of scanning and interpretation.[11]

Managerial Work, first published in 1973.[12] In this work, Mintzberg categorises managerial roles into ten different types – figurehead, leader, liaison, monitor, disseminator, spokesman, entrepreneur, disturbance handler, resource allocator and negotiator. The function of scanning falls within the 'manager as monitor' role insofar as it relates to scanning for information about events and trends in the external business environment, and is therefore confirmed as a key top ten managerial activity.

As well as understanding reasons for senior managers' general lack of awareness of scanning behaviour and related activities, our research also highlighted that senior managers have a lot of discretion as to how they scan. Senior managers – which we defined to include first, second and third tier managers – are in a position to exercise a lot of discretion as to how they meet their goals and manage their time and activities, including staying in touch with changes in the business environment. This level of freedom or discretion leads to many and varied scanning behaviours across the population of senior managers.

After years of experience of exercising discretion as to how to scan, managers appear to develop routines or work patterns that are particular to them. By routine, we mean an unvarying or habitual method or procedure. *Managers develop routinised work patterns in ways of gathering external business information, monitoring the environment, and making sense of it.* Over time, managers develop work patterns connected with learning about events and trends in the environment outside their organisation. Ways of gathering external business information, monitoring the environment and making sense of it, eventually become routinised.

If these routines become more than transient habits and instead become well established patterns that are not readily influenced, then we refer to the routines as 'embedded'. Embedded routines are well established work patterns that are not obviously strongly related to changes in extraneous factors. Embedded scanning routines encompass biases or preferences that ultimately reflect the manager's own preferred way of learning about the business environment. Another way of expressing this idea is that over time a manager will likely develop a favoured means of scanning that will be consistently enacted.

In order to change our behaviour to be more effective, we need firstly to understand it. This is as true for scanning behaviour as for other types of behaviour. Hence, the next section of this chapter focuses on testing your understanding of the business environment and making explicit your individual scanning practices in order that we can analyse them and their impact.

Application point: How self aware are you of your scanning behaviour?

Accepting that scanning is an important activity, describe your current scanning behaviour. What aspects are easy to describe? What aspects are difficult to describe? To what extent does your scanning reflect basic ingrained behaviours versus something you do with conscious awareness?

Test your understanding

A diagnostic approach is helpful to assess how well you understand the business environment and is a necessary step prior to offering tailored advice on how to improve your environmental scanning behaviour and systems. The remainder of this section is designed to test your understanding of significant environmental factors and the degree of attention that you pay to different environmental sectors.

Test your understanding of the remote environment

The first area we'll test is your understanding of the 'remote environment'. The remote environment is a well established term in management literature and refers to environmental factors that are 'far away, not near, or distant in respect to time and place'.

These remote factors are key events or trends that may affect the strategic position and performance of a business at some stage in the future. Remote factors are sometimes readily identifi-

The remote environment refers to environmental factors that are far away or distant in respect to time and place.

able as definite events and trends, and hence are reasonably straightforward to include in an analysis of the business environment. However, remote factors may also start off as very discreet and low profile events, or begin as weak trends that belie easy identification. Over time, these weak trends may grow in strength, or may indeed change in nature. Identifying, monitoring and analysing remote factors is a challenge that many managers shy away from as it is very difficult.

A well established type of analysis to identify significant factors in the remote business environment is PEST analysis. PEST itself is an acronym for Political, Economic, Social and Technological factors. PEST is a widely taught and well known framework often used when conducting a market analysis to support business planning or strategy development.

A PEST analysis can be helpful as a checklist of remote factors to look for and consider and can help to identify market potential, market direction such as growth or decline and market attractiveness.

The presentation of PEST analysis is often done using a two-by-two matrix which creates four discrete sections to list out political, economic, social and technological factors. A short description of each factor is shown in Figure 3.1.

The PEST acronym is also sometimes presented as STEP which represents those same factors. There are also several variations of the PEST model which claim to extend the categories of factors to consider. Examples of other categories include legal (L), ecological (E), ethical (E) and Demographic (D). The more common variations on the PEST acronym are STEEP and PESTLE.

Political factors	**Economic factors**
political factors that could be important influences on regulations, law, business requirements and incentives	economic factors that could impact on the level of demand for products and services and costs of production, promotion and distribution
Social factors	**Technological factors**
social factors that impact on how business is conducted and specific requirements concerning management of resources, and human resources in particular	technology advances that may open up opportunities for innovations in products and services or change the relative competitiveness of businesses that exploit technology advances

Figure 3.1 *PEST analysis descriptions.*

In Chapter 1 we introduced the SLEPT acronym. However, based on our experience in using a tool to diagnose managers' understanding of the remote environment, we found that using a simplified tool built around the four categories of political, economic, social and technological was most effective. This works, as the PEST analysis can incorporate the additional categories listed above: legal factors (L) can be listed under political factors (P) as they result from a political and legislative process; ecological and ethical factors (E) can be listed under any of the four headings depending on their impact; and demographic factors (D) can be listed under social factors (S).

The PEST model directs the researcher to conduct an environmental analysis from four major perspectives. Arguably the additional categories above are sub-categories as they are not as strategically significant and can be incorporated into the four main categories of PEST.

The power of PEST analysis is that it provides a checklist of items to consider what could be important and ultimately affect the position and performance of your business.

The power of the PEST analysis is that it provides a checklist of items to consider what could be important and ultimately affect the position and performance of your business. Examples of the types of factors to consider when assessing the remote environment are outlined in Table 3.1.

To help test your understanding of the remote environment, a set of a self assessment questions is presented in Box 3.3. Under each of the PEST categories are listed some typical questions to consider.

Prior to considering these self assessment questions, you will find it helpful to rephrase them to be more specific to your market and firm situation as appropriate. For example, under the Political factors category (P) is the generic question 'What is the state of relations with other key countries?' This should be re-phrased to specify the countries that are 'key' to your situation. These key countries will likely be, for example, neighbouring countries, major trading countries, world leader countries, countries that exert a specific influence on your home country, countries that represent a significant threat and emerging countries.

As you review the questions, ask yourself whether you think they are of sufficient interest and relevance to your firm to warrant addressing them. You may conclude that some questions are not applicable for the purposes of a meaningful remote environment analysis for your firm in its current

Table 3.1 *PEST factors.*

Political factors	Economic factors
• Environmental regulations	• General economic growth
• Corporate taxation	• Industry specific economic growth
• Employee taxation	• Government spending
• Employment law	• Government economic priorities
• Trade regulations	• Monetary policy
• Consumer protection regulations	• Consumer confidence
• Business conduct standards	• Inflation rates
• Competition regulation	• Foreign exchange rates
• Pricing practices	• Taxation regulations
• Government guidelines	• Interest rates
	• Unemployment policy
	• Business cycle
Social factors	**Technological factors**
• Demographics	• Innovations and developments
• Population age distribution	• R&D investment levels
• Population growth projections	• Changes in internet
• Lifestyle trends	• Changes in telecommunications
• Education	• Change in mobile telephony
• Fashion	• Costs of data transfer
• Health and safety	• Cost of data storage
• Work–life balance preferences	• Computing processing power
• Labour availability	• Rate of transfer of technology
• Wealth distribution	• Government technology investment

Box 3.3 PEST self assessment questions

Political factor self assessment questions

- What environmental regulations exist, or are emerging, that impact on the sourcing and management of input resources and production processes?
- How stable is the political environment?
- Which Government policies may significantly impact the business environment?
- What trading agreements is the Government signed up to or seeking to create?
- What is Government policy on key areas of economy, taxation, free markets, national interests, culture, social welfare and trade?

- What is the state of relations with other key countries?
- What other countries are considered to be allies, neutral, or threats?
- What is the level of threat from established military forces or terrorist groups?
- Does the 'rule of law' apply?
- What is the extent of corruption among Government officials?
- What regulations exist to protect intellectual property?
- Who are favoured trading partners?
- What is the degree of Government oversight into market practices?
- What Government bodies and regulations affect competition and pricing?
- What is/are the taxation policy, rates and incentives?
- What is the labour policy covering wages, work and overtime?
- What is the extent of health and safety regulations?
- What mechanisms exist to protect consumer rights?

Economic factor self assessment questions

- What is the Central Bank's interest rate?
- What are projected levels of inflation?
- What is the Government monetary policy and impact on the economy?
- What are the prospects for GDP per capita?
- What are target areas for Government investment and spending?
- What type of economic system is in place?
- What is the level of Government intervention in the free market?
- What is the unemployment rate?
- What is the economic growth rate?
- What is the general state of the economy (e.g. buoyant, recession etc.)?
- What is the level of discretionary income?
- What is the cost of labour?
- What is the skill level of the workforce?
- What are the relative strengths and weaknesses of the labour force?
- What is the quality of infrastructure and utilities?

- What is the relative strength of the exchange rate?
- What are the country specific competitive advantages?

Social factor self assessment questions

- What are attitudes to nationals and foreigners?
- What is the level of tolerance for diversity?
- What is the mix of religious beliefs and affiliations?
- What is the work to life balance?
- What are the common shared values of mainstream population?
- What is the impact of gender on social status and opportunities?
- What is the age distribution among population?
- What is the wealth distribution among population?
- What issues does the population feel most strongly about?
- What are the demographics?
- What class structures exist?
- What is the level of education?
- To what extent are entrepreneurial activities encouraged?
- What are the prevailing attitudes to work, leisure, health and environment?
- What are the common leisure interests?

Technology factor self assessment questions

- What technologies are emerging that may allow products to be made at lower cost?
- What technologies may enable a more effective way of delivering services?
- What are the breakthroughs in communications and connectivity technologies and how will they help?
- What technological innovations will emerge and be valuable to customers?
- What technologies will permit businesses to be more successful?
- What are the recent technological developments?
- What is the impact of technological developments on value chain and cost structure?

situation. For example, if your firm was small to medium sized, based in a first world country that has leading edge infrastructure and utilities, operating in a Government regulated environment to ensure competitive pricing practices among utilities entities, then the generic question of 'What is the quality of infrastructure and utilities?' under the Economic factor (E) heading, may be inapplicable.

Obviously the list of questions in Box 3.3 is not intended to be exhaustive. Rather the questions should prompt you to gauge your degree of understanding about potentially significant factors. As you read through these questions, it's worth thinking about how to tailor them to make them more relevant to your situation. For example, under the Social factors category (S) there is a generic question 'What are the prevailing attitudes to . . . environment?' The global environment is a subject that is getting increasing attention and attitudes towards it may prove significant and worth further exploration. For example, what might be the impact of sympathetic environmental attitudes on shareholder communications, investment strategy and product development? For firms that produce significant waste or carbon dioxide (e.g. heavy manufacturers) or for firms that make 'environmentally friendly' substitute products (e.g. solar panel manufacturers) then the questions concerning environmental trends and implications are especially relevant and worth tailoring and elaborating upon.

As these self assessment questions show, PEST is a broad type of analysis. When undertaking a PEST analysis you should expect that some areas of query will be fruitful while others may be interesting to know but ultimately not relevant. As with any piece of quality research you should pose the 'so what' question, i.e. So what are the implications of a particular insight? If you can't answer this, or the answer is insignificant, then arguably no insight has been gained and the resources invested in the exercise have been wasted.

Remember to pose the 'so what' question: So what are the implications of a particular insight? If you can't answer, or the answer is insignificant, arguably no insight has been gained.

Our discussion of the questions in Box 3.3 has concerned you and your individual understanding. In practice, it is likely that the responsibility for researching and developing insights into the remote environment will fall not just on one individual but on a broader team and among the most senior management. Hence, it is important that the top team gain a shared understanding of remote environment. This requires working together and, through discussion and debate, developing a shared view on how well the team understands the key political, economic, social and technological factors and their implications for firm success.

For your benefit, an interactive tool to help assess your knowledge of the remote environment is provided at www.stratevolve.com and www.pragmedic.com. This tool summarises the PEST categories, lists out the PEST factors, sets out all of the self assessment questions listed above and provides an area where you and your top team can input your shared answers or comments. The tool will also provide a rating of your overall level of understanding of the remote environment, and suggest ideas on how to build further knowledge and understanding. The tool can be completed online or it can be downloaded as an excel spreadsheet for use on your own personal computer. Any queries on the operation of the interactive tool or suggestions for enhancement can be sent to info@stratevolve.com.

Application point: How well do you understand the remote environment?

Reflecting on the PEST tool described above, how well do you understand remote political, economic, social and technology factors? What remote factors are most significant and why?

Test your understanding of the task environment

The next area to test is your understanding of the 'task environment'. The task environment is also a well established term in management literature and refers to the immediate environment to the organisation. The task environment encapsulates the organisation's immediate external environment. For example, the type of information that resides in the task environment includes customer preferences and behaviour, competitor events and intentions, changes affecting sales and distribution channels and supplier outputs and terms. The task environment, or micro environment, is often simplified conceptually into four areas – customer, competitor, channel and supplier.

The task environment is often simplified conceptually into four areas – customer, competitor, channel, and supplier.

It can be helpful to think of the remote and task environments as different points on a continuum of perspective, rather than discrete categories of information. Conceptually, the narrowest perspective is the task environment comprising internal information concerning the organisation's effectiveness, and the broadest perspective is the remote environment comprising distant events with no obvious impact on the immediate business environment.

A summary description of each of the four major areas of the task environment – customer, competitor, channel and supplier – is outlined in Figure 3.2.

Many managers argue that understanding customers is the most important research activity of a firm. It's a commonly held view that understanding customers is critical to success. *Customer analysis typically focuses on target segments – Who are they? What are their needs? What is their value?* Regardless of whether your business is B2C or B2B, understanding your customers' needs and buying criteria is critical to successfully selling products and services and creating satisfied customers.

Customer analysis will typically focus on being clear about who our target segments are, their needs and what value can be captured through serving them. More advanced analysis often covers the means and costs of customer acquisition, retention and attrition. Advanced financial analysis of

Customer factors	**Competitor factors**
Customer factors refer to the needs of actual and potential customers and especially the way needs translate into market segmentation	Competitor factors refer to alternate ways of satisfying the needs of the target customer segment
Channel factors	**Supplier factors**
Channel factors refer to issues regarding the delivery of the offer, or any part of it, to the market	Supplier factors refer to the influence of suppliers on the availability of inputs, costs of inputs, terms of sourcing and conferring sourcing advantages

Figure 3.2 Task environment area descriptions.

customers considers items such as share of customer spend, customer profitability and ROI, and potential for cross-selling to improve ROI.

After customer analysis, most managers rate competitor analysis as the next most important area of the task environment to understand. Competitor analysis has long been accepted as an important part of the strategic planning process. Competitor analysis broadly aims to help management to understand competitors' current and future strategies, relative advantages and disadvantages, and to prompt thinking about how to gain competitive advantage.

Another critical area to understand in the task environment is channels to market. Bringing products and services to market in an effective and cost efficient manner is critical to organisational success. A thorough analysis of channels to market will help identify

Competitor analysis helps managers understand competitors' strategies, relative advantages and disadvantages, and prompts thinking about how to gain competitive advantage.

channel strengths and weaknesses and prompt ideas on how to deliver more products and services, more securely or exclusively, at lower cost or more advantageous terms, to our chosen markets.

Channel analysis should make explicit the costs of using various channels and other key characteristics such as complexity, administrative effort, regulatory burden, security, risk and timeliness. Further, the analysis

Channel analysis should make explicit key characteristics such as channel costs, complexity, administrative effort, regulatory burden, security, risk, and timeliness.

should identify where value is created and where value is captured throughout the channel to market. In other words, it is useful to identify how much profit margin is being taken by each stakeholder in the channel to market and assess whether it is proportional to their role in the channel.

Channel analysis is also an opportunity to consider how to reconfigure channels and stakeholders to secure a competitive advantage. This often involves identifying strategically key channel stakeholders and reflecting on what type of relationship (e.g. alliance, partnership, joint venture, joint ownership etc.) could be developed that would build loyalty, competitive advantage and create greater economic value.

Supplier analysis is also needed to complete your understanding of the task environment. Supplier factors are a significant influence on operational viability and ability to generate profit. A starting point for supplier analysis is to be clear on who are your strategic versus commodity suppliers; what is the state of current supplier relations and what opportunities present themselves for improvement; and what

In supplier analysis, begin by identifying who are your strategic versus commodity suppliers. What is the state of current supplier relations and what opportunities are there for improvement?

potential there is for supplier consolidation and innovations in arrangements that secure a sourcing advantage.

As with the remote environment, for all of the task environment areas, it is helpful to have a checklist to help ensure that your analysis is comprehensive and that it addresses all important items. A checklist of factors to consider when assessing the task environment is given in Table 3.2.

To help test your understanding of the task environment, a set of self assessment questions is presented in Box 3.4. Under each of the major task

Table 3.2 *Task environment area factors.*

Customer factors	Competitor factors
• Customer segmentation	• Competitor identification
• Value of segments	• Emergent competitors
• Target customers	• Competitor profiles
• Customer wants and needs	• Competitor objectives
• Customer accessibility	• Competitor threats
• Share of customer	• Competitor successes and failures
• Customer migration	• Competitor strengths and weaknesses
• Customer ROI	
• Customer cross-sell potential	
• Customer acquisition	
• Customer retention	
• Customer attrition	

Channel factors	Supplier factors
• Channel strengths and weaknesses	• Strategic suppliers
• Channel options	• Supplier prioritisation
• Channel exclusivity	• Supplier selection criteria
• Channel value	• Supplier management
• Channel reconfiguration	• Supplier relationship goals
• Channel partnerships	• Supplier management indicators
• Channel partner bargaining power	• Supplier cost and contribution
• Channel substitutes	• Supplier substitutes
• Channel competitive advantage	• Supplier consolidation
	• Supplier partnerships
	• Supplier innovation

Box 3.4 Task environment self assessment questions

Customer self assessment questions

- How well do you understand the heterogeneity of customer needs?
- How well do you understand customer purchasing behaviour?
- How do customers first learn about your business?
- What leads to customers first considering your firm as a potential provider?
- Who are your target segments?
- How do we distinguish among target segments?
- What are the needs for each target segment?
- What is the value of each target segment?
- What is your prioritisation of segments?
- What is the cost of customer acquisition?
- What is the cost of customer retention?
- What is the rate of customer acquisition?
- What is the rate of customer retention?
- What is your share of customer spend?
- Who are your most profitable customer groups?
- What is the ROI for your customer segments?
- How effective are you at identifying and capitalising on cross-selling opportunities?

Competitor self assessment questions

- What are the revenues and returns for each competitor firm?
- What are business results by business division, brand, geography etc.?
- What is the competitor's cost structure?
- What is the market share of key competitors?
- How is the competitor firm organisationally structured?
- What is the management structure of the competitor?
- Who are the competitor's top management team?
- What are the strengths and weakness of the competitor's top team?
- What are the competitor's advertising messages and implications?
- What are customer attitudes to competitor firms?

- How successful are competitors at customer acquisition and retention?
- What are competitor distribution channels and associated costs?
- What new competitor products and services are likely to come to market?
- How loyal is the competitor's customer base?
- What is the nature and scale of current and announced competitor investments?
- What strategic partnerships exist and on what terms?
- What are competitor arrangements and terms with top suppliers?
- What are product and service features among the competitor group?
- How do these product features interact to provide value?
- How does your firm value offering compare to competitor offerings?
- How does your firm rate, in term of customer satisfaction, on each feature?
- What product features are superior, equivalent, or inferior compared to competitors?

Channel self assessment questions

- What are the strengths and weaknesses of existing channels?
- What are emerging or alternative channels to market?
- What is the cost of each channel to market?
- What is the revenue and net contribution associated with each channel?
- What parts of the channel to market are most vulnerable to disruption or cost increases?
- What is the potential to develop or secure exclusive channels to market?
- What impact do current and emerging technologies have on channels to market?
- What changes may occur as communications technologies further improve?
- What are current inefficiencies or bottlenecks in channels to market?
- What is the relative bargaining power of each channel stakeholder?

- What is the potential to substitute channel stakeholders or broker lower costs?
- What channels do competitors use and what is the consequence?
- What alternative channel configuration might confer competitive advantage?
- What are the needs – both met and unmet – of channel stakeholders?
- What are win-win potential ideas for your firm and channel stakeholders?
- What is the potential to consolidate channel stakeholders into fewer strategic partnerships?
- What type of relationship – alliance, partnership, joint venture, joint ownership etc. – may confer competitive advantage?
- What opportunities exist to improve relations with existing channel partners?
- What will keep channel partners loyal?
- How can channel partners be used to sell more, increase distribution and generate more revenue?
- What useful points of differentiation can be incorporated into channels to market?

Supplier self assessment questions

- Who are your strategic suppliers?
- What suppliers are key to your operations?
- What are the key input components or technology needed in your business?
- For your strategic suppliers, what are the criteria for selection (e.g. quality, speed, uniqueness, etc.)?
- What are the differences in how to manage commodity suppliers versus strategic suppliers?
- What types of relationships should be developed with various suppliers and supplier groups?
- What are your supplier management goals?
- Who is responsible for supplier strategy and supplier management?

- What type and scale of resources should be invested in supplier management?
- What are the different approaches to supplier management based on procurement value, supplier availability and supply risk?
- What buyer power does your firm have?
- What additional profitability can be realised through leveraging buyer power?
- Who are alternative suppliers?
- What substitute supplier products and services exist?
- Which category of supplies has the most potential for supplier consolidation?
- What additional tracking measures should be applied to which top suppliers?
- What is the potential to work closely with suppliers to reduce cost?
- What is the potential to establish a joint quality improvement programme?
- What types of arrangements have suppliers entered into with other firms?
- What is the potential for more proactive involvement with suppliers in areas of design, development, innovation, quality assurance and pay-for-performance standards?

environment categories – customer, competitor, channel and supplier – are listed some specific questions to consider.

Through reflecting on the above questions you will now have a sense of the extent to which you understand the task environment across the four areas labelled customer, competitor, channel and supplier. You should now reflect on the factor list in Box 3.4 and self assess the level of organisational data, information and knowledge that exists for each factor. It's worth noting that the list of factors presented is a concise list, in view of the many thousands of words published in management texts concerning what to pay attention to when analysing the business environment. Hence, if your organisational knowledge on any of the listed factors is limited then it suggests a weakness to address.

While the self assessment questions can be used just to test your own individual understanding of the task environment, it is more helpful to do this exercise as a management team and therefore assess how well the organisation as a whole understands that task environment.

For your benefit, an interactive tool to help assess your knowledge of the task environment is provided at www.stratevolve.com and www.pragmedic. com. This tool states each of the four areas of the task environment, lists out the task environment factors, sets out all of the self assessment questions listed above and provides an area where you and your top team can input your shared answers or comments. The tool will also provide a rating of your overall level of understanding of the task environment, and suggest ideas on how to build further knowledge and understanding. The tool can be completed online or it can be downloaded as an excel spreadsheet for use on your own personal computer. Any queries on the operation of the interactive tool or suggestions for enhancement can be sent to info@stratevolve.com.

Application point: How well do you understand the task environment?

Reflecting on the task environment as described above, how well do you understand customer, competitor, channel and supplier factors? Which factors will have the most significant impact in the short term on creating and capturing value?

We have now tested your understanding of both the remote and task environment. Of course, no self assessment is entirely satisfactory and you have probably identified other important factors and questions that are not covered in this self assessment exercise. Hopefully, however, the self assessment exercise has led to some useful reflections – some in direct response to the questions posed and others that are prompted by the exercise itself – on the business environment. The end result should be a sense of those areas in which you have a thorough understanding and those areas in which your understanding is weak. With these insights, we can begin to address those critical weak areas. This is a necessary but not sufficient state from which to tackle the challenge of gaining genuine market insight. In order to make effective recommendations about positive changes in your scanning behaviour, we need firstly to understand key dimensions of your scanning behaviour which we'll cover in the next section.

Scanning mechanism

Our next step toward understanding the business environment is to understand more about 'scanning mechanisms' – the key dimensions of your scanning behaviour and the consequences of that behaviour on the ability to gain market insight.

Understanding scanning behaviour requires making it explicit so it can be analysed. This was the goal in our recent research. We set out to understand and make explicit what managers actually do when they enquire into and assess the business environment.

What are the key differences among scanning behaviour?

To understand key differences among scanning behaviour, we began by reflecting on major prior studies that set out to describe scanning behaviour and then to further group or categorise scanning behaviour. In particular, we referred to *Scanning the Business Environment*, by Francis Aguilar, which, as we explained in our technical note in Box 3.2, is the most influential prior study in this area.

By explicitly describing the scanning process (in terms of what, where and how managers conduct their scanning of the business environment), Aguilar's work analysed the types of external information that managers observe and examine. An important output of this research was his suggestion that there are four alternative approaches to scanning, or 'modes' of scanning behaviour. To recap, the four modes are as follows:

- **Undirected Viewing**
  General exposure to information where the viewer has no specific purpose in mind with the possible exception of exploration.
- **Conditioned Viewing**
  Directed exposure, not involving active search, to a more or less clearly identified area of type of information.
- **Information Search**
  A relatively limited and unstructured effort to obtain specific information or information for a specific purpose.

- **Formal Search**
  A deliberate effort usually following a pre-established plan, procedure or methodology, to secure specific information or information relating to a specific view.

While this typology of scanning modes was useful to hint at ways to discern among scanning behaviour, it was never empirically validated. In other words, there was no supporting evidence to show whether managers could actually relate to these modes, nor any data showing the adoption rate of each mode. The modes were developed through a qualitative assessment process and are more akin to hypotheses about scanning behaviour than to observed managerial behaviour. A further limitation was that it relied on a single choice among just four partial descriptions of scanning behaviour.

In short, Aguilar's study provided only partial descriptions of scanning behaviour and was not corroborated through further research or testing in a practical management environment. Hence, the results of the prior study were not sufficient to discern among *Research for this book focused on dimensions of behaviour rather than separate, defined 'modes'. Analysis revealed four significant dimensions: formality, personal, completeness and breadth.* actual scanning behaviour in practice. We therefore adopted an alternative approach in our research which was to derive key scanning dimensions that underpin individual scanning behaviour, with the expectation that these could be used to discern among scanning behaviour.

The alternative approach we adopted was to create a long list of scanning behaviours, to ask managers to what extent these behaviours reflected what they did, and to analyse the results to identify significant areas of differences among the responses. The long list of different scanning behaviours was created based on prior management research and a pilot study of managers' scanning behaviour in the workplace. The final refined list comprised 44 different statements of scanning behaviour. We then asked managers to indicate to what extent each of the statements reflected their own behaviour. Based on analysing the responses, using an analytical technique of Principal Components Analysis, there emerged four components or dimensions of scanning behaviour that are particularly significant. For those interested in further details on the principal components analysis undertaken, refer to the technical note in Box 3.5.

Box 3.5 Technical note concerning principal components analysis

Principal Components Analysis ('PCA') was undertaken to identify some significant underlying dimensions or components of scanning behaviour. The output of PCA provided a means to differentiate among scanning behaviour.

In our research, PCA was applied to responses to 44 statements concerning scanning behaviour. In our survey, managers were asked to rate to what extent each of the 44 statements reflected their current behaviour on a 1 to 7 Likert Scale. Information to construct the 44 statements about scanning behaviour was gathered from a number of sources, including: prior scanning questionnaires used in management research; the outcomes of an in-depth pilot study of scanning behaviour of practising managers in actual work environments; and scanning behaviour related literature.

The 44 statements were designed to gather information on key aspects of scanning behaviour. For example, some statements about scanning behaviour that emerged through the pilot study were as follows: 'I often feel uneasy because I can't deal with the massive amounts of information I come across'; 'I tend to limit the information I'm exposed to when I feel overwhelmed'; and 'I will usually change the information mediums I use when I feel overwhelmed by the amount of information I come across'.

Further examples of statements about scanning behaviour based on prior management studies included: 'I usually seek out clearly identified types of information'; 'I usually have a formal or structured plan or process to gather the information I consider I need'; and 'I would describe my approach to scanning for key information about the environment as very systematic'.

PCA was then used to explore the scanning behaviour items on one half of the sample, and then to validate that structure on the other half of the sample. The first half of the sample comprised 197 cases randomly chosen. Prior to exploring the structure of scanning behaviour items, two tests were run to determine the suitability of the data for structure detection. The first test was the Kaiser-Meyer-Olkin Measure of Sampling Adequacy which produces a statistic that indicates the proportion of variance in the variables that might be caused by underlying factors. The second test employed was Bartlett's test of sphericity. This tests the hypothesis that the correlation matrix is an identify matrix, which would indicate that the variables are unrelated and therefore unsuitable for structure detection. The results of both tests indicated that factor analysis may be useful for structure detection.

An initial solution was then determined using the PCA method of extraction and varimax as the method of rotation of the component matrix. The initial solution identified 15 components that each had eigenvalues greater than 1. An analysis of the scree plot, which shows the percentage of variance among the variables that is explained by each individual component in the initial solution, suggested that the number of components in the final solution would likely be four components. An analysis of the rotated component matrix for the initial solution confirmed the potential to reduce the number of variables to feature in the final solution. The variables that were substantially loading on two or more components were removed, as were the single item factors. Variables with loadings less than 0.3 on all or any components were also removed as non-significant. Once these variables were removed, another solution was computed and the associated scree plot examined. It was decided that the four component solution made the most conceptual sense and accounted for a reasonable level of variance.

The labels given to the four components were: 1) formality, 2) personal, 3) completeness and 4) breadth. These components, which emerged from the first half sample analysis, were then cross validated against a second half sample. The results served to validate the four component solution identified through analysing the first half solution. Based on this cross validation exercise, there appeared to be four components that were conceptually clear and contributed to explaining a reasonable amount of variance among the variables in the final solution.

Finally, a PCA was conducted on the entire data sample of 394 cases. The components identified and the loadings almost mirrored those identified in the solutions produced, based on the first half and second half data. Based on the commonalities of the computed solution for the first half sample, the identified components were judged to be robust.

A summary of the final four significant components of scanning behaviour and a short description of their meaning is set out in Box 3.6.

For each scanning component – formality, personal, completeness and breadth – it is possible to assess your own behavioural tendencies. A self assessment exercise is set out in Table 3.3. Under each scanning component heading, we have set out illustrative representative statements of scanning behaviour. For each of the statements, consider to what extent the statement reflects your behaviour – the greater the extent of agreement with the statements, the greater your adoption of the stated behaviour.

The purpose of these self assessment questions is to point out that there are a number of important components to scanning behaviour, and it is helpful to know what these are, to gauge your behaviour against each of them. This is a first step in building your self awareness of how you scan the environment.

Box 3.6 Four major components of scanning behaviour

1. Formality

The first scanning dimension was labelled 'Formality' which implies a high degree of formality and planning with respect to scanning behaviour. This dimension reflects behaviour that involves stating upfront a set of scanning related purposes, defining the type of information to be sought that would help fulfil the stated purposes and identifying the means by which the required information will be gathered, analysed and reported.

'Formality' implies a high degree of formality and planning with respect to scanning behaviour.

2. Personal

The second scanning dimension was labelled 'Personal' and concerns the means by which information is gained or communicated. This dimension stresses the importance of personal sources and dialogue as a preferred means of both gathering information and assessing the significance of that information. Scoring

'Personal' concerns the means by which information is gained or communicated; it stresses the importance of personal sources.

high on the 'Personal' dimension suggests that you value an informal mode of communication more than a formal mode. The dimension reflects a preference to individualised, verbal and personal means of information gathering and dialogue.

3. Completeness

The third scanning dimension was labelled 'Completeness' and reflects the extent to which a manager is able to find all of the desired strategy information and, further, the extent

'Completeness' reflects the extent to which a manager finds all the desired information, and the extent to which that information is helpful.

to which received information is helpful. The main meaning of this dimension is the degree of satisfaction with the type of information acquired. The information acquired may not be sufficiently informative on matters of strategic importance or it may be missing altogether. The dimension differs in nature from the others as it is not an obviously observable behavioural trait. Instead, it reflects a state of mind – the extent to which a manager thinks that information acquired is adequate. This may in part be due to the quality of information acquired, but it may also be due to the subjective assessment of the manager regarding the adequacy of the information. In this way, this dimension is more subjective and specific to individual managers than the other dimensions.

4. Breadth

The fourth scanning dimension to emerge was 'Breadth' that essentially concerns the scope or broadness of scanning behaviour. The dimension incorporates the act of scanning broadly over time to be able to recognise important trends

'Breadth' concerns the scope of behaviour, including scanning broadly over time to recognise important trends as a cumulative effect of processing many items of information.

which may result from the cumulative effect of processing many items of information. It also captures the idea of scanning broadly through learning all that is possible about the events and trends in the environment that are strategically relevant. Scanning broadly implies embarking on a general exploration of information in the outside environment rather than gathering information specific to a particular business purpose only.

Table 3.3 *Self assessment of scanning behaviour: four key components.*

Scanning Component	Self Assessment Statement
1. Formality	I would describe my approach to scanning for key information about the environment as very systematic. I usually have a formal structured plan or process to gather the information I consider I need. I am usually very clear on what type of information I am seeking and for what purpose. I have a very fine grained screening criteria to discern which information I should pay further attention to.
2. Personal	I consider that information gained through my personal sources, versus public sources, to be the most valuable. I consider that information that is communicated informally versus formally to be the most valuable. I consider that dialogue versus one-way information is critical to assessing the significance of information.
3. Completeness	I often cannot find all the strategic information that I want. I often receive information that is not helpful to me.
4. Breadth	I don't consciously scan for information unless I have a particular business purpose in mind. I am motivated to learn all I can about the events and trends in the environment that are strategically relevant to my organisation. I think that it is important to scan broadly over time to be able to recognise important trends through the cumulative effect of processing many items of information.

For now, it is sufficient for you simply to gain a greater self awareness of how formally you scan, your preferred means of information gathering, the extent to which you think you have all the information that you need, and the breadth of factors in the environment to which you pay attention.

Self-assessment helps you gain a greater self-awareness of how formally you scan, your preferred means of information gathering, the extent to which you think you have all the information that you need, and the breadth of factors in the environment to which you pay attention.

The point here is to be aware that each of the above scanning components can be thought of as a spectrum of behaviour. For example, low ratings on the first component reflect very informal, ad hoc behaviour; and high ratings reflect a highly formal and systematic approach to scanning. So no matter where you rate yourself, there is the potential opportunity to adjust your behaviour to a different point in the spectrum. Further understanding of scanning behaviour in action will be discussed in Chapter 5, which concerns what real managers do to understand the business environment.

For your benefit, an online self assessment tool covering scanning behaviour is available at www.stratevolve.com and www.pragmedic.com. The tool states each of the above scanning behavioural statements and asks you to rate the extent to which each statement reflects your own behaviour on a scale of 1 (strongly disagree – almost never applies to me) to 7 (strongly agree – almost always applies to me). The tool will provide a numerical output reflecting your degree of scanning behaviour for each of the four scanning components – formality, personal, completeness and breadth. The tool can be completed online or it can be downloaded as an excel spreadsheet for use on your own personal computer. Any queries on the operation of the interactive tool or suggestions for enhancement can be sent to info@ stratevolve.com.

Application point: What are your distinctive scanning characteristics?

In light of the discussion on scanning behaviour, what aspects of your scanning are different from those of your managerial colleagues? How formal is your scanning? To what extent do you use personal information sources? How satisfied are you with external information obtained? How broadly do you scan?

By now you should have greater self awareness of how well you understand your business environment. The self assessment questions on the remote and task environments should provide insight as to how well you understand each significant environmental factor – political, economic, social, technological, customer, competitor, channel and supplier – and the degree of attention that you pay to different environmental sectors.

You should also have an appreciation of some key aspects of scanning behaviour, and a view on how formally you scan, your preferred means of information gathering, the extent to which you think you have all the information you need and the breadth of factors in the environment to which you pay attention.

As we said earlier, the market is increasingly complex and turbulent, and managers' self awareness of scanning behaviour is generally low. Hence, we expect that the self diagnostic will highlight gaps in your knowledge of the business environment and start you reflecting on the link between some of your scanning behaviours and gaining market insight.

With this improved self awareness, you are better placed to consider what changes you could make to improve your effectiveness at gaining market insight. Chapters 4 and 5 focus on making clear what it is that we are trying to achieve and what scanning behaviour may be most effective in different circumstances.

Powerpoints

- A sensible starting point to gain market insight is to assess your current understanding of the business environment.
- Greater self awareness of your understanding of the business environment and scanning behaviour will help determine needed changes.
- The business environment can be conceived of as the remote environment and the task environment.
- When analysing the remote environment pay attention to political, economic, social and technology factors.
- When analysing the task environment pay attention to customer, competitor, channel and supplier factors.
- There are four key dimensions of scanning behaviour that concern formality, preferred means of gathering information, the extent to which you have all the information you need, and broadness of attention.
- Greater self awareness of a) gaps in market knowledge, and b) distinguishing features of your scanning behaviour, is a prerequisite to gaining market insight.

4

What does market insight look like?

'The willing, destiny guides them, the unwilling, destiny drags them.'
Seneca

In his hugely successful self-help book, *The 7 Habits of Highly Effective People*, Stephen Covey summarises the second habit as 'Begin with the End in Mind', and urges us to form a strong picture of what we want to achieve before we even think about how we get there. This idea, although wonderfully expressed by Covey, is neither very new nor limited to the realm of personal development. The same concept was expressed by the 1st century Roman philosopher, Seneca, in the quote at the head of this chapter. It is also captured in anonymous aphorisms which are familiar to most of us, such as 'If you don't know where you're going, any road will take you there'. The idea that goals are easier to achieve if they are preconceived was also the sentiment that lay behind Louis Pasteur's most quoted saying 'Chance favours the prepared mind'. In short, if you know what you're looking for, you're more likely to find it. By the time we had completed our research into this area we had concluded that the same is true when trying to uncover market insight. So this chapter is aimed at painting a picture of market insight, not so that you will be able to copy and use that picture in your firm, but so that you will be able to recognise and use market insights that are relevant and useful in the particular context of your firm and market.

The chapter begins therefore by building on the Smith wheel, the iterative process that generates insight and value from data, which we introduced in Chapter 2, and elaborates on the sort of knowledge that is not insight, because it does not have the VRIO characteristics of an organisational strength. The following section then looks at how insight arises, emphasising the point that market insight is a precious thing precisely because it is so hard to extract from the complexity and turbulence of the market. The penultimate section presents a taxonomy of market insights, because taxonomies help us to understand, identify and differentiate different species, be they insights, flora or fauna. The chapter closes with some conclusions about what the nature of insight implies for firms wishing to become more effective at finding it.

When is an insight not an insight?

In business, hyperbole is a modern plague. To impress customers and peers, words are often used to make an impact rather than to communicate. It is easy to tire of 'mould-breaking' new business models, 'radical' concepts and, especially, 'strategic' roles. The loose use of the word 'insight' is a further manifestation of this hyperbolic disease and, to make progress, we need to be clear and to differentiate between what is real insight and what is described as insight in order to further the interests of those responsible for less insightful knowledge. At this point, it might be useful for the reader to flick back to the Smith wheel model in Chapter 2 (p. 46), and to re-appraise him- or herself with the definition of insight derived from the resource-based view of the firm.

In business, hyperbole is a modern plague.

Whatever the sales pitches of CRM companies, market researchers and data warehouses, data is not insight. It is merely one ingredient towards it. Nor is information, which is merely organised data. Only when information is contextualised and synthesised with other information does it become knowledge. Only some of that knowledge has the properties of value, rarity, inimitability and organisational usefulness that constitute true insight. Non-insightful knowledge is still

Non-insightful knowledge is still useful, often essential, in running the business; but we do need to differentiate between knowledge that is insight and that which is merely useful.

useful, often essential, in running the business; but we do need to differentiate between knowledge that is insight and that which is merely useful. To illustrate this point, consider the example of one of our case studies. This global firm synthesised information about purchase patterns and profitability to create a knowledge set about the profitability of each customer. This knowledge was useful for account managers and, at a gross level, strategic planners. However, it was only when this work was synthesised with the profitability of all other customers that an insight emerged, namely that there was a point of inflection at which customer profitability rapidly increased as a function of sales. That piece of information was an insight, in that it was valuable, rare and inimitable and the organisation was able to act on it.

As this and other cases told us, the Smith wheel involves a number of tasks, but they vary in both difficulty and value of output. By and large, the tasks of gathering data and organising it into information were, in the context of established companies with reasonably good people and systems, laborious but not difficult. Proportionately, the information that was the output of these tasks was useful but only in an 'entry stakes to the game' way, to quote one of our research respondents. More difficult was synthesising those multiple sources and types of information into knowledge, but even that seemed easily within the capabilities of the, admittedly, established and successful firms we interviewed. The point at which the tasks of the Smith wheel got beyond the reach of most firms was in the separation of insight from knowledge.

From the firms that succeeded, we learnt that the critical step towards finding insight is learning to separate routine, functional knowledge by the application of the tests of VRIO. However, a key learning for us was that this application was not simplistic, automatic or mechanical, but subtle, manual and judgemental. It is the lessons of this very human process that the next four sections try to capture.

Application point: What's your insight and what's your knowledge?

Based on the discussion above, list what you perceive to be the most important knowledge sets that your organisation has generated. Then rank them in importance, trying to differentiate between what is useful knowledge and that which might be insight.

An insight is not an insight if it is not valuable

The value test is a contentious and difficult one to apply to a piece of knowledge. Taken literally, of course, all knowledge is valuable to some degree, since it all costs money to make and much of it could be sold to someone else for some amount of money. However, we must recognise that we are trying to sort out the truly valuable wheat from the merely useful chaff. In the reality of a corporate setting, we must also realise that the value of any knowledge is in part imputed by its origins and promoted by its originator. In other words, a politically astute manager will often assert the value of the knowledge he creates or owns, independent of any objective value it may have. We observed in practice that this 'everything is valuable, especially the knowledge I own' perspective hinders the sorting process. To get around this problem of 'politically hindered winnowing', we observed that effective companies define 'valuable' in a certain way. Although these definitions varied in detail between cases and were often implicit or not articulated, there emerged from them a common definition of what valuable means in the context of market insight:

The value of any knowledge is in part imputed by its origins and promoted by its originator.

> Knowledge is valuable if it informs or enables actions that will either increase customer preference or increase the efficiency of serving the customer base. Knowledge is useful if it informs or enables the execution of existing activity

Or, in simple terms, knowledge is valuable if it enables us to change something, rather than maintain things, and that change is valuable to either the customer or to the firm.

Examples of valuable knowledge abound. For example, the telecoms industry has known for years that the cost, inconvenience and extent of travelling to business meetings has created a need for videoconferencing. It has also known that the majority of opportunities lie with large, multinational firms. Yet for years, its penetration has been limited, relative to the size of the opportunity. This is now changing, with the advent of telepresence, an advanced form of videoconferencing that creates a more realistic experience, with identical rooms, life-size screens

Knowledge is valuable if it enables us to change something, rather than maintain things, and that change is valuable to either the customer or to the firm.

and only very small delays between each transmission. New entrants like HP and Cisco as well as existing players such as Polycom and Tandberg are now penetrating this market with new products that offer a much enhanced experience, compared to traditional videoconferencing. The knowledge that made this change possible was not the quantitative data about market size, although that was useful in substantiating business cases, but the qualitative data about the videoconferencing experience. Once it was understood that non-verbal signals, sight and sound work together to make the experience realistic, it informed the development of new products.

The telepresence example is one of creating customer preference. The earlier example of the company that synthesised customer profitability information to discover an inflection point in the sales/profit curve is an example of value deriving from increased efficiency. That firm (who asked to remain anonymous) sold electrical components to many tens of thousands of customers, ranging from small development firms to huge manufacturing companies. An important part of its business model was to optimise the cost of serving this huge customer base and to maximise the profitability of each customer. Amongst the huge amount of knowledge it held about its customers, most of it was merely useful, enabling the operation of its efficient operations. From careful analysis and synthesis of this knowledge, however, emerged the knowledge that the volume/profit relationship was non-linear. Not only that, but that the point of inflection, beyond which customer profit rose exponentially with sales volume, could be calculated for different firms. It was therefore not just a single fact but a complex body of knowledge. Armed with this, the firm was able to focus its sales and customer service activity, effectively prioritising those customers where relatively little sales activity was rewarded with a moderate sales increase but a large increase in profitability. The actions that followed did not change the offer significantly and had no large effect on customer preference, but they created value for the firm by significantly increasing the efficiency of its customer facing activity. In their case, that knowledge was valuable and therefore, potentially, an insight.

Application point: How much of your knowledge is valuable?

Based on the definition above, consider the various kinds of knowledge that your organisation owns or creates. What parts of it are truly valuable and which are merely useful?

An insight is not an insight if it is not rare

If value is not always a clear cut property of some knowledge, then rarity is sometimes even harder to determine, in that it means making a judgement not only about what knowledge your organisation has, but also that which might be held by the your competitors. Knowledge is rare, in this sense, if it is a piece of knowledge that you have but that is not shared by your competitors. In practice, the rarity of some

Knowledge is rare if it is a piece knowledge that you have but that is not shared by your competitors.

piece of knowledge, or a knowledge set, sits somewhere along a continuum: the majority of knowledge is common knowledge amongst anyone who is active in the industry, a tiny amount is sometimes held by just one firm in the sector, and in between lies a small amount of knowledge that a firm may hold uniquely within its competitive set. In this last case, the knowledge is also held by other firms in the sector, but not those that form your direct competition, so that knowledge can be almost as important as a truly unique piece of knowledge.

Examples of knowledge with different degrees of rarity correspond to the frequency with which they exist. There are therefore lots of examples of knowledge that is common within the sector. Often, these relate to knowledge about the remote environment. In the music industry, for example, it is common knowledge that CD sales are tumbling and that other sources of income, such as online sales, concert revenues and merchandise are becoming much more important. Another example, although slightly more remote, comes from the life and health insurance sector of the financial services industry. Here, it is seen as inevitable that personal genetic profiling and personalised medicine, flowing from the sciences of genomics and proteomics, will radically change the industry. However, this knowledge lacks rarity, in the sense that all of the major players have it. Its commonality reduces its applicability, along with the fact that the enabling legal and regulatory context is not yet established.

At the other extreme lie knowledge sets that have often been carefully crafted and are only truly understood by the firms in which they originated. Such, at the time of writing, seems to be the basis for Tesco's planned assault on the US market. Faced with strong, entrenched competition from the world's largest retailer Wal-Mart, Tesco has chosen to adopt an indirect approach based on its understanding of shoppers' needs. Its 'Fresh and Easy' concept aims at a middle market, between Wal-Mart and wholefood stores, with relatively small stores offering convenience and quality. This strategy arose not just from analysis of commonly held knowledge about where American families shop, but rare knowledge gained partly from Tesco executives living with real families.

In between these two extremes of common knowledge and almost proprietary knowledge, lies knowledge which is not restricted in its availability, but in its applicability. An example of this lies in Luxoticca, the Italian eyeware company. Its knowledge that the sunglasses market has shifted from a functional market to a luxury market is shared amongst other eyeware companies, such as Safilo. However, the resource set needed to make use of this knowledge, to develop and manage luxury brands, is huge. At four times the size of its nearest competitor, Luxoticca has a kind of working monopoly on this knowledge.

This range of 'rareness' that knowledge can exhibit is problematic for those of us trying to understand and create market insight. Not only is rareness not 'binary' (i.e. knowledge is unique to us or not, but can be in between) it is also time dependent. The rareness of a piece of knowledge decays over time as competitors find it for themselves or it leaks out, through employee transfer or through the work of researchers and writers. Further, this time dependence is not straightforward. Rare knowledge may diffuse throughout an industry, but the ability to use it may not diffuse at the same rate. For example, few executives have not heard of Tesco's use of its club-card data, but no-one has yet emulated its application. A smaller scale but less well known example lies with Carpigiani, the Italian firm that dominates the world market for ice-cream making machines. Its knowledge of customer service requirements and product needs is observable to its competitors as soon as it is acted upon, but its applicability is somehow protected by Carpigiani's culturally-embedded ability to understand the ice-cream market.

As with value, our studies of the rarity of knowledge have helped us to define it based upon both the explicit and the tacit understanding of our case companies:

Knowledge is rare for so long as only one firm has embedded and appreciated that knowledge to a degree significantly greater than the other firms in its competitive set. Knowledge is common if it is already embedded and appreciated by firms in the same competitive set.

> *Knowledge is rare if no-one else worth worrying about has it or can use it.*

Or, in simple terms, knowledge is rare if no-one else worth worrying about has it or can use it.

Application point: How much of your knowledge is rare?

Based on the definition above, consider the various kinds of knowledge that your organisation owns or creates. Whereabouts on the rarity spectrum do these pieces of knowledge sit?

An insight is not an insight if it is easily imitable

As with value and rarity, the imitability of a piece or set of knowledge is not a simple question. In extremis, of course, all knowledge is imitable. A competitor can buy research or invest in a programme of activity to gain the

> *'Practical inimitability' means that a piece of knowledge can not be imitated within a timescale or cost that is affordable to competitors.*

same knowledge as your firm. Copying a firm's knowledge, especially tacit knowledge, can often be achieved by poaching key employees or even acquiring the firm itself. So in a literal sense, little or no knowledge is truly inimitable and so, by these tests, no knowledge can be called insight. But Barney's original description of imitability referred to the cost and time taken to copy an organisational strength and these factors provide a more realistic guide to assessing imitability. In our study of firms who had found market insights, none of the firms saw that insight as permanently unique to them. When questioned, they referred to 'practical inimitability', meaning that it could not be imitated within a timescale that mattered or for a cost that was affordable to their competitors.

An example of imitability was provided by one of our research cases, Sky, the dominant player in the UK satellite broadcasting market. Sky has, over the long-term, invested huge resources into gathering data on

24 million UK households, which is, effectively, the entire population. This data, from a vast array of sources, has been synthesised to create a knowledge set about what factors predispose a household to subscribe, upgrade and lapse. In practical terms, this knowledge has enabled Sky to target not only those households that do not have a satellite subscription, but focus on those unsubscribed homes with a propensity to subscribe. The outcome of this is that some 8 million UK homes, a third of the total, are now Sky customers. As Sky revealed in our research interview, the data they gather is accessible to other firms and their processes could be replicated by their competitors. For them to do so, however, would require such a large investment and would take so long to generate a return that it is, in effect, inimitable.

Nor are such examples limited to huge, consumer oriented companies like Sky. Rackspace, Europe's leading managed-hosting company, host the websites and internet applications of about 3000 companies. They see customer service as the main strand of their competitive advantage and, within a strong culture that can best be described as 'fanatical', gather large amounts of data about usage, customer satisfaction and aspirations. In comparison to Sky, Rackspace buy relatively little data and have data analysis systems appropriate to their smaller volume of customers. However, they invest heavily in structures and systems that gather information about the complex needs of their customers. These include quantitative methods, such as questionnaires, and qualitative methods, such as user groups. All of this effort, which is proportionately of a similar magnitude to Sky, gives Rackspace a knowledge set about the existing and future needs of their current and potential customers, details of which were revealed in the research interviews but which are commercially sensitive and have been reserved at the firm's request.

The remarkable thing about Rackspace is the passion with which this data is used and the prominence the resulting knowledge has at the highest levels of the company. As with Sky, they do nothing which is patented or otherwise protected, but in practice it would be very hard for their competitors to copy, not least because it is embedded in the Rackspace culture.

Both of these examples illustrate the idea of 'practical inimitability' spoken of by our research interviewees. From the experience of those firms, it is possible, as with value and rarity, to construct a working definition of inimitable in this context:

Knowledge is inimitable if, to recreate it, a competitive firm would need to invest resources that would not generate a positive return within the normal planning cycle of the industry. Knowledge is imitable if it can be recreated, copied or acquired by an investment that would generate a positive return within the normal planning cycle of the industry.

If knowledge can't be copied profitably in the next planning period, it is practically inimitable.

In other words, if the knowledge can't be copied profitably in the next planning period, it is practically inimitable.

This working definition not only captures the idea of practical inimitability but also recognises that it is influenced by the nature of the sector. A knowledge set that can be imitated in 3–5 years may be practically inimitable in a fast moving sector, such as fashion goods, but the same timescale may represent imitability in an industry with longer planning cycles, such as pharmaceuticals.

Application point: How much of your knowledge is inimitable?

Based on the definition above, consider the various kinds of knowledge that your organisation owns or creates. How easy would it be for a competitor to recreate that knowledge? What, if any, of your knowledge is practically inimitable?

An insight is not an insight if it is not organisationally aligned

The final criterion that market knowledge must meet if it is to be classed as an insight is that the organisation is capable of acting upon it. As with value, rarity and inimitability, there is a degree of judgement needed here. In theory, a firm could reinvent itself to act on a piece of insight. In practice, however, this is more a judgement of the firm's responsiveness in the face of the realistic constraints placed on the firm by its current situation and strategy. Of course, as with value, rarity and inimitability, it is possible to stretch this assessment. At one extreme, knowledge is only organisationally aligned if the firm can use it without any change, which is hardly ever the

In reality, only knowledge that can be acted upon with a reasonable amount of change meets the criterion of being organisationally aligned.

case. At the other extreme, some knowledge might imply major strategic change to achieve organisational alignment. Two contrasting examples make the point.

In the automotive industry, Toyota presciently understood that two remote environment trends combined to create an opportunity for them. The development of hybrid (petrol and electric) power systems and social attitudes toward 'green' issues converged to create the market opportunity into which they positioned the Prius, which has achieved an almost cult status as well as strong sales. They were, however, not alone in seeing this. In particular, German manufacturers such as Audi had an early lead in technology and most of the major players saw the opportunity to differentiate. However, various factors combined to limit the ability of these companies to use this knowledge: The advanced state of alternative strategies, such as focusing on diesel engines; the 'performance' positioning of their brands, their internal champions for alternatives such as 'start-stop' or 'mild' hybrids. As anyone who has worked at senior level in a company will recognise, the decision not to act on some market knowledge is often not because that opportunity is unappealing, but because alternative opportunities are more appealing. Whatever the specifics of the case, Toyota's organisation was more aligned to act on their knowledge about hybrid cars than its competitors were.

The second example concerns the UK grocery industry, in which Iceland has long held a specialised position as a relatively downmarket retailer of frozen foods, mostly through own label products. In the late 1990s, whilst exploring ways to grow beyond this well defined segment, it came to see that, compared to mainstream brands, its products could make strong claims regarding lack of additives and genetically modified ingredients. Under the leadership of Malcolm Walker, it therefore sought to use this knowledge by launching an 'organic only' strategy. The failure of this strategy was followed by the resignation of Walker and his Managing Director. What they had failed to appreciate was that, despite the advantages they could claim, Iceland's extant strategy, positioning, structure and resources were not aligned to use them. Their stores, brand and existing customer franchise were, arguably, the opposite of what one would choose to support an 'organic only' strategy. In plain English, the cost conscious convenience shoppers who shopped at Iceland did not care much about organic foods, and those relatively upmarket people who did want organic food would not see Iceland as their brand of choice. Hence the knowledge that an 'organic only' opportunity existed was not organisationally aligned to Iceland.

Both of these examples illustrate the idea that organisational alignment is a practically constrained construct. The degree of practical constraint is contextually variable of course. Knowledge that offers huge opportunity may justify a more radical realignment of the company than knowledge which offers a small incremental growth opportunity. Similarly, business pressures may play a part. A firm that is performing satisfactorily will have less motivation to change, in order to act on new knowledge, than a firm that is struggling. These considerations make it possible, as with value, rarity and inimitability, to construct a working definition of organisationally aligned in this context:

Knowledge is organisationally aligned if the firm can act on it within its current situation or a development of that situation that seems realistic within the foreseeable business context. Knowledge is not organisationally aligned if, in order to act on it, the firm would need to change its current strategy or structure at a cost disproportionate to the benefits of that change.

If, to act on knowledge, a firm has to change more than it thinks possible or necessary, the knowledge is not organisationally aligned.

In other words, if, in order to act on the knowledge, a firm has to change more than it thinks possible or necessary, the knowledge is not organisationally aligned.

Application point: How much of your knowledge is organisationally aligned?

Based on the definition above, consider the various kinds of knowledge that your organisation owns or creates. How easy would it be for you to act on that knowledge? What, if any, of your knowledge is organisationally aligned?

The origins of market insight

The discussion and examples in the preceding section were intended to help the reader differentiate between market insight and other knowledge, which may still be useful, by the judgemental, rather than mechanistic, application of the VRIO tests and a working definition of each term. In doing so, we hope that another feature of market insight will have become clear: True market insight, that knowledge which

The exquisiteness of market insight arises by the need to meet all four criteria at once, which is indeed rare and, ultimately, is what makes true market insight so hard to find.

meets all four VRIO criteria, is exquisite, in the old sense of that word that included a sense of rarity. This exquisiteness is the compound result of the four criteria. For a piece of knowledge to be actionable so as to create value is uncommon, as it is for knowledge to be relatively unique to the firm. Similarly, for such knowledge to be hard to copy is unusual, whilst it is quite common for a firm to be constrained in its ability to act on some knowledge. The exquisiteness of market insight arises by the need to meet all four criteria at once, which is indeed rare and, ultimately, is what makes true market insight so hard to find.

This exquisiteness of market insight begs a question, expressed best in a metaphorical discussion with a research interviewee. The interviewee made the metaphor between a piece of market insight and a rare jewel. Like a jewel, he said, insight was valuable, rare and hidden in a lot of less valuable, but useful to some, rock (his metaphor for other market knowledge). But the metaphor extends further, in that geologists who hunt for jewels do not do so in a random manner. They have learnt to look for indicative but easily identified geological features and mineral deposits that are associated with, say, diamonds, because they were formed by the same geological events. This metaphorical story led to us probing for such 'indicators' of market insight that would suggest where it might be found. There seem to be three such indicators.

Market insight is associated with market turbulence

As discussed, in Chapter 3, market contexts vary greatly in their complexity and turbulence. Even the most stable markets, however, have some degree of turbulence or change going on, even if it is only in a limited part of the task or remote environment. It is in these pockets of turbulence that market insight is often found. An example of this can be seen in the personal computer market, which by many traditional measures is now mature and stable.

Growth in this market has slowed to about half its peak rates, market share is consolidated and core product differentiation is now very small. The text book would suggest that commoditisation is the next stage in this sector's life cycle. Within this overall picture, however, home and small office users are showing important changes in their purchase drivers. With functional needs met, many are now looking to issues of design and convenience. One consequence of this is a shift from desktops to laptops, whilst another is a preference for a 'hands-on' purchase experience. By chance or design, this has favoured HP, with its range of distribution channels, but hindered Dell, with its direct model. The point, however, is that, even in a mature market such as this, a pocket of turbulence was an indicator of where some insight lies.

Market insight is associated with market complexity

Just as markets vary in turbulence, they also vary in complexity. Further, pockets of complexity form in markets that appear relatively simple markets. Coca-Cola, although hardly a simple firm, has, by absolute standards, a relatively simple range of relatively simple products with relatively simple (albeit powerful) brand propositions and a relatively simple (which is not to say easy) competitive environment. Amidst this, however, lie particularly complex aspects of the market environment in channels to market, where local bottlers make and distribute the products. It is this area where Neville Isdell, Coca-Cola's CEO, found insight. By recognising the potential in these partners (who Coca-Cola either owns or has stakes in) and allowing them to work with other firms, he has been able to address the growth in the health conscious sector.

Market insight is associated with 'soft' factors

The third, but by no means least important, indicator of where to look for insight lay in the nature of the data, information and knowledge that was used. Sometimes, as in the case of the customer-profitability inflection point example discussed earlier, or in the case of Sky, market insight does arise from the manipulation of hard, quantitative data about things that can be measured, be they sales, or physical characteristics of the customer, such as family size or income level. However, the most valuable insights we came across seem to be associated with 'soft' data that was either not amenable to number crunching or, if it was, was often not gathered initially. A strong example of this lay with one of earliest case studies, Littlewoods, a dominant player in the UK mail order market. Its target segment is low income households and, although it ostensibly sells a wide range of goods, it is in fact a competitor in the credit market, since its goods are bought through low weekly or monthly payments. In such a business, profitability arises from balancing sales growth with credit control and minimising defaulters. To achieve this, Littlewoods synthesises lots of knowledge that many firms would never consider, such as the neighbourhood of the customer, purchasing patterns and relationship with the 'principal' who acts as Littlewoods' agent. Using this, they are able to gain precious insight into which customers to target in both sales and in credit control. A further example lies in the luxury goods business, in which Patek Philippe, an independent Swiss watchmaker, competes with strong brands such as Rolex and Breitling. Despite such strong competition, Patek Philippe has been able to build a distinctive position, based on the insight that many potential customers, especially men, regard such an expensive purchase as indulgent, selfish and at odds with their family-oriented values. As a result, Patek Philippe positions itself by the strapline, and associated creative advertising, 'You never actually own a Patek Philippe, you merely look after it for the next generation'. What is remarkable about this piece of market insight is that it is based not on the number crunching of some CRM system, but qualitative insight gained from many meaningful conversations with their target customers.

Hence signs of complexity, turbulence and 'soft' factors point to where to look for market insight. Whilst these three indicators of where to look for market insight emerged unexpectedly from our research, their logic is consistent with the diamond metaphor. If diamonds were plentiful and easy to find, they would be as valuable as granite or marble. If market insight were not hidden by complexity, if it did not emerge from change and if it were always found simply by applying huge amounts of computing power to the obvious data, then every organisation would have it in abundance and it would no longer be, by our definition, market insight.

> *Signs of complexity, turbulence and 'soft' factors point to where to look for market insight.*

Considering the points made in this section, where might you look for market insight? Where is there turbulence in your market? Where is there complexity? Where might you find 'soft' factors driving the market?

A taxonomy of market insight

Although the term is thrown around loosely, we can pin down the meaning of market insight. We can also distinguish it from the concepts with which it is most frequently confused. Market insight is not the same as data, information, or market knowledge. It is a certain kind of market knowledge which we can assess to be valuable, rare, inimitable and organisationally aligned, within the practical limits described above.

Such clarity is useful and indeed necessary in understanding and creating market insight, but it is not sufficient for really effective insight creation. In order to really 'begin with the end in mind', it helps to know if all market insights look the same or if there are 'species' of market insight. If there are, and we have some idea of what these species of market insight look like, we stand a better chance of discovering them in the cluttered, swirling market environment. To stay with the zoological metaphor for a moment, zoologists categorise animals according to similarities and differences in anatomy (e.g. vertebrates have backbones, mammals have mammary glands etc.) and just such a set of defining characteristics emerged from our examination of the market insights created by the firms in our study. Although, at a very detailed level, all market insights differ from one another, three broad distinguishing features emerged.

Narrow vs. broad insight

An important differentiator between different types of market insight is the breadth of knowledge involved. That is, does the knowledge relate to a single, relatively specific and focused, feature of the market or to a broader set of trends in the market? Two very disparate examples illustrate the difference.

Royal Numico is a Dutch food company, the bulk of whose sales come from specialised foods for babies and toddlers. This is a difficult market, characterised by strong customer loyalty, making share growth difficult, and demographic decline, making market growth hard to find. Although Numico has done well in this market, the most interesting example of its market insight lies in its relatively small Clinical Nutrition division. Here, the company created insight that eluded its larger, less specialised rivals from the food sector, such as Nestlé and Heinz, and those from the pharmaceutical sector, such as Novartis. This insight was that clinical food choice was driven less by clinicians or purchasing managers, than by the patients themselves. This insight led Numico to innovations such as more convenient packaging and more concentrated food.

Compare this with the insight of MGA Entertainment, the privately held firm that chose to take on Mattel, the global giant toy company. Mattel has dominated its sector with Barbie dolls for almost 50 years, constantly renewing its appeal with minor variations to accessories and advertising of the classic Barbie design. Yet by 2005, MGA was making significant inroads into Mattel's share with Bratz, a very different looking doll; pouting, made-up and, to parents' eyes, much less wholesome. Mattel had failed to spot that Barbie was becoming a byword for uncool amongst its target segment of pre-pubescent girls. MGA's strategy was based on the market insight that little girls are very different to their peers of half a century ago. Their Bratz dolls were much more in line with the attitudes and mores of the media influenced girls of today.

Whilst both Numico and MGA gained market insight, those insights differed in breadth. Numico's was tightly defined and directly connected to one aspect of their offer to the market. MGA's was broad and far-reaching, dictating not only the design of the doll but the whole offer; market positioning, communications, packaging and merchandising. The former insight arose from a relatively simple set of data about customer needs; the latter insight arose from a synthesis of social and industry trends since the 1960s.

Market insights may not be narrow 'facts' about the market, but may also be broad views about the way the market is evolving.

The lesson to draw from this is that market insights may not only be narrow 'facts' about the market, but may also be broad views about the way the market is evolving. That is not to value one type of insight above the other (their value is a function of much more than breadth); but this lesson implies that executives must open their minds to both types of market insight.

Continuous vs. discontinuous insight

A second differentiator between types of market insight lies in their coherence with existing knowledge. That is, does the insight reinforce and extend existing knowledge and beliefs about the market, or does it open up new ideas and perspectives? Again, two contrasting examples illustrate the point.

The first is an example of continuous insight. A major house building firm, one of our case studies that chose to be anonymous, had long had the policy of allowing customers to choose from a limited range of fittings such as bathrooms, external doors and so on. In its qualitative research, however, it uncovered that the desire to 'customise' was not a minor driver of customer preference but a very significant one, sometimes outweighing factors such as location that had been thought to be more important. As a result of this, the firm both extended the customer choice and, more importantly, enhanced the customer experience of customisation, making full use of what was possible within the practical and cost constraints of this market.

The second is an example of discontinuous insight. CPF, a medium sized firm of agricultural merchants, had long supplied farmers with everything from fertiliser to hardware in a relatively low margin, price sensitive market. As a distributor with little product differentiation, it was hard put to find growth in this market. However, CPF had, for a firm of its size, a relatively sophisticated CRM system and a management team able to make good use of the information it provided. By comparing customer purchase records, an insight into market segmentation was uncovered. Not all its customers were price sensitive farmers.

The CRM data clearly revealed at least two other segments: a domestic consumer segment, who bought outdoor clothing and pet goods; and another segment, nicknamed the 'lawyer and pony' segment, who bought consumer goods as well as small quantities of agricultural goods for the smallholdings that had become their

Market insights may complement or diverge from existing thinking and lead to either the development of the existing strategy or a significant change in the choice of target customer and the offer made.

rather expensive second homes. Both of these non-farming segments offered faster growth, higher margins and greater loyalty than the traditional farmer segment. To access these segments, CPF's strategy had to change quite radically, changing stores, product range, pricing, staff recruitment and training and almost every other aspect of its offer.

The lesson to draw from these contrasting cases is that market insights may complement or diverge from existing thinking and lead to either the development of the existing strategy or a significant change in the choice of target customer and the offer made. Again, this is not to value one type of insight above the other (both can be valuable), but this lesson implies that executives not only open their minds to insights that contradict received wisdom but also welcome less radical, more incremental insights.

Transient vs. lasting insight

A third and final differentiator between types of market insight relates to their longevity. That is, how long the knowledge remains current and therefore useful, which is a function of the turbulence of the market. Turbulence and therefore transient insight is often, but not always, seen in markets in which technology is important as the following two contrasting examples illustrate.

The games console market is a fierce, three-way battle in which brand and scale are as important as technology development. Sony, Microsoft and Nintendo fight it out in this market and each round of their fight is characterised by new technologies which leapfrog their predecessors. Given this competitive intensity, market insight is extremely valuable and may dictate which of the players stays in the fight and which is relegated to an 'also ran'. In this context, Nintendo seem to have created market insight which has, surprisingly, eluded Sony and Microsoft. Whereas the latter two seem to believe that the hardcore gamers are the innovators who lead the market, Nintendo has identified non-gamers as the critical segment. From their perspective, the growth opportunity lies outside hardcore gamers and with families, women and other people who have not traditionally played console games. It is this market insight that has underpinned Nintendo's positioning of Wii, a games platform based on a motion-sensitive device.

Compare the console games example with another technology driven market. For some years in the late 1990s and early 2000s, new technology seemed on the verge of transforming education. Educational publishers, such as Thomson, have spent much time and energy trying to gain advantage from this trend but a rash of divestments reflects the fact that most attempts to tap into this huge market have been unsuccessful. Counter to this trend is Pearson who have invested huge sums developing a 'blended' value proposition that integrates educational software with assessment and lesson planning. Pearson's strategy is based on the insight that politics, demographics and technology have come together in a rare, fleeting nexus to create the opportunity for such an offer.

Market insights may reflect lasting opportunities or chances that will pass quickly.

These contrasting cases, although both reflect technological turbulence, demonstrate that market insights may reflect lasting opportunities or chances that will pass quickly. Nintendo's insight into the market looks set to change the shape of that market for a long time to come, perhaps dividing into 'hardcore' and 'fun' sub-sectors. Pearson are exploiting an insight that was not there before and will evaporate once 'blended' approaches become the norm, which appears to be happening quickly. However, as with the previous categories, the terms 'transient' and 'lasting' should not be taken as value judgements. The value of each insight is determined by many factors, not just its longevity.

These characteristics of market insight add up to a taxonomy, summarised in Figure 4.1.

Whilst the taxonomy of Figure 4.1 helps us to understand and differentiate between market insights, it is better understood with the incorporation

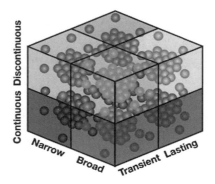

Figure 4.1 *Taxonomy of market insight.*

of two more findings of our research. Firstly, insights are not polarised between each of the three dimensions, but populate the spectrum between transience and longevity, breadth and narrowness, continuity and discontinuity. Secondly, although the three dimensions are distinct, they are not entirely independent. There appear to be weak associations between, for instance, breadth and longevity, and narrowness and continuity. In graphical terms, these two observations mean that, if all possible market insights were fitted into Figure 4.1, they would not form eight tight little clusters, one in each box. Instead, they would spread out in a manner that was neither totally even nor tightly clustered, but in which the clusters were uneven in size.

Application point: What kind of market insights might you look for?

Considering the taxonomy of market insights discussed in this section, what sort of market insights might you expect to see? Would they be transient or lasting? Broad or narrow? Continuous or discontinuous? How would you classify any insights you currently have?

The end in mind

In the first part of this book, Chapters 1 to 3, we described the importance of market insight, the difficulties that make its creation such a rare skill and shed some light on your current practice for making sense of the market environment. In this fourth chapter we have tried to create a 'picture' of what market insight looks like, the better to enable the creation of insights. What remains now is to guide the reader towards an appropriate process for doing so. We say 'appropriate' rather than 'best' way because, as the rest of this book will describe, there is no one right way. The most effective way of creating market insight is contingent on the complexity and turbulence of the market in which you operate. In the second half of this book, therefore, we describe first how managers in practice scan their business environment. We then go on to how they assess the complexity and turbulence of a market in preparation for the design and implementation of the optimal market insight creation process for any particular situation.

Powerpoints

- Market knowledge is different from data and information.
- Only market knowledge which is VRIO can be called market insight.
- Non-VRIO market knowledge is still useful.
- The VRIO tests are not clear cut, but can be defined for practical application.
- Market insight has its roots in market complexity, turbulence and soft factors.
- Market insight can be characterised along dimensions of breadth, continuity and longevity.
- Market insights cluster unevenly according to these three dimensions.

5

What do real managers do to understand the environment?

'The effort really to see and really to represent is no idle business in face of the constant force that makes for muddlement.'
What Maisie Knew, Henry James

Chapter 4 emphasised the importance of 'beginning with the end in mind' through being very clear on what environmental scanning should deliver. The key idea is that the outcome of environmental scanning

At best, scanning provides data and information which is organised and then synthesised into knowledge, of which some will be genuine insight.

should connect with and inform your strategy development efforts. At a minimum, effective scanning should identify externally originated opportunities to gain competitive advantage and it should surface threats to achieving your firm's business goals. At best, as happens in leading firms, scanning provides data and information which is organised and then synthesised into knowledge, of which some will be genuine insight.

Keeping the end outcome in mind is important, as it provides a basis for judging whether your scanning behaviour is effective. An effective scanning effort should result in an improved understanding of both the remote environment and the task environment. Although remote environmental factors are distant and not likely to impact until the medium or long-term, it is important to be aware of them as they may significantly affect the strategic performance and position of a business in the future.

While some managers shy away from analysing the remote environment because it is very difficult, others deliberately downgrade their remote environmental scanning efforts in favour of analysing the task environment. Managers often think that ana-

Managers often think that analysing the firm's organisational environment and its immediate external environment is relatively more valuable as it will provide short-term actionable insight.

lysing the firm's organisational environment and its immediate external environment – covering customers, competitors, channels and suppliers – is relatively more valuable as it will provide short term actionable insight.

As we undertook our research into market insight, it became clear that understanding what managers actually do and why was critically important for two reasons. First, it would help explain why, on average, managers' understanding of the task and remote environment is somewhat limited. Our initial research results confirmed that most managers do not understand the business environment very well, or not as well as they would like to. This insight was based on analysing hundreds of responses to assessment questions similar to those presented in Chapter 3. Second, understanding the major ways in which managers scan will allow us to identify the associated pros and cons. Now that we are clear on what environmental scanning should deliver, we can discern what is helpful to achieving market insight and what may hinder gaining this insight.

This chapter aims to provide you with a collective understanding of what real managers do to understand

Scanning is generally ad hoc, informal, and unsystematic.

the business environment. Through focusing on what real managers actually do, we will be able to distil what is good current practice, versus develop some 'ivory tower' prescriptions. We will begin by reflecting on some key observations of managerial scanning

Scanning is an embedded behaviour and hard to manage.

behaviour. The headline messages are that scanning is generally ad hoc, informal and unsystematic; scanning is an embedded behaviour and hard to manage; and scanning is typically under-resourced, unmeasured, and unrewarded. Further elaboration, anecdotes and examples supporting these observations will be provided throughout this chapter. These obser-

Scanning is typically under-resourced, unmeasured, and unrewarded.

vations suggest that many managers are in fact struggling with the task of understanding the business environment. The quote at the beginning of this chapter is meant to point out that the ability to see or to derive insight is a significant challenge in light of market complexity and turbulence and that most managers are in fact 'muddling through' as best they can. In this context, 'muddling through' refers to not adopting a considered and premeditated approach to scanning and deriving market insight.

Following on from sharing key observations, the next section in this chapter will present the results of our analysis that clusters together various managers, based on similar scanning behaviours. Based on detailed information of scanning behaviour from 394 managers, there emerged four major groups that each had distinctive scanning behaviours. These groups were named: Analysts, Categorists, Monitors and Viewers. We detail the major behavioural traits of each group, including commenting on preferred methods of gathering information, the degree of structure applied to scanning efforts, the capacity to process information and the ability to analyse and derive market insight.

The ability to see or to derive insight is a significant challenge in light of market complexity and turbulence – most managers 'muddle through' as best they can.

Finally, this chapter concludes by highlighting the importance of understanding the pros and cons of each group of managers in different market contexts with varying degrees of complexity and turbulence.

Scanning is generally ad hoc, informal and unsystematic

There is continued puzzlement about the adoption of formal systematic scanning versus ad hoc informal scanning within organisations. A complex and turbulent business environment would seem to call for the increased use of sophisticated scanning practices and systems. Yet, despite the fact that executives can put in place formal scanning practices, invest in supporting systems and

Despite investment in formal scanning practices, supporting systems and technologies to gain business environment insights, most knowledge at top levels is gained through informal personal sources.

technologies, and commit significant resources to gain business environment insights, most knowledge at top levels is gained through informal personal sources.

Numerous management studies have commented on the ad hoc nature of senior managers' scanning practices. 'Ad hoc' is a Latin phrase which means 'for this purpose' and is often used to reference a solution that has been custom designed for a specific problem and is therefore non-generalisable and cannot be adapted to other purposes. However, ad hoc is also used in another sense to mean a makeshift solution, inadequate planning or improvised events. When we use the term ad hoc with respect to scanning behaviour, we mean to imply that the behaviour is makeshift and, in the absence of guidance on what constitutes effective scanning practices, it may well prove to be inadequate to understand the business environment and gain market insight.

Our study highlighted the ad hoc nature of current scanning practices. Ad hoc scanning behaviour is characterised by an upfront lack of clarity on what data and information is being sought and why. Managers who scan in an ad hoc manner will often scan through information without having a particular business purpose in mind. An ad hoc approach is reflected in the absence of fine grained screening criteria to discern what information to pay attention to.

> *Ad hoc scanning behaviour is characterised by an upfront lack of clarity on what data and information is being sought and why.*

Another characteristic of ad hoc scanning behaviour is the use of different methods or media to obtain information. Ad hoc scanners will often switch among four major information sources: external personal networks (i.e. individuals that are outside the organisation); internet (including online search engines, websites and email news services); mass media (i.e. television, radio, newspapers, business periodicals); and internal networks (i.e. formal and informal relationships with individuals within the organisation). However, ad hoc scanners did exhibit a preference for verbal communication and dialogue, often with known individuals within internal and external personal networks, over mass media.

In short, an ad hoc approach implies a lack of formal structure, plan or process to gather information about the business environment, interpret that information and derive meaning. It also implies a general lack of managerial scanning routines or regular ways of going about understanding the environment. Ad hoc scanners are unpredictable with respect to their approach to gathering information, use of information and degree of scrutiny.

As well as highlighting the ad hoc nature of current scanning practices, our research also highlighted the related finding that current practices tend to be more informal than formal. By informal, we mean lacking in structure and without agreed actions and outcomes. An informal search for information refers to a relatively limited and unstructured effort to

A senior manager is more likely to learn of new business environment information through corridor conversations, coffee room remarks, work breaks, and social functions than through formal meetings, market analysis reports, competitor monitor summaries or trend reports.

obtain specific information or information for a specific purpose. In an informal mode, managers often use their intuition to direct attention to certain types of information or content.

A most striking finding concerned managers' strong preference and use of informal communication channels. Informal communication refers mostly to verbal communication which is often individualised. On average, a senior manager is more likely to learn of new business environment information through corridor conversations, coffee room remarks, work breaks and social functions than through formal meetings, market analysis reports, competitor monitor summaries or trend reports!

Our study captured data on the use of different information channels covering information received from superiors, peers, subordinates, company information reporting systems, external consultants, external market research professionals and external industry commentators. As well as analysing how frequently each channel was used, we also determined whether the communication was done on a formal or informal basis. Across all of the above information channels we found that the informal means of communication was statistically significantly higher than the formal means.

In particular, the highest utilised sources of information were informal meetings inside the company. This preference for internal, informal meetings indicates the heavy reliance that executives place on their personal communication networks. This reliance is understandable as personal communication with company personnel and colleagues can be a very efficient way to communicate, receive, or dialogue on business environmental matters of interest. Also, close proximity to company personnel increases the opportunities for interaction and there often develops a credibility and trust among individuals that facilitates the exchange of information. Information sourced through company personnel is additionally valuable as it has been partially processed or assessed as to its relevance and value. As information received from certain company personnel proves itself to be salient and significant, the credibility and trust assigned to that person increases. This in turn may contribute to further information exchange and increased frequency of use as a source of external business information.

So although some scanning practice elements, such as gathering information, may be informal in nature it does not mean that they are without value. Indeed, the type of information exchange described above can be very helpful to direct managers to areas of interest which may ultimately lead to insights being incorporated into strategy formulation.

By now it will come as no surprise that other management studies have come to the same conclusion we did – that current scanning practices are predominantly unsystematic. This description goes hand-in-hand with ad hoc and informal characteristics already commented upon. An unsystematic approach to scanning implies that managers do not have fine grained screening criteria to discern which information they should pay attention to, nor do they have a structured plan or process to gather the information they consider they need.

Managers who are unsystematic in their scanning efforts are likely to be motivated to scan by ad hoc personal interests, at least as much as any business goals.

We found that managers who are unsystematic in their scanning efforts are likely to be motivated to scan by ad hoc personal interests, at least as much as any business goals. The unsystematic managers we observed were not overly orientated to market events nor broad market trends; they were not orientated or interested in the external business environment for the most part.

These research findings are surprising, even puzzling. Managers in our research acknowledge the importance of scanning the environment and recognise that, when managers misin-

Our research conclusion was consistent with prior studies – scanning behaviour among senior managers is ad hoc, informal and unsystematic.

terpret changes in the environment, or fail to notice changes that turn out to be important, they may not make necessary adjustments to an organisation's strategy or structure. If analysis of the environment is critical, since environmental change may change the significance of resources to the firm, then you might expect firms to develop sophisticated environmental scanning practices and systems. Instead, our research led to a conclusion consistent with numerous prior studies – that scanning behaviour among senior managers is fundamentally ad hoc, informal and unsystematic.

Application point: Is your scanning behaviour generally ad hoc, informal and unsystematic?

Reflect on the research findings outlined above and consider the extent to which you and your firm have adopted formal systematic scanning practices versus ad hoc scanning practices. Are you clear on what data and information is being sought and why? How do you learn of developments in the business environment? What motivates you to scan?

Scanning is embedded and hard to manage

Given that current scanning practices appeared to be highly individualised and unsystematic, we were interested in what circumstances or events might significantly impact upon an individual manager's scanning behaviour. If we could identify these significant

Current scanning practices appear to be highly individualised and unsystematic, so what circumstances or events might significantly impact upon an individual manager's scanning behaviour?

influences it could provide a basis for developing some rules about how to predictably affect scanning behaviour.

A thorough review of prior managerial studies into scanning behaviour revealed that a wide range of variables had been tested for their influence on the interrelated tasks of scanning and interpretation. All told, 19 variables were identified (see Figure 5.1). These variables can be broadly grouped into four categories: individual perceptions, objective environmental characteristics, individual job characteristics and organisational characteristics. For those who are interested in the sources of these 19 variables, please refer to the note in Box 5.1.

In our research we tested for strength of associations among the four variable types – individual perceptions, objective environmental characteristics,

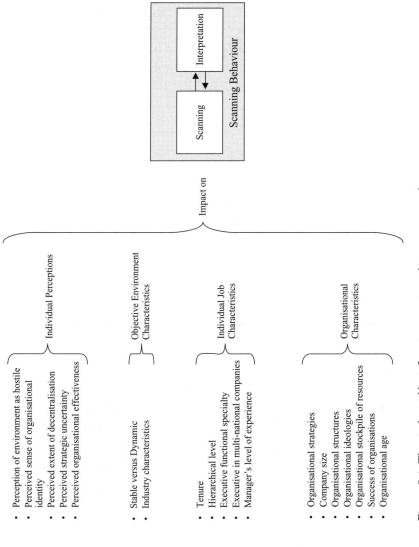

Figure 5.1 *Theorised variables influencing scanning and interpretation tasks.*

Box 5.1 Variables influencing scanning behaviour

Nineteen variables were identified, as illustrated in Figure 5.1. The source references for these variables are listed at the end of the book (pp. 305–6), cross referenced as follows:

- perception of environment as hostile;[1]
- perceived sense of organisational identity;[2]
- perceived extent of decentralisation;[2]
- perceived strategic uncertainty;[3]
- perceived organisational effectiveness;[2]
- stable versus dynamic environment;[4]
- industry characteristics;[5]
- tenure;[6]
- hierarchical level;[7]
- executive functional specialty;[8]
- executives in multinational companies;[9]
- manager's level of experience;[7]
- organisational strategies;[10]
- company size;[11]
- organisational structures;[12]
- organisational ideologies;[12]
- organisational stockpile of resources;[12]
- success of organisations;[13]
- organisational age.[11]

individual job characteristics and organisational characteristics – and scanning behaviour. Overall, a set of significant relationships did not emerge and hence the results were inconclusive, a result consistent with prior studies. Our analysis for relationships identified a set of weak associations only.

For those who are interested in the approach and statistical tests applied to test for the significance of key independent variables upon scanning behaviour, please refer to the technical note in Box 5.2. Alternatively, feel free to skip over this technical note and read on about the embedded nature of scanning behaviour.

Box 5.2 Technical note concerning testing for statistically significant influencing variables

Our approach to testing for significant statistical relationships between key influencing variables and scanning behaviour was as follows. First, we reviewed all of the management studies in which any of the 19 independent variables listed in Figure 5.1 were tested for their impact on scanning and interpretation tasks. Then we identified a subset of variables among the 19 that consistently featured in multiple studies or had demonstrated potential for a significant relationship to scanning behaviour. In other words, we identified those independent variables that had the greatest validity and reliability according to prior studies.

Specifically, the independent variables identified with relatively greater validity and reliability were company size, hierarchical level, functional roles, age (as a proxy for tenure), cross-functional experience and organisational strategy from a strategy process perspective. These were the variables that we subsequently tested for strength of relationship to scanning behaviour. In addition, we theorised that two further variables – industry affiliation and post graduate education in business and management – may significantly impact on scanning behaviour and, hence, we included these for testing.

The set of variables for further testing was then categorised into two major groups – individual experiential variables and contextual variables – for ease of analysis. Individual experiential variables included hierarchical level, functional roles, age, cross functional experience and postgraduate education in management. Contextual variables included company size, industry affiliation and organisational strategy.

Next, the concept of scanning behaviour was operationalised to enable the associations between the individual experiential and contextual variables, and scanning behaviour to be empirically tested. The concept of scanning behaviour was broken down into three sub-parts: 1) how managers gather external business information (i.e. scanning modes); 2) what external business information managers pay attention to; and 3) where managers source external business information from.

The first sub-part of the concept of scanning behaviour (i.e. how managers gather external business information) was operationalised using the four modes of scanning: undirected viewing, conditioned viewing, informal search and formal search. These modes are essentially differentiable by purposefulness of search and specificity of information sought. Refer to Chapter 3 for an elaboration on the meaning of each scanning mode.

The second sub-part of scanning behaviour (i.e. what external business information managers pay attention to) was operationalised through a typology of various environmental sectors. In our research the environmental sector typology used was more granular than in prior studies and comprised 13 sectors as follows: macro level economic information; trends within your company's industry; functional specialist information; major business leader commentaries; emerging technologies with potential to impact business; management techniques; innovation in a competing product or service; customer companies; supplier companies; joint venture or alliance partners; spending priorities of other companies; regulatory, governmental and legislative information; and competitor companies.

The third sub-part of the scanning behaviour (i.e. where managers source external business information from) was operationalised using four sources as follows: personal networks of individuals outside your company; internet sources including search engines, company websites, email information subscription services; traditional media such as television, radio, newspaper, business magazines, etc.; and company personnel such as superiors, peers and subordinates.

Statistical analysis was then undertaken to identify major associations among the independent variables and the operationalised sub-parts of scanning behaviour. The types of statistical analyses applied were chi-square tests to determine whether there was a significant effect of influencing variables on scanning mode adoption; correlation analysis of certain statements of scanning behaviour and scanning mode adoption; a one-way ANOVA to test for significant effects on the scanning attention paid to the 13 environmental sectors; post-hoc comparison tests; independent t-tests to test whether certain independent variables had a significant effect on scanning attention paid to various environmental sectors; and a one-way ANOVA to test for significant effects on the frequency of use of each of the four major sources of information.

The statistical analysis showed the following. The major influencing variables on predominant scanning mode adoption remain unclear for the most part. Based on our analysis, there did not emerge any unequivocal empirically validated influencing variables. The result is consistent with a pattern of results of similar studies dating back to the late 60s and early 70s. Further, only a limited number of significant associations between influencing variables and level of attention paid to various environmental sectors emerged. The more significant determinants of attention identified in this research, and generally supported in other studies, are functional role, hierarchy and size of company. Finally, there is insufficient evidence of any significant association between most of the independent variables tested and usage across the four information sources of personal networks, internet, traditional media and company personnel. One exception was the finding of the high use of the internet as the most frequently utilised source by senior managers and a tendency for higher use of the internet by MBA graduates.

Overall, the results of our statistical tests were inconclusive as a series of statistically significant relationships did not emerge; this result was consistent with prior studies. Weak associations only emerged between individual experiential and contextual variables and scanning modes, attention paid to environmental sectors and sources of information.

Given the lack of significant associations between influencing variables and scanning behaviour, consistent with prior studies, we reasoned that either scanning behaviour is of such a nature that it is not simply determined by the above independent variables, or

Either the nature of scanning behaviour is such that it is not simply determined, or the phenomenon of scanning behaviour has not previously been well understood and operationalised.

that the phenomenon of scanning behaviour has not been sufficiently well understood and operationalised. In either case, it suggested that our research efforts be redirected into understanding more about actual individual managerial behaviour. This was a case of taking a step backward in order to better figure out how to move forward!

The fact that the influencing variables are only weakly associated with scanning behaviour suggests that the behaviour itself is embedded. By embedded behaviour we mean individualised routines that reflect personal biases or preferences. The idea that scanning behaviour is embedded or ingrained is supported by the evidence of a large range of behaviours

The existence of highly individualised routines suggests that scanning is complex and ingrained and is not dependent on a few exogenous variables.

that we observed among managers; we observed many and varied types of scanning behaviour which suggested a high degree of individualised and idiosyncratic behaviour. We observed this individualised behaviour across many industries and across different sized firms. In all manner of different contexts, the existence of highly individualised routines suggested that scanning is sufficiently complex and ingrained to avoid being dependent on a few exogenous variables.

Our research found that individual senior managers have typically developed their own particular way of enquiring into and learning about the business environment. The more senior the managers, the more likely

A main reason why senior managers lack self awareness of scanning behaviour is that the process is so familiar it is almost taken for granted.

they are to have developed their own pattern of scanning behaviour. Once a pattern of scanning behaviour becomes embedded it is all the more difficult to make explicit and to change that behaviour. As previously mentioned, one of the main reasons for senior managers' general lack of self awareness of scanning behaviour and related activities is that the process is so familiar it is almost taken for granted! Scanning represents a basic behavioural aspect of managers' activity and it is not always done with conscious awareness. This is especially true as the behaviour becomes more routinised and embedded.

Overall, our research did lend support to the idea that individuals develop scanning routines or embedded work patterns connected with learning about events and trends in the environment outside their organisation. One major implication of this view is that developing an organisational scanning capability requires developing practices around individuals rather than assuming strategy processes will shape individual behaviour. However, to suc-

Organisational scanning capability practices need to be developed around individuals rather than assuming strategy processes will shape individual behaviour.

cessfully develop practices 'around individuals' means firstly appreciating an individual's predominant scanning mode and the environmental sectors that the individual manager pays attention to. If scanning behaviour is embedded as an established routine, then the development of scanning practices and systems should account for these established behavioural biases.

Application point: What individual scanning routines have you developed?

As our research indicates, managers tend to develop individualised scanning routines. As you reflect on your scanning behaviour, what aspects require conscientious action and what aspects are done out of habit? What aspects tend to change and what remain the same? What, if anything, causes changes in your scanning behaviour?

A valid line of research enquiry to further understand the scanning phenomenon was to undertake a more detailed analysis of the underlying scanning behaviour of managers. We attempted to identify and describe common sets of behaviour – clusters of behaviour – that were meaningfully differentiable and could fairly describe some of the major scanning behavioural characteristics of a large set of senior managers. While this set of clusters of behaviour may not necessarily illuminate new associations between influencing variables and scanning behaviour, it should help to better understand the major embedded routines and work patterns that managers adopt. The results of our cluster behaviour analysis are presented later in this chapter.

Scanning is typically under-resourced, unmeasured and unrewarded

The senior managers in our study reported that it is rare for there to be a separate budget dedicated to gathering information and generating intelligence about the business environment. While marketing heads may have separate budgets for market research, this is not the same as a budget for scanning the environment.

Instead of establishing a separate unit to analyse the environment, often this responsibility is implied to be shared among the top team and 'part of everyone's day job'.

Our study reflected that organisations don't generally maintain a separate business unit or division dedicated to analysing the external environment. Some multinational organisations do maintain a dedicated Strategy Unit that will conduct regular business environment analysis. However, this is the exception rather than the norm. Instead of establishing a separate unit to analyse the environment, most often this responsibility is implied to be shared among the top team and 'part of everyone's day job'.

Despite many advances in IT and business reporting and transaction systems, most notably major ERP (enterprise resource planning) systems, we noted a lack of dedicated systems to support business environmental information gathering and analysis.

On the whole, systems utilised by firms to understand their environment were not orientated to business environment analysis.

Some systems contributed to understanding parts of the environment, e.g. CRM systems to help understand customer attributes and behaviours, but on the whole the systems utilised by firms were not orientated to business environment analysis. Of the available technologies, senior managers identified the internet as a tool useful to learn about external events and trends and news; however its use was ad hoc, informal and unsystematic. Many managers used the internet to search for news of external events that they were personally interested in as frequently as they used it to search for information that was clearly linked to a business objective.

Consistent with this lack of resourcing to support business environment analysis, it is no surprise that the scanning practices are usually not formally documented in process maps. This further obscures the activities and outputs of business environment analy-

If scanning practices were formally documented and assessed it might help to highlight under-investment and under-resourcing in light of the strategic significance of effective scanning.

sis. A well mapped business process can be reviewed for degree of effectiveness, the value of its outputs and the cost incurred in producing those outputs. This can lead to an informed analysis of the level of resourcing that is appropriate for a process. The point is that if scanning practices were formally documented and assessed it might help to highlight the degree of under-investment and under-resourcing in light of the strategic significance of effective scanning.

Our research highlighted that there are limited internal resources directed to scanning and analysing the business environment. Rarely is there a separate budget for scanning, nor is there a dedicated business unit, system, or formalised processes. We also confirmed that there are generally limited external resources engaged to help with scanning. We did not uncover explicit arrangements with third parties to outsource aspects of external information gathering and analysis, i.e. a watch offering. Of course, there were many third parties providing broadcast external information via traditional channels, such as TV, radio, newspapers, business journals and internet news sites. However, there were very few instances of expert third parties providing tailored information and analytical services linked to specific business domains. This reinforced our view that scanning practices are generally under-invested in and under-resourced.

One explanation offered for under-resourcing of the scanning function is that there is lack of clear accountability; no one person is formally assigned with the role of 'effective scanning'. This may be because scanning is very difficult to isolate and so assign responsibility. Or, it may be that senior management have just not explicitly considered the possibility of assigning responsibility. We have seen that scanning represents a basic behavioural aspect of managers' activity and is not always done with conscious awareness. This lack of awareness may obfuscate the need to better manage this activity.

Scanning represents a basic behavioural aspect of managers' activity and is not always done with conscious awareness . . . which may obfuscate the need to better manage this activity.

Occasionally, there are circumstances when greater investment is made and resourcing put in place connected to effective scanning of the business environment. This usually happens when the Board initiates a project to formulate strategy, update the existing strategy, review the market for opportunities, or review competitor capabilities. This is helpful, but still intermittent, and therefore is inadequate as a substitute for a continuous, real-time scanning capability.

Most managers are familiar with the adage 'You can't manage what you can't measure'. They also appear to have taken this adage to heart when you consider the vast amount of management reporting that takes place in the average firm. In management, there are a myriad of common reports created, such as actual to budgeted spend, sales revenue, volume throughput, customer satisfaction etc. Yet, in our study we uncovered virtually no measures specifically associated with scanning practices and outcomes. This is not so surprising given that scanning appears to be an ill defined phenomenon, an embedded activity and largely undertaken in an informal manner. If more management teams set out to create competent scanning capabilities, perhaps as a result of digesting the findings in this book, then proper measures to help gauge process effectiveness and quality of market insight will no doubt follow.

Application point: How is your individual scanning behaviour influenced by your firm's performance management system?

As discussed above, it is usual for management teams to assume that colleagues adopt a scanning role as a matter of course. How clear is your scanning role? Are scanning activities and outcomes part of your performance evaluation? What role do performance systems play regarding scanning behaviour?

It directly follows that as scanning is ad hoc, informal and unsystematic; embedded behaviour that is hard to manage; and under-resourced and unmeasured, it is also not explicitly rewarded. Generally, specific scanning roles and outcomes are not built into senior managers' performance statements and targets. This is a conundrum as managers readily acknowledge the importance of business environmental analysis and prior management studies have shown that the role of 'information monitor' is, in practice, one of the top ten roles that managers perform.[14]

Scanning is ad hoc, informal and unsystematic, hard to manage, under-resourced and unmeasured; it follows therefore that it is also not explicitly rewarded.

At the time we conducted our research it was clear that rational expectations about how managers go about scanning the business environ- ment were just not being met. Management is not investing in building scanning capabilities; dedicated resources are not being allocated; managers are not being tasked with scanning specific goals; scanning practices are not being formalised into processes; scanning systems are not being upgraded;

Rational expectations about how managers scan the business environment were not being met.

performance targets concerning market insights are not in place; and report-ing metrics to gauge scanning effectiveness are non-existent. Clearly, what real managers do to understand the business environment is not being guided by rationally constructed management text book prescriptions! Hence, it seemed to us that we needed to get a much better understanding of what managers actually do as a starting point to understand what is driving their behaviour and to assess the implications on effective scanning.

There are four major behavioural clusters of business environment scanning

It's clear that we needed to gain a more in-depth understanding and repre-sentative view of scanning behaviour. Our initial in-depth understanding of scanning behaviour came through Phase 1 of our research, which comprised in-depth interviews with a selection of senior managers, conducted in their work environments. The purpose of Phase 1 was to better understand the phenomenon of scanning and to inform Phase 2. To recap on our research approach, refer back to Chapter 3, Box 3.1, Market Insight Research Parameters (p. 56).

Phase 1 confirmed that the subject of scanning behaviour is difficult to research because, amongst other reasons, scanning represents a basic behav-ioural aspect of a manager's activity and is not always done with conscious awareness.[15] This was evidenced by one research subject who stated:

> I can't articulate how I scan, or what is salient. A lot of stuff isn't salient, but I've never been that sort of person that I'll only go for the stuff that is directly related to my job . . .

Thus, part of our research challenge was to help senior managers articulate and make explicit their scanning behaviour so we could begin to analyse it. Phase 1 was useful to identify the areas of scanning behaviour that needed articulation. For example, the pilot study highlighted the need to better understand which parts of the environment managers pay attention to. An analysis of the pilot study transcripts identified a list of 13 environmental sectors that managers pay attention to as follows: trends within your firm's industry; functional specialist information; competitor companies; customer companies; macro level economic information; regulatory, governmental and legislative information; major business leader commentaries; emerging technologies with potential to impact business; innovation in a competing product or service; joint venture of alliance partners; supplier companies; management techniques; and spending priorities of other companies. This information was factored into Phase 2, the survey research.

Phase 1 also identified information overload as an important issue affecting scanning behaviour. This was unexpected as it hadn't featured as a finding in prior studies. Different managers employed different tactics to manage information overload, such as not delving into too much detail on a particular subject until it had come to their attention multiple times. Another tactic was to network with knowledgeable people rather than seeking to acquire knowledge first hand. Hence, we developed specific statements concerning information overload and incorporated these into the broad based scanning survey. Examples of statements concerning information overload included: 'I think information overload is a greater issue now than two years ago'; 'I think the capacity of an individual manager to absorb information via scanning falls far short of the volume of information available and is a limiting factor to effective scanning'; 'I often feel uneasy because I can't deal with the massive amounts of information I come across'; 'I tend to limit the information I'm exposed to when I feel overwhelmed'; and 'I will usually change the information media I use when I feel overwhelmed by the amount of information I come across'.

Managers employed different tactics to manage information overload, such as not delving into too much detail until a subject had come to their attention multiple times.

The internet offered a high degree of credibility because of the ability to access multiple online information sources and then to cross-reference or triangulate them.

Researching current scanning behaviour highlighted the high use and reliance on the internet as an information source. The internet was often described as useful firstly to detect items of interest and secondly to 'drill down' into the information. Interestingly, a high degree of credibility was associated with the internet because of the ability to access multiple online sources of information and then to cross-reference or triangulate information sources. Hence, consideration of the role of technology on scanning behaviour was factored into the survey. In the survey, specific questions were developed that related to the frequency of receipt of information from internet sources including search engines, company websites and email information subscription services, compared to personal networks of individuals outside the firm, traditional media such as television, radio, newspaper and business magazines and company personnel.

Another interesting finding of the pilot study concerned the frequency of scanning activity. Participants in the pilot study indicated a wide range of frequencies of scanning covering daily, weekly, monthly, a few times a year or less than once a year; although we observed in our study that most managers undertake scanning very frequently – usually daily or at least weekly. As the frequency of scanning could distinguish managers' scanning behaviour, we incorporated some related questions into our scanning survey.

Other aspects of scanning behaviour that were identified in the pilot study and were elaborated into a set of questions for input into the survey included: the extent to which managers networked; drive to acquire knowledge and learn; salience of information from a personal and business perspective; capacity to absorb information; interpretative ability; congruence with work role; available time; deliberateness of search; degree of formality of approach; and specificity of information sought.

Again, the purpose of the pilot study was to understand in-depth managers' scanning behaviour as a first step to distinguish different behaviours that could help to develop a set of scanning profiles. The focus groups provided qualitative information on scanning behaviour that was in-depth and indicative of the range of behaviours. However, this qualitative information was not sufficient as a valid representation of the behaviour across the population of senior managers. To achieve a statistically valid representation of all senior managers' scanning behaviour required a quantitative approach using a survey to obtain data that could be statistically analysed and whose results could be extrapolated in accordance with sound statistical principles.

Therefore, we created a survey that included a section specifically concerning scanning behaviour from the perspective of an individual senior manager. This section of the survey comprised a set of statements, expressed in the first person, that covered a wide range of scanning behaviours. Against each of the statements we attached a 7 point Likert scale for respondents to identify to what extent the statement reflected their own individual behaviour. A score of 1 indicated 'strongly disagree' and a score of 7 indicated 'strongly agree'. In our survey we set out 44 statements of scanning behaviour for respondents to assess and rate themselves. For those who are interested, these statements are listed in Box 5.3.

Next, we analysed the results of responses to the 44 statements about scanning behaviour. More specifically, we did an exploratory analysis to

---

Box 5.3 Survey statements concerning scanning behaviour

Scanning Behaviour

Respondents were asked to indicate the extent to which they agreed with the following statements from (1) 'strongly disagree' to (7) 'strongly agree'.

1 I usually seek out clearly identified types of information.
2 I am usually very clear on what type of information I am seeking and for what purpose.
3 I use many and varied sources of information.
4 I have very fine grained screening criteria to discern which information I should pay further attention to.
5 I am typically able to individually assess the significance of certain information I am exposed to.
6 I think that effective scanning of the environment should be very broad (e.g. industry, general economic, political and social level analysis) and adopt a medium to long-term outlook.
7 I usually have a formal structured plan or process to gather the information I consider I need.
8 I would describe my approach to scanning for key information about the environment as very systematic.
9 I consider that information gained through my personal sources, versus public sources, to be the most valuable.
10 I consider information that is communicated informally, versus formally, to be the most valuable.
11 I consider that information needs to be received almost immediately for it to be valuable.
12 I consider information received verbally to be more valuable than in printed form.

13   I consider that dialogue, versus one-way information, is critical to assessing the significance of information.

14   I substantially change the type of information I pay attention to in different circumstances.

15   I substantially change the way I gather information according to different circumstances.

16   I have changed the way I gather information because of the internet.

17   I think information overload is a greater issue now than two years ago.

18   I could scan (i.e. gather relevant information in the business environment) more effectively.

19   I usually seek out information that is primarily relevant to strategic decisions as opposed to operational decisions.

20   I tend to scan broadly for information, mindful that any piece of information could bear on a strategic problem.

21   I usually seek out information that helps me to solve complex problems requiring innovative solutions, versus routine solutions that relate to recurrent problems.

22   I discern information that is strategic – useful for considering how to ensure competitiveness – from non strategic information.

23   I often can not find all the strategic information that I want.

24   I often receive information that is not helpful to me.

25   I believe that individual scanning is more effective when organisations provide support resources (e.g. systems, etc.).

26   I think that effective scanning – securing relevant information – is a largely individual and intuitive activity.

27   I think effective scanning of the environment should be focused on the local market and adopt a short term to medium term outlook.

28   I think that scanning for relevant strategic information in the environment will always be an incomplete and imperfect process, for the environment is too extensive and complex to be completely analysable.

29   I think the capacity of an individual manager to absorb information via scanning falls short of the volume of information available and is a limiting factor to effective scanning.

30 I spend much more of my time attuned to internal information concerning my organisation's level of effectiveness than to external information.

31 I trust broadcast media information received directly from external sources more than I trust information from company personnel.

32 I often feel uneasy because I can't deal with the massive amounts of information I come across.

33 I don't think data or information by itself is important unless it is relevant to some particular purpose.

34 I don't consciously scan for information unless I have a particular business purpose in mind.

35 I tend to limit the information I'm exposed to when I feel overwhelmed.

36 I think that it is important to scan broadly over time to be able to recognise important trends through the cumulative effect of processing many items of information.

37 I scan not only for information relevant to my job and organisation, but also for my personal interests.

38 I will usually change the information media I use when I feel overwhelmed by the amount of information I come across.

39 I am not really able to assess the significance of new information on subjects that I'm not familiar with.

40 I do not have much available time to scan for relevant external information given my job responsibilities.

41 I am now expressly rewarded or penalised based on my scanning behaviour.

42 I am motivated to learn all I can about events and trends in the environment that are strategically relevant to my organisation.

43 I am very aware that the information I receive from outside the organisation may be distorted both unintentionally and deliberately.

44 I have developed a routine whereby I focus on a few familiar sources that meet my information needs.

detect groups of managers that exhibited similar scanning behaviour. The outcome was the identification of four 'clusters' of managers that exhibited similar behaviour within their clusters.

For those interested in the approach and statistical tests to identify 'clusters' of managers who had similar scanning behaviours, please refer to the technical note in Box 5.4. Otherwise, feel free to skip over this technical

---

Box 5.4 Technical note concerning cluster analysis of scanning behaviour

In our research, we were interested in doing an exploratory analysis to detect potential groups of managers that exhibited similar scanning behaviour and thereby elicit a typology of scanning behaviour. The data upon which we conducted our analysis comprised responses from 394 managers, who each indicated the extent to which they agreed with 44 statements of scanning behaviour from 1 (strongly disagree) to 7 (strongly agree). The 44 statements are set out in Box 5.3 above.

The statistical technique chosen to explore this data was cluster analysis, a multivariate procedure for detecting case groupings in data. Both the hierarchical cluster analysis and the k-means cluster analysis were considered. The k-means cluster analysis method begins by using the values of the first k cases in the data as temporary estimates of the k cluster means, where k is the number of clusters specified by the user. Initial cluster centres are formed by assigning each case in turn to the cluster with the closest centre and then updating the centre. Then, an iterative process is used to find the final cluster centres. At each step, cases are grouped into the cluster with the closest centres, and the cluster centres are recomputed. This process continues until no further changes occur in the centres or until a maximum number of iterations is reached. The k-means method is particularly well suited to situations where there is a sound basis for estimating the likely number of meaningful clusters that will emerge from the data analysis. In this research, there was a theoretical and empirical basis for estimating that the likely number of meaningful clusters to emerge would be four, based on prior management studies.

A further reason for preferring the k-means cluster analysis over the hierarchical cluster analysis was that it handles large problems (greater than 200 cases) more easily.

Our analysis began by transforming all scores on all 44 statements or variables into Z scores where each variable has a mean of 0 and a standard deviation of 1. This was helpful to analyse and interpret the results. By providing the distance from each case to its cluster centre, k-means clustering characterises whether or not a case is too close to the others within its cluster or is an outlier. The size of the F statistic in a k-means one-way ANOVA is useful for identifying variables that drive the clustering and those that differ little across the clusters.

Final cluster centres were determined when the k-means cluster analysis was run assuming the four clusters would emerge. Cluster centres report the means of the standardised variables for each cluster. The means for each cluster determine the cluster centre. Distances between the final cluster centres were also calculated. In addition an ANOVA calculation was done. For each standardised variable, a one-way analysis of variance using the final clusters as groups was done. The ratio of the between-cluster mean square and the within-cluster mean square is the usual ANOVA F statistic. The range of ANOVA F statistical results was as follows. The mean of responses to the statement 'I would describe my approach to scanning for key information about the environment as systematic' differed the most ($F = 55.372$). In comparison, the means of responses to the statement 'I trust broadcast media information received directly from external sources more than I trust information from company personnel' differed the least ($F = 1.570$).

The final number of cases in each of the four clusters was as follows: Cluster 1 contained 50 cases; cluster 2 – 88 cases; cluster 3 – 100 cases; and cluster 4 – 66 cases. As each cluster contains a substantial number of cases, this lends some support that four clusters is a defendable outcome. (The missing 90 cases are accounted for by a case being excluded if one or more responses to the 44 statements was not valid.)

For purposes of comparison, analyses were also attempted using different cluster values of six, five, three and two to identify the appropriate cluster value. When a k-means cluster analysis was run for six clusters, the number of cases in clusters five and six were very low at 1 and 13. A k-means cluster analysis for five clusters attracted just two cases into the additional cluster. The outcome of a k-means cluster for three clusters, and then two clusters, proved difficult to meaningfully interpret. Therefore, it seemed likely that the most reasonable and defendable number of discernibly meaningful clusters was four.

An exercise was then undertaken to analyse the final cluster centre, the more significant ANOVA results, and the profile of the individual survey respondents within each cluster. This analysis enabled a descriptive profile of each cluster of scanning behaviour as set out in the next section of this chapter.

note and read on for a description of each of the four major clusters of behaviours.

Based on the cluster analysis, there emerged four distinct clusters or groups of managers that reported similar scanning behaviour within clusters. These four clusters were labelled Analyst, *Four 'clusters' of managers exhibiting similar behaviour to each other were identified and labelled Analyst, Categorist, Monitor and Viewer.*

Categorist, Monitor and Viewer. A qualitative description of each cluster is provided below.

Analyst

An 'Analyst', for the purposes of this research and with respect to scanning behaviour, refers to a manager who is deliberate in his or her scanning efforts, systematic and structured in terms of approach to gathering and interpreting information and has higher than average ability to process significant levels of information and effectively interpret that information.

Analysts are quite deliberate in their efforts to obtain certain types of information. They usually have well developed views on the type of information or information topics which are important and therefore worth paying attention to. If they do not have clearly articulated information topics to attend to, then they will often have clear criteria to help them discern which information they should pay attention to.

A strong characteristic of an Analyst is the adoption of a systematic and structured approach to gathering and interpreting information. These types of managers are usually deliberate in their efforts to obtain information using established and formalised methods and approaches, often drawing upon specialist resources or tasking resources with specialist tasks. Gathering the targeted information is usually done in a structured way through executing a structured search in accordance with an explicit plan, which may or may not be documented.

More so than other managers, Analysts report that they are regularly presented with or come across large volumes of information. Further, they are personally comfortable with dealing with large volumes of information and are generally confident in their ability to assess the significance of such information and derive meaning and insight.

Analysts exhibit other characteristics, including varied use of information media and a sense that the vast majority of information received is helpful. They have confidence in their ability to assess the significance of information on subjects with which they are not familiar and a sense of

Analysts are systematic, rational, business objective orientated, information hungry problem solvers, capable of processing information and confident of their capability to interpret data.

coherence between gathering and interpreting information in the external business environment and their job roles and responsibilities. They understand that information can be important even though it's not immediately recognised as relevant to a specific business purpose. They consider that the business environment can be effectively scanned and analysed and believe that effective scanning should cover both the task and remote environment and not just focus on local market short term events and trends. Their personal self assessment is that they are scanning the business environment effectively, successfully managing the threat of information overload. They attempt to orientate themselves as much to external information as to internal information concerning a firm's effectiveness and make relatively high use of the internet such as search engines, and email information subscription services over alternative sources of company personnel and traditional media. Their view is that they are ultimately rewarded or penalised based on their effectiveness at scanning the business environment.

In short, Analysts are systematic, rational, business objective orientated, information hungry, deterministic and knowledgeable about business management techniques. They are problem solvers, capable information processors and confident and capable in data interpretation.

Application point: To what extent does your scanning profile match that of an Analyst?

Reflecting on the above description, consider how closely your scanning behaviour matches that of an Analyst. How deliberate are your scanning efforts? How systematic and structured is your approach to gathering and interpreting information? Do you have above average abilities to process significant volumes of information and effectively interpret information you gather?

Categorist

A 'Categorist' refers to a type of manager who is also very systematic in his or her approach to scanning for key business environment information. Unlike the Analyst, however, a Categorist is sceptical about his or her ability to absorb and effectively interpret significant volumes of business environment information, and conservative about his or her ability to derive genuine market insight.

Categorists are, in fact, the most systematic in their scanning efforts among all the managers. They are deliberate in their efforts and accordingly have very fine grained screening criteria to discern which information they should pay attention to. This translates to having in place a structured process, that is often documented, to achieve scanning and market insight goals.

A strong distinguishing characteristic of Categorists is their scepticism about their ability to absorb and effectively interpret significant volumes of business environment information. Categorists think that the capacity of an individual manager to absorb information via scanning falls far short of the volume of available information and is a definite limiting factor to effective scanning. Linked to a view about the lack of capacity to absorb large volumes of information is a high sense of unease when dealing with large volumes of information. Categorists admit that the information they acquire is not necessarily 'absorbed' or 'processed'. In fact, Categorists will limit the information they are exposed to when they feel overwhelmed.

Categorists are conservative about their ability to effectively interpret business environment information and derive insight. They acknowledge that they find it difficult to assess the significance of new information on subjects with which they are not familiar. Categorists report that they often receive information that is not helpful to them, while acknowledging that they are not very confident in their assessment of helpfulness! Part of their discomfort in dealing with large volumes of information is their view that information overload is increasingly becoming a significant issue.

A somewhat subtle and yet important point concerns Categorists' areas of confidence. They do claim confidence in being able to systematically scan the environment and identify significant and relevant topics of information or headlines items. However, their confidence wanes when it comes to effectively absorbing and interpreting the information they have gathered.

Other characteristics of Categorists include their deliberate use of many and varied information sources, changing the means of gathering information as required to suit the circumstances. They also hold the view that information needs to be received almost immediately for it to be valuable and tend not to scan for information unless they have a particular business purpose in mind since they consider data or information by itself to be unimportant unless it is recognised as relevant to some particular purpose. They acknowledge that they could be more effective in assessing the business environment although they do have an ability to discern information topics that are strategic or otherwise important. The Categorist's view is that it is important to scan broadly over time to identify recurrent themes and hence important topics, acknowledging that deriving business environment insight will always be an

Categorists are formal in their information gathering efforts, well organised, mindful of business objectives, and capable researchers and information synthesisers.

incomplete and imperfect process, for the environment is too extensive and complex to be completely analysable.

In brief, Categorists are formal in their information gathering efforts, well organised, mindful of business objectives and capable researchers and information synthesisers.

Application point: To what extent does your scanning profile match that of a Categorist?

Reflecting on the above description, consider how closely your scanning behaviour matches that of a Categorist. How systematic is your approach to scanning? How sceptical are you about the ability to effectively interpret significant volumes of information about the business environment? Are you conservative about claims to derive genuine market insight?

Monitor

A 'Monitor' refers to a type of manager who is moderately systematic but will generally not develop and adhere to a formal business environment scanning process. A Monitor does not have fine grained screening criteria but will pay attention to information items that are brought to their attention using a few trusted information sources.

Monitors are only moderately systematic in their scanning practices. They are unlikely to be following a formal business scanning process and are less likely again to be following a formally documented process. However, they are likely to develop established ways or routines regarding inquiring into the business environment. As they are likely to adopt established patterns of behaviour we can justify describing them as 'moderately systematic' in their approach.

Related to being moderately systematic in their scanning practices, Monitors will usually not possess or be able to articulate fine grained screening criteria to discern what information to pay attention to. Instead, they will notice items that come to their attention through exercising their established routines.

Part of a Monitor's established routine is the use of a few trusted sources of information. Monitors report a high degree of unease in dealing with large amounts of information they may come across. Perhaps as a tactic to try and restrict exposure to too much information, Monitors use fewer and less varied sources of information than other managers.

Other characteristics of Monitors include claims that they have limited skills only in assessing the strategic significance of information and their view that they rarely receive information that is not helpful (which may be due to use of a few trusted information sources). Their perception is that there is only limited time available that can be used for external scanning given other job role requirements. They tend not to favour the internet and online sources over other sources, exhibiting

Monitors have rigid but clear scanning practices, investing enough effort to obtain sufficient information to identify major changes, but limiting scanning if information becomes overwhelming.

a lack of change to the way they gather information in different circumstances. They consider their current scanning behaviour to be effective and, perhaps as a result, are generally reluctant to change their scanning behaviour. Monitors have a tendency to scan for information that is relevant to their job and firm as opposed to personal interests, in particular, with the view that effective scanning should be focused on the local market and adopt a short term to medium term outlook.

In short, Monitors are likely to be rigid in their scanning practices; be reasonably clear on what information seems helpful and how it links to business purpose; limit scanning if information becomes overwhelming; and invest enough effort to obtain a simplified view of the local environment sufficient to identify major changes.

Application point: To what extent does your scanning profile match that of a Monitor?

Reflecting on the above description, consider how closely your scanning behaviour matches that of a Monitor. Are you moderately systematic in your approach to scanning? Do you avoid adhering to a formal scanning process? Do you lack fine grained screening criteria? Do you use a few trusted information sources?

Viewer

A 'Viewer' refers to a type of manager who approaches scanning the business environment in an ad hoc manner but who is uncertain about his or her ability to process large volumes of information and assess significant information. Viewers tend to spend more of their time attuned to internal information concerning the organisation's level of effectiveness than to external information.

Viewers' approach to scanning for key information about the environment is the least systematic of all types of managers. Consistent with an ad hoc approach to scanning, Viewers do not have a structured process to gather the information they think they need, nor do they have established criteria to discern what information they need in the first place.

The clear opinion expressed by Viewers is that their capacity to absorb information via scanning falls far short of the volume of information available and is a limiting factor to effective scanning. Moreover, Viewers consider that they are typically not able to assess the strategic significance of information they are exposed to. The profile of Viewers' scanning behaviour that begins to emerge is a somewhat hapless state of scanning!

Viewers report that they spend more time attuned to internal information concerning internal matters, such as an organisation's effectiveness or efficiency, than to external information. When they do cast an eye out to the external environment, albeit intermittently, they may use all and any selection of many and varied sources.

Other characteristics of Viewers are their adoption of the internet as a useful source of information and their tendency to change their scanning behaviour in different circumstances. Viewers also consider that scanning activities are likely to be discrete events and to differ from prior efforts. They do not insist that information needs to be immediately current to be valuable and may intermittently scan for information with no particular business purpose in mind since they consider that data or information by itself can be important even though it is not recognised as relevant to some particular purpose. Viewers recognise that they could scan more effectively and consider that scanning for relevant strategic information in the business environment will always be an incomplete and imperfect process. Unlike Analysts, their perception is that there is a lack of reward or penalty associated with their scanning behaviour.

In brief, Viewers are very unsystematic scanners; not attuned to the significance of information; commit limited time and effort to scanning; are mostly inwardly focused; and generally lack clarity about what to scan and how to use the results to progress achieving business purposes.

Viewers are unsystematic scanners, not attuned to the significance of information and generally lacking clarity about what to scan and how to use the results.

Application point: To what extent does your scanning profile match that of a Viewer?

Reflecting on the above description, consider how closely your scanning behaviour matches that of a Viewer. Is your approach to scanning mostly ad hoc? Are you uncertain about your ability to process significant volumes of information and assess significance? Do you spend more of your time attuned to internal information concerning organisational effectiveness than to external information?

Each of these groups – Analysts, Categorists, Monitors and Viewers – have distinctive and differentiable behavioural traits in terms of preferred methods of gathering information; degree of structure applied to scanning efforts; capacity to process information; and ability to analyse and derive market insight. This typology of scanning behaviour (i.e. the systematic classification of the types of scanning behaviour according to their common characteristics) is very useful to further understand the major scanning behavioural characteristics across the senior manager population.

Analysts, Categorists, Monitors and Viewers each have distinctive behavioural traits in terms of information gathering methods, structure in scanning efforts and capacity and ability to analyse information and derive market insight.

The next logical question that follows is: how effective are each of these groups in scanning the business environment and deriving market insight? Furthermore, how effective are organisations that utilise different mixes of Analysts, Categorists, Monitors and Viewers to scan the business environment? We can begin to answer these questions by considering the pros and cons of the scanning behaviour of each group on achieving desired scanning outcomes.

However, before we consider the advantages and disadvantages of the scanning behaviour of each of our four groups, let's reflect on market context. This is important as we're aware that market context will impact on the effectiveness of different types of scanning behaviour. We're also aware that understanding the market is very difficult because of market complexity and market turbulence in general, as elaborated upon in Chapter 2. So how can we assess the different levels of market turbulence and market complexity? What are the different levels of turbulence and complexity to appreciate?

What is the general effect of different levels and combinations of turbulence and complexity on effective scanning? These are the questions that are addressed in Chapter 6. The content in Chapter 6 will allow us to be much clearer in describing various market contexts and thereby offer a more refined contextual analysis of effective scanning practices.

Once we have developed a framework for representing different market contexts, we will return to the question of how different market contexts impact on effective scanning behaviour in general. We will also specifically consider the pros and cons of the scanning behaviour of Analysts, Categorists, Monitors and Viewers in different market contexts. These market contextual assessments and implications will be considered in detail in Chapter 7. But before we can do this, we need to develop a framework for different market contexts. Hence, the next chapter is concerned with how to assess market complexity and market turbulence.

Powerpoints

- Understanding how managers scan is a necessary first step to identify how to improve scanning effectiveness.
- Actual managerial scanning behaviour is largely ad hoc, informal and unsystematic.
- Scanning practices and process are generally under-resourced and unmeasured.
- Managers develop their own scanning behaviour which becomes routinised and embedded over time.
- There are four groups of managerial scanning behaviour – Analysts, Categorists, Monitors and Viewers.
- These four groups differ in terms of preferred means of gathering information, degree of structure applied to scanning efforts, capacity to process information and ability to analyse and derive market insight.
- The effectiveness of each type of scanning behaviour will vary by market context.

6

Understanding and assessing the complexity and turbulence of a market

'There is an objective reality out there, but we view it through the spectacles of our beliefs, attitudes and values.'
David G. Myers

In Chapter 5, we reviewed our research into how real-world managers make sense of their environment, scanning it in different ways to collect the data that they then organise into information. The various classes of information are then synthesised into knowledge. Some, but by no means all, of that knowledge is valuable, rare, hard to copy and capable of use by the organisation, such that it can be called market insight. The key lesson of Chapter 5, however, is that there is no single, optimal, way of scanning the business environment. Managers and firms differ in how systematically and how widely they scan, trading off time and other costs against the benefits that their approach gives them. Although scanning behaviour varies widely, it does not vary uniformly and, when their behaviour is measured and placed on a chart, managers can be seen to cluster into groups that share similar scanning behaviours. Importantly, none of these clusters of scanning behaviour can be said to be 'better' or more effective than another in any absolute sense. What we observe is a contingent model, in which some scanning behaviours work better in one situation than in another. In other words, what works is what fits.

Significantly, the effectiveness of any one scanning behaviour is not a function of the sector or organisation size per se. Rather, different scanning behaviours cope better or less well

What works is what fits the complexity and turbulence of the market, not what fits with the label attached to the sector.

with different levels of market complexity and market turbulence. So, not only is it a case of what works is what fits, but what works is what fits the complexity and turbulence of the market, not what fits with the label attached to the sector.

In short, a manager seeking to understand his or her market environment cannot simply look for 'best practice' or copy from an apparently successful role model. Instead they must begin by making an objective assessment of how complex and how turbulent the market is in which they operate, and select the approach to scanning that best fits those conditions. To do this well, however, that manager has to overcome the 'beliefs, values and attitudes' that the social psychologist David Myers alluded to in the quote that heads this chapter. The harsh fact is, as many management researchers have found, that practising managers have strong biases in how they perceive the world, biases that distort reality. These vary, but in the case of assessing market complexity and market turbulence, a clear pattern arises. Generally speaking, the majority of managers perceive their market to be rather more complex than it really is, whilst a minority see it as being rather more simple than in fact it is. Very few managers manage to accurately assess the complexity of their market. A similar but not identical pattern emerges with respect to market turbulence. Most managers overestimate the turbulence of their market and a minority underestimate. It is extremely rare for managers to accurately assess either the complexity or turbulence of a market in which they are closely involved. This lack of objective judgement seems to be the result of the very closeness to the market that is both necessary to and an inevitable outcome of doing their day-to-day job. Put simply, when you are so close to a market that you observe every detail and every change, it inevitably seems complex and turbulent. As one executive put it during a workshop:

> We're like microbes on a marble slab. What seems smooth to an outsider seems very rough to us.

It is to this problem of objectivity that this chapter speaks. It untangles what we mean by complexity and turbulence, then suggests ways to assess each in an objective, evidence based way. No assessment can ever be completely objective or accurate, of course, but this approach, developed out of work with very many firms, provides a practical, approximate solution to a problem that is not completely solvable.

What is a market?

The first step in understanding and assessing the complexity and turbulence of a market is to understand what we mean by market. 'The market' is what academics call a 'complex construct'. What this wonderfully arcane

The market is a 'complex construct' and, to understand it, we need to dismantle and measure it along multiple dimensions.

and typically academic phrase means is that a market is not made up of one factor that can be measured along one dimension. Rather, a complex construct is one that is made up of multiple sub-constructs and, to understand it, we need to dismantle that aggregation and measure it along multiple dimensions.

A simple construct would be something like market value or market volume. These can be characterised by one or two simple and agreed dimensions, such as currency units or units of sale. By contrast, we can't accurately measure the complexity or turbulence of a market by one or two simple units, because it has many dimensions. If it helps your understanding, think of a simple construct as a cube of wood (which can be characterised by width, height and length) whilst a complex construct is more like a tree. The three dimensions begin to describe the tree, but only in a simplistic way.

It follows therefore that, if the market is a complex construct, then both market complexity and market turbulence must also be. Our challenge is to improve on subjective judgement of those in the market in a practical but non-simplistic way.

The concepts we have explored in earlier chapters help here by dividing 'the market' into its component parts. In addition, observing what it is that managers, in practice, gather data about when they scan also helps. In the following sections, both market complexity and market turbulence are examined and understood as the aggregate of several component complexities and turbulences.

Understanding market complexity

By observing what types of complexity managers find they need to pay attention to, we can see that market complexity has five primary components:

1. customer complexity;
2. channel complexity;
3. competitor complexity ;
4. remote environment complexity;
5. value proposition complexity.

These five subcomponents have still further levels of detail, as summarised in Table 6.1 and Figure 6.1. It is worth spending a moment considering the table and figure before reading the next section, which describes market complexity in more detail.

Customer complexity

Customer complexity is that component of market complexity that exists in any market in which the customers are not identical to each other or do not make simple decisions on their own. Hence, all real markets have at least some degree of customer complexity, made up of three contributing factors: segment complexity, decision making unit complexity and buying process complexity.

Segment complexity

Segment complexity arises when customers are not all identical, that is, the market is heterogeneous. In some markets, especially niches for luxury goods or in some highly specialised technical products or services, the differences between customers are small and insignificant. In most markets, however, customers fall into a small number of segments which represent a moderate level of market complexity. In some large markets, especially mature ones such as food retailing, for example, there are many distinct segments (as a rule of thumb, more than ten is many), contributing to a high level of market complexity. It is important to note here that we are referring to real segments and therefore differences in customers' needs, motivation and behaviour. We do not mean segment in the sense of a classification or categorisation

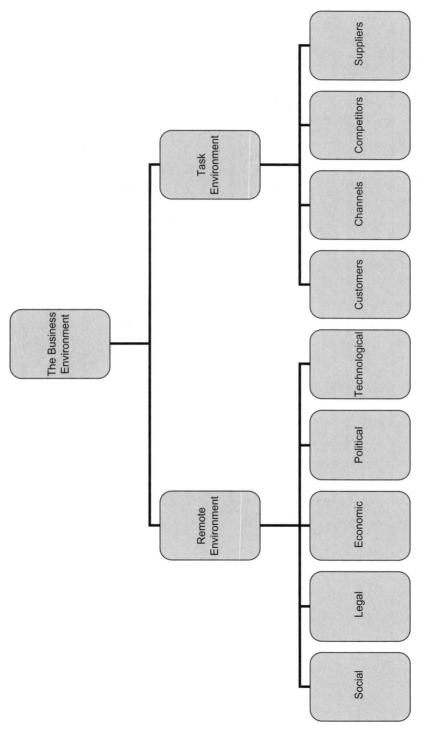

Figure 6.1 *Components of market complexity.*

Table 6.1 *The nature and implications of market complexity.*

Subcomponent of market complexity	Complexity factors	Typically observed implications of failing to cope with this aspect of market complexity
Task environment – Customer complexity	Segment complexity: the number of substantially different market segments.	Failure to differentiate between the needs of distinct segments; conflation of the needs of distinct segments.
	Decision making unit complexity: the number of significant contributors to the decision making unit.	Failure to identify and address adequately all the significant contributors to the decision making process or to allow for their needs in the value proposition.
	Buying process complexity: the length and number of distinct stages in the buying process.	Failure to identify and address adequately all the stages of the decision making process with subsequent failure of selling process.
Task environment – Channel complexity	Channel type complexity: the number of different types of channel to market.	Failure to identify and address adequately the needs of the channels to market, leading to a failure to understand their needs or the interactions between channels.
	Channel length complexity: the number of different tiers in the channel to market.	Failure to identify and address adequately one or more levels within the channel to market, leading to a failure to understand the needs or value adding activity of each level.
	Channel value complexity: the extent to which the channel to market adds to the value proposition.	Failure to understand and address adequately the way in which the channel to market adds or destroys value.
Task environment – Competitor complexity	Competitive force complexity: the number of different competitive forces significant in the market.	Failure to identify and address adequately the implications of indirect threats, especially new or emergent competitive forces.
	Industry rivalry complexity: the number of different strategic sets into which direct competitors may be classified.	Failure to identify and address adequately the implications of direct competition, especially from outside the firm's competitive set.

Remote environment complexity	Social complexity: the extent to which sociological factors have significant impact on the market.	Failure to identify and address adequately the implications of social factors, especially the combined implications of multiple social and other factors.
	Legal complexity: the extent to which legal factors have significant impact on the market.	Failure to identify and address adequately the implications of legal factors, especially the combined implications of multiple legal and other factors.
	Economic complexity: the extent to which macro-economic factors have significant impact on the market.	Failure to identify and address adequately the implications of economic factors, especially the combined implications of multiple economic and other factors.
	Political complexity: the extent to which political factors have significant impact on the market.	Failure to identify and address adequately the implications of political factors, especially the combined implications of multiple political and other factors.
	Technological complexity: the extent to which technological factors have significant impact on the market.	Failure to identify and address adequately the implications of technological factors, especially the combined implications of multiple technological and other factors and technological factors outside of the firm's core technology environment.
Value proposition complexity	Range complexity: the number of different product components offered to the market.	Failure to understand and address adequately the value added or destroyed by different components of the value proposition.
	Technical complexity: the technological complexity inherent in developing, supplying and selling the value proposition.	Failure to understand and address adequately the implications of technology in the development, delivery and communication of the value proposition.
	Extended product complexity: the extent to which the value proposition extends beyond the core product into higher benefits.	Failure to understand and address adequately the value added or destroyed by the non-core parts of the value proposition.

of customer description, which is what *The implications of failing to*
passes for segmentation in some com-   *understand segment complexity*
panies. There is not necessarily a cor- *can be fundamental.*
relation between market complexity
and a wide variety of customer descriptors (size, age, industry category, etc.).
Some 'commodity' products, such as paper towels in washrooms, go to lots
of different types of customers but with very little segmentation in the
market. The implications of failing to understand segment complexity can
be fundamental. A scanning behaviour that does not cope with it (i.e.
understand the differences between customers within a market) is unlikely
to create insight or value propositions that are sufficiently segment specific.
Even if it does, appropriate targeting of effort is very difficult without understanding the complexity of segmentation within a market.

Decision making unit complexity

Decision making unit complexity is that component of market complexity
that exists in any market in which individual customers do not make the
buying decision alone. In industrial, technical and business to business
markets, the decision is almost always made by a group rather than an individual. Even in consumer markets though, the complex interplay of friends
and family influences apparently solo choices. Those readers with children
will be familiar with 'pester power' and the parent–child decision making
unit. Between the extremes of the spectrum, there are many levels of decision making unit complexity. A scanning process that does not cope with
decision making unit complexity is unlikely to address all the needs of the
market. In this case, the complexity of customers' needs increases in proportion to the complexity of the decision making unit and contributes to overall
market complexity.

Buying process complexity

Buying process complexity is that component of market complexity that
exists in any market where the purchase decision is not instant and standalone. Hence, anything but the most impulse of impulse buys has some level
of buying process complexity and most markets have significant amounts of
it. It is important to remember, of course, that the buying process does not
always end with purchase. In many markets, the buying process continues

in the form of affirmation of decision and continuing contact between sup-plier and customer. At the extreme of buying process complexity are major capital purchase decisions such as cars and houses for consumers and plant,

The complexity of customers' needs increases in proportion to the complexity of the decision making unit and contributes to overall market complexity.

equipment and service outsourcing for businesses. Again, there are innumer-able levels between the extremes of, say, a chocolate bar and a power station. A scanning behaviour that does not cope with buying process complexity may gather data about only one part of the buying process and fail to appre-ciate important features of the rest of the process. Any business to business marketer who has been perplexed by an apparently keen user who is 'not allowed' to buy what he or she wants has fallen victim to the complexities of the buying process.

Application point: What are the main sources of complexity in your customer environment?

Bearing in mind the discussion in this section, what do you see as being the main sources of complexity in the customer environment? Is it segment complexity, decision making unit complexity, buying process complexity or some combination of the three?

Channel complexity

Channel complexity is that component of market complexity that exists in any market in which the product or service does not go directly from the supplier to the customer via one single route with little or no addition of value. Some markets are very simple in this respect whilst others are hid-eously complex. Channel complexity is the aggregate of three aspects of channel intricacy: channel type complexity, channel length complexity and channel value complexity.

Channel type complexity

Channel type complexity arises when the market is addressed by more than one channel. At the simplest extreme, for instance, a management consul-tancy delivers its value directly to its customers and through only that direct channel. Its near competitor, a business school, by comparison, might deliver its value directly, via overseas partners or via distance learning. Each different channel adds a level of complexity through its different requirements.

Each different channel adds a level of complexity through its different requirements.

Failure to address that complexity adequately may result in a failure to grasp important implications for the business. Typically, firms whose scanning process doesn't cope with channel type complexity fail to deliver value because of absent or sub-optimal use of channels. Good examples of this are 'clicks and bricks' operations that combine online and 'real' outlets. The habit of some customer segments to browse online whilst still wanting to purchase from a real store makes each channel complementary rather than conflicting, an important piece of knowledge in this market that, if not common to all competitors, may be a useful insight.

Channel length complexity

Channel length complexity arises when multiple levels exist in the channel to market. A manufacturer of agricultural chemicals might use a logistics firm to move products physically from the factory to localised specialised distributors. This distributor

Levels of channel complexity can exist in several different channels at once and contribute to overall market complexity through the different demands of each tier.

may then deliver the herbicide to the farmer. The wholesale chain in FMCG markets is another example. Levels of channel complexity, which can exist in several different channels at once, contribute to overall market complexity through the different demands of each tier. A scanning behaviour that fails to cope with channel length complexity may, typically, miss important aspects of how the channel is adding or destroying value, especially at the interfaces between channel levels. This is seen, for example, in markets where large numbers of different products are involved, such as book sellers and automotive parts. Here, a distributor 'leanness' strategy can conflict with a retailer's strategy of availability superiority, destroying value.

Channel value complexity

Channel value complexity arises when the value proposition is partly created by the chain, as opposed to entirely by the manufacturer (or equivalent). In practice, almost all channels add some value but the extent of this varies greatly. In simple commodity markets, the value adding role of the channel is limited to little more than physical logistics and perhaps breaking down or bundling product. More valuable channels add support, service and other forms of knowledge. The most valuable chains, for example some value adding resellers (VARs) of IT systems, design and manage the business process into which the product or service fits. A scanning behaviour that does not cope with this complexity may fail to see value being destroyed or created in this way. An example of this was provided by David Lloyd, a UK chain of health and fitness clubs. They failed to grasp that much of the value in this market was created by the personal relationships between the staff and the regular customers. As a result, and in an attempt to increase staffing efficiency, they changed their employees' contracts to make them 'multi-task'. So, for instance, fitness instructors would double up serving coffee. The resultant loss of valued staff forced David Lloyd to make a near complete reversal of this policy.

The more that channels add value, the more the activity involved in making this happen creates channel value complexity. This aggregates with the channel type and channel level complexities into overall channel complexity and thence market complexity. A scanning behaviour that does not cope with channel value complexity will often fail to deliver the value proposition to a greater or lesser extent.

Application point: What are the main sources of complexity in your channel environment?

Bearing in mind the discussion in this section, what do you see as being the main sources of complexity in the channel environment? Is it the types of channel, the levels of the channels or the way in which they add value?

Competitor complexity

Competitor complexity is that component of market complexity that exists in any market in which more than one competitive force or direct competitor exists. As with the other components of market complexity, a broad spectrum of competitor complexity exists across different markets.

Competitor complexity is the aggregate of two parts: competitive force complexity and industry rivalry complexity.

Competitive force complexity

Competitive force complexity arises when competitive pressure comes from more than one direction (e.g. from suppliers, new entrants, substitutes etc.). Rarely does the only significant competitive pressure come from the industry rivalry of direct competition.

Failure to comprehend the significance of competitive force complexity leads to competitive disadvantage, normally as the result of being 'blindsided' to new threats.

More usually, competitive pressures come from two or more of: industry rivalry, substitutes, new entrants, buyer pressure and supplier pressure. Rarely, the entire gamut of competitive forces impacts significantly on the market. Again, small or embryonic niches tend to be at the simpler end of the spectrum whilst larger and more mature markets are usually more competitively complex. Failure to comprehend the significance of competitive force complexity naturally leads to competitive disadvantage, normally as the result of being 'blindsided' to new threats.

Industry rivalry complexity

Industry rivalry complexity arises when direct competitors exist in more than one strategic set. That is, they compete via more than one strategy. In the simplest case, all of the direct competitors differ in detail but compete on the same basis, for instance on product performance. The most common scenario is of moderate levels of industry rivalry complexity, in which there are two strategic sets. An example of this is prescription pharmaceuticals, where the only two significant strategic sets are research-based ethicals and cost-based generics. Rarely, there are three or four strategic sets, each consisting of competitors focusing on one of: price, performance, service, distribution density or other forms of competitive advantage. The market for lifestyle magazines is an example of industry rivalry complexity, with multiple different strategic sets each based around a different basis of competition. In these cases, the more strategic sets there are, the greater the industry rivalry complexity. This contributes to competitor complexity and thence to overall market complexity. Failure to appreciate the complexity of industry rivalry is manifested by overly simple responses to competitive activities, which address only one but not all of the strategic sets.

Application point: What are the main sources of complexity in your competitive environment?

Bearing in mind the discussion in this section, what do you see as being the main sources of complexity in the competitive environment? Does the complexity come from multiple types of competitive force or from different strategic sets within industry rivalry?

Remote environment complexity

Remote environment complexity is that component of market complexity that arises from the remote, rather than the task, environment. That is, the factors in the market place that *The imperceptibility of remote environmental changes can mask the importance of their bearing on the market.* impact less directly on the market than competitors and customers, such as social trends and technological development. That is not to say that this less direct impact is less important. Like global warming or demographic change, the imperceptibility of remote environmental changes can mask the importance of their bearing on the market. All markets are to some degree complicated by remote environmental forces but, again, markets range from the simple to the complex in this respect. Remote environmental complexity can be thought of as the aggregate of five subcomponents: social, legal, economic, political or technological complexity.

Social complexity

Social complexity arises when social factors influence the market. Examples of this might be tangible, such as changes in demographics, or harder to discern, such as the decline in deference to authority commonly observed in westernised societies. An interesting current example of social complexity is the housing market in many countries, influenced as it is by both demographics, the growing number of single adult households and changing expectations about independence and even personal wealth management. The more such social factors impact on the market, the greater is the level of social complexity that contributes to remote environment complexity.

Legal complexity

Legal complexity arises when legal factors influence the market. Examples of this might be direct, such as industry regulation in financial services, or indirect, such as the harmonisation of duty on alcoholic drinks which has affected 'duty free' markets at ports and airports. The more such legal factors impact on the market, the greater is the level of legal complexity that contributes to remote environment complexity.

Economic complexity

Economic complexity arises when macro-economic factors influence the market. Again, these influences can be direct, such as when recession impacts on the purchase of discretionary purchases such as holidays, or indirect as when oil prices make alternative energy more or less competitive. In the latter case, this impacts indirectly but strongly on, for instance, the makers of composite materials for wind turbines. The more such economic factors impact on the market, the greater is the level of economic complexity that contributes to remote environment complexity.

Political complexity

Political complexity arises when political forces influence the market. Examples of this are most common in sectors such as transport, health, education and defence, in which public spending has a more direct impact than in other sectors. Similarly, the impact of political attitudes towards trading agreements or 'trade and aid' arrangements. For instance, the market for water treatment infrastructure projects is heavily influenced by political factors around aid to developing countries. The more such political factors impact on the market, the greater is the level of political complexity that contributes to remote environment complexity.

Technological complexity

Technological complexity arises when the development and application of new technologies has an impact on the market. Although nowadays 'technology' is used as a loose synonym for information and communications technology (ICT), technological complexity actually has broader origins. It can arise from ICT enabled factors, such as the emergence of e-tendering in some commoditised markets like packaging, or the ability of customers to compare propositions on the web, as is common in consumer financial services. More widespread, though, is the complicating impact of new technologies that relate to the market directly. One single technological development by Du Pont, namely Lycra (or Spandex), impacted hugely on the clothing market, especially in casual clothing sectors. Similarly, the development of genomics and proteomics is currently enabling the development of 'personalised medicine', which will, in time, change the face of the market for medical diagnostics and treatment. The more such technological factors impact on the market, the greater is the level of technological complexity that contributes to remote environment complexity.

Application point: What are the main sources of complexity in your remote environment?

Bearing in mind the discussion in this section, what do you see as being the main sources of complexity in the customer environment? Is it social, legal, economic, political, technological or some combination of these?

Value proposition complexity

Value proposition complexity is that component of market complexity that exists in any market when the value proposition is more than a simple and unelaborated commodity. Almost all markets, even those superficially commoditised, have some level of value proposition complexity. As with the other components of market complexity, a broad spectrum of value proposition complexity exists across different

Almost all markets, even those superficially commoditised, have some level of value proposition complexity.

markets and it is, in this case, the aggregate of three parts: range complexity, technical complexity and extended product complexity.

Range complexity

Range complexity arises when the value proposition requires the provision of multiple component products or services. It can exist in both product markets (for instance, companies which supply the car parts market) and in the service sector (for instance, in contract research organisations which must offer a wide range of technical services). Range complexity is, therefore, simplistically correlated to the thickness of the catalogue, but the relation is more sophisticated than

Holding a thousand types of screw does not contribute to range complexity to the same degree as providing even a few different types of pathology services.

this, as multiple products are grouped into fewer basic types. Holding a thousand types of screw does not contribute to range complexity to the same degree as providing even a few different types of pathology services. Product range adds to value proposition complexity by making it necessary to achieve proposition coherence across the range, always a difficult thing in practice. From the point of view of scanning behaviour, range complexity adds to difficulty by making it necessary to gather data and insight about a wider range of customer segments and their needs.

Technical complexity

Technical complexity arises from the technology inherent in developing, supplying and selling the value proposition. Even the simplest markets (breakfast cornflakes, for example) are rarely as technically simple as they seem, but there is clearly a wide gap in technology between those and, say, some IT, complex financial derivatives or other technically complex markets. It is important to note here that technical complexity is not synonymous with scientific technology. Many legal, financial and other service markets are technically complex even without much of what we traditionally think of as technology. The application of advanced mathematics in financial derivatives is as much a technology as the application of advanced electronics by engineers. Technical complexity increases the number of factors that might be relevant or valuable to the scanning process. It is often coincidentally related to decision making unit complexity, as 'technical' propositions are generally bought by units, not individuals. Failure to grasp the technical complexity of the market, often seen when new entrants make mistakes in entering a technically complex market, hinders the formulation of a compelling value proposition. From the point of view of scanning behaviour, technical complexity adds to difficulty by making it necessary to gather data and insight about a wider range of technical developments.

Extended product complexity

Extended product complexity arises when the value proposition extends beyond the core product or service. The least complex value propositions (again, usually commodities) offer benefits derived only from the functionality of the product. More common, and more complex, are the value propositions that offer additional benefits associated with service. The convenience of a local store is an example of this moderately extended value proposition. The highest levels of extended product complexity arise when the value proposition appeals to functional, service and emotional needs. Examples of this are those service or product/service combinations that rely heavily on relationships either with individuals (for instance, an advertising agency account handler) or with a brand. Failure of the scanning process to understand extended product complexity leads to simplistic and incomplete value propositions. In everyday experience, the restaurant which excels in every way but for its surly staff is an example of an incomplete value proposition. From the point of view of scanning behaviour, extended product complexity adds to difficulty by making it necessary to gather data and insight about a wider range of customer needs and how well the value proposition and its competitors are meeting them.

Market complexity is therefore a very complex construct indeed. To form an objective judgement of our own position on the simple-to-complex

We need to understand that market complexity is multi-factorial.

market spectrum, we need to understand that it is multi-factorial. As outlined above, our research identified five components and sixteen subcomponents that aggregate to form overall market complexity. Often, but not always, we can make some generalisations. Market complexity is associated with market maturity, business to business, technical and large markets. Simpler conditions are more likely to apply in embryonic and growth markets, smaller niches, impulsive consumer markets and those which do not depend on technology. However, these generalisations are not strong enough for us to make good guesses. In practice, each market must be assessed for complexity in a systematic manner. That is the goal of the following section.

Application point: What are the main sources of complexity in your market?

Bearing in mind the discussion in this section, what do you see as being the main sources of complexity in your market? Is it the remote environment, the task environment or a combination? Which components of the market contribute most to complexity in your case?

A process for evaluating market complexity

In simple terms, evaluating market complexity is no more than the aggregation of the complexity implied by the five contributing factors of customers, channel, competition, remote environment and value proposition. However, we need to be cautious about simplistic approaches. The consequences of over- or underestimating the complexities of the market are serious, since they lead to inappropriate design of scanning processes. Our research observations were that it was common to either underestimate market complexity or to overstate it, and rare to assess it accurately. In cases of underestimation, companies stick with less rigorous and less systematic scanning behaviours, which are not up to the task of extracting data and thence insight from the market environment. Overestimating market complexity can also be catastrophic to insight creation. It leads companies to over-engineer their scanning and planning process and to get bogged down in bureaucracy. In both cases, the resultant understanding of the market is weak and so, inevitably, is their resultant strategy.

Our research observations were that it was common to either underestimate market complexity or to overstate it, and rare to assess it accurately.

To evaluate market complexity in a more sophisticated way requires the incorporation of two further findings from our research. Firstly, almost all markets exhibit tangible characteristics, such as the number of competitors or channels, which can be used to create a graduated complexity scale for each of the five subcomponents. Secondly, these five subcomponents do not all contribute equally to market complexity, so that simply adding up the complexity due to each doesn't give a true picture. These two findings imply that the accurate, objective assessment of market complexity involves two stages: quantifying the components of market complexity and then calculating a weighted aggregate, as opposed to a simple average, of those values.

Quantifying the components of market complexity

In short, quantifying the components of market complexity involves estimating where our market sits along each of five scales. Each scale represents one of the five market complex-

Quantifying market complexity involves estimating where the market sits along each of five scales.

ity factors described above and runs from simple to complex. To do this, however, means assessing the level of market complexity arising from each subcomponent. Table 6.1 (see p. 148 at the beginning of this chapter) summarised these components and subcomponents. Table 6.2 uses our research findings to create an assessment scale for them. In Table 6.2, each level of complexity is described in general terms not restricted to any market. Hence by looking along the description, one can estimate a level of market complexity for each subcomponent. The average of these subcomponent estimates forms the basis of estimating the complexity due to each of the five factors. This may seem a disproportionately long winded way of assessing market complexity, but it has two significant merits when compared to less comprehensive approaches. Firstly, it ensures that all factors are considered. The sheer number of factors contributing to market complexity can easily overwhelm a simpler approach, which leads to the relative neglect of key factors and hence a false judgement of market complexity. Secondly, breaking down the estimate into, effectively, 16 smaller estimates that are then aggregated has the effect of reducing errors. This is because errors in each of the 16 judgements tend to be made in both directions and therefore combine to cancel each other out.

Table 6.2 *Graduated scales of market complexity.*

Subcomponent of market complexity	Complexity factors	Simple (1)	Moderately simple (2)	Median complexity (3)	Moderately complex (4)	Complex (5)
Customer complexity	Segment complexity: The number of substantially different market segments	There is only one significant, real segment in the market	There are two or three substantially different segments in the market	There are four to six substantially different segments in the market	There are six to ten substantially different segments in the market	There are more than ten substantially different segments in the market
	Decision making unit complexity: the number of significant contributors to the decision making unit	The decision making unit consists of only one person with little external influence	The decision making unit is one person but with significant influence from one or two other people	The decision making unit consists of two or three people, each with direct influence on the decision	The decision making unit consists of three to five people, each with direct influence on the decision	The decision making unit consists of more than five people, each with direct influence on the decision
	Buying process complexity: the length and number of distinct stages in the buying process	The buying process is near instantaneous with no discernable stages	The buying process is of significant duration but in only one discernable stage	The buying process is protracted but not formalised and has one or two discernable stages	The buying process is protracted but not formalised and has three or more discernable stages	The buying process is both formalised and protracted with three or more discernable stages

Channel complexity					
Channel type complexity: the number of different types of channel to market	There is only one significant channel to market	There are two or three significant channels to market, but one is much more dominant than the others	There are two or three significant channels to market. They are all of significant importance, but they differ from each other in only minor ways	There are two or three significant channels to market. They are all of significant importance and they differ from each other in significant respects	There are four or more channels to market, each of which differs significantly from the others and each carries significant volume
Channel length complexity: the number of different tiers in the channel to market	There are no tiers in the channel to market; it is entirely direct	There is only one tier in the channel to market and that channel only accounts for a small proportion of the business	There is only one tier in the channel to market and that channel accounts for a large proportion of business	There are two or three tiers in the channels to market but one channel is dominant	There are two or more tiers in the channels to market and those channels are all significant to the business
Channel value complexity: the extent to which the channel to market adds to the value proposition	The channels to market add no value other than physical distribution	The channels to market provide physical distribution and some minor value such as stockholding and order processing	The channels to market provide selection and usage advice as well as stockholding and order processing	The channels to market tailor the product significantly as well as providing other value	The channels to market incorporate your value proposition into a broader offer

Table 6.2 (*Continued*)

Subcomponent of market complexity	Complexity factors	Simple (1)	Moderately simple (2)	Median complexity (3)	Moderately complex (4)	Complex (5)
Competitor complexity	Competitive force complexity: the number of different competitive forces significant in the market	Only one competitive force (usually industry rivalry) is significant in the market	There are two or three competitive forces acting on the market, but one is much more significant than the others	There are two significant competitive forces acting on the market	There are three or more competitive forces acting on the market but two are dominant	Four or five competitive forces impact significantly on the market
	Industry rivalry complexity: the number of different strategic sets into which direct competitors may be classified	There is only one significant competitor and they occupy the same strategic set as yourselves	There is only one significant competitor and they occupy a different strategic set to yourselves	There are two strategic sets each containing two or more competitors	There are three or more strategic sets but each containing only one competitor	There are three or more strategic sets each containing two or more competitors
Remote environment complexity	Social complexity: the number of different social factors which impact significantly on the market	The market is largely immune to social factors	The market is only susceptible to one or two tangible social factors such as population size and structure	The market is susceptible to a number of tangible social factors	The market is susceptible to a number of either tangible or intangible social factors, such as fashion and attitudes, but not both	The market is susceptible to multiple social forces both tangible and intangible

Legal complexity: the number of different legal factors which impact significantly on the market	The market is largely immune to legal and regulatory factors other than the basic legal structure	The market is influenced to a small extent by legal and regulatory factors from a single authority	The market is influenced to a significant extent by legal and regulatory factors from a single authority	The market is influenced to a significant extent by legal and regulatory factors from a single authority and to a minor extent by other authorities	The market is heavily influenced by the legal and regulatory frameworks of multiple authorities
Economic complexity: the number of different macroeconomic factors which impact significantly on the market	The market is largely immune to macroeconomic factors	The market is influenced to a small extent by macroeconomic factors but only in a single economic entity, such as a nation state or trading bloc	The market is influenced to a significant extent by macroeconomic factors from a single economic entity	The market is influenced to a significant extent by macroeconomic factors from a single authority and to a minor extent by other economic entities	The market is heavily influenced by the macroeconomic factors of multiple economic entities
Political complexity: the number of different political factors which impact significantly on the market	The market is largely immune to political factors	The market is influenced to a small extent by political factors but only in a single political entity, such as a nation state or trading bloc	The market is influenced to a significant extent by political factors from a single political entity	The market is influenced to a significant extent by political factors from a political entity and to a minor extent by other political entities	The market is heavily influenced by the political factors of multiple political entities

Table 6.2 (*Continued*)

Subcomponent of market complexity	Complexity factors	Simple (1)	Moderately simple (2)	Median complexity (3)	Moderately complex (4)	Complex (5)
	Technological complexity: the number of different technological factors which impact significantly on the market	The market is largely immune to both ICT related and industry specific technological developments	The market is influenced to a small extent by either ICT related or industry specific technological developments	The market is influenced to a significant extent by either ICT related or industry specific technological developments, but not both	The market is influenced to a significant extent by either ICT related or industry specific technological developments and to a lesser extent by the other	The market is influenced to a significant extent by both ICT related and industry specific technological developments
Value proposition complexity	Range complexity: the number of different product components offered to the market	The product or service range consists of a single product or service or has only minor variants	The product or service range consists of a small number of products or services with similar or complementary applications	The product or service range consists of a large number of products or services with similar or complementary applications	The product or service range consists of a small number of products or services with dissimilar or unrelated applications	The product or service range consists of a large number of products or services with dissimilar or unrelated applications

Technical complexity: the technological complexity inherent in developing, supplying and selling the value proposition	The value proposition is not technologically complex at any stage of the value chain	The value proposition has elements of technological complexity in some, but not all, stages of the value chain	The value proposition has elements of technological complexity in all stages of the value chain	The value proposition has significant technological complexity in some stages of the value chain and some in other stages	The value proposition has significant technological complexity in all or most stages of the value chain
Extended product complexity: the extent to which the value proposition extends beyond the core product into higher benefits	The value proposition is entirely or mostly built around the core product or service	The value proposition is entirely or mostly built around the core product or service, but with minor contributions from the extended product or service	The value proposition is mostly built around the core product or service, but with significant contributions from the extended product or service	The value proposition is partly built around the core product or service, but mostly from the extended product or service	The value proposition is derived entirely or mostly from the extended and augmented product

Adapted from Smith. Reproduced by permission of Elsevier from *Making Marketing Happen* by Smith, Brian D, 2005. Copyright © 2005 Elsevier

So the first stage of the process to evaluate market complexity is to use Table 6.2. Look along each line and make an estimate of which situation best describes your market. Clearly, this is best done with reference to any data you have and is also enhanced by doing it as a group exercise. However, even if done alone and using only tacit market knowledge, these multiple judgements are a better assessment of a complex construct than a simple estimate along one dimension.

Having made the sixteen estimates, combine the subcomponent estimates into the five factors to make an estimate of the market complexity due to customers, channels, competitors, the remote environment and the value proposition. At this level, weighted averages seem an unnecessary complication. It is enough simply to look at your judgements for the subcomponents and make a judgement as to the combined complexity of each of the five factors. The output of this first step, therefore, is five numbers, one for each factor. Although the scale is in five steps, you will find it useful to make the assessment on a scale of one to ten, enabling you to 'shade' your answer to reflect your assessments of the subcomponents. For instance, if your assessment of the five subcomponents of remote environment complexity is a combination of twos (moderately simple) and threes (median complexity), then your judgement of remote environment complexity might be 2.5. The end result of this first part of the process for assessing market complexity is five numbers between one and ten. The next step is to combine them into a way that is straightforward without being simplistic.

Application point: What are the market complexity factor scores for your market?

The first stage in objectively assessing the complexity of your market is to make a good judgement of the scores for each of the five factors. This means considering each of the subcomponents and then making a reasoned judgement. Use Tables 6.1 and 6.2 to assess your five component scores before you proceed further.

Aggregating market complexity

As alluded to earlier, each of the five factors (customers, channels, competitors, remote environment and value proposition) contributes to market complexity, but they do not do so equally. In short, the five different factors do not only vary in magnitude but in the degree to which they contribute to market complexity. Partly, this is a function of the firm's strategy. For example, a firm following an undifferentiated, cost-led strategy may think that the complexities of customer segments and competitive sets are less relevant than would a firm adopting a carefully differentiated strategy. Similarly, two firms with similarly broad product ranges may not see product range complexity as equally important if one firm has its sales dominated by one product. The relative importance of the five factors is also a function of the market. Some markets, such as advanced IT sectors or fashion markets, are heavily and quickly influenced by the remote environment. Other markets, perhaps stationery or certain sectors of publishing, are only slowly and indirectly affected by the remote environment.

This explanation of how internal and external factors influence the contribution of the five factors to market complexity is important. It means that two companies in the same market may not have exactly the same level of market complexity because it is determined partly by internal factors. It also means that markets with apparently similar remote environments may be very different. These two considerations help to explain why one approach to scanning behaviour does not fit all firms and why the process for creating insight must be tailored and not simply copied.

The second stage in assessing market complexity, therefore, is to estimate the relative contribution each of the five factors makes. If each of the five factors contributed equally, then market complexity would be a simple average of our five assessments. In practice, they impact differently on the complexity of the market because of the internal factors mentioned in the preceding section. Because of this, a simple average is inadequate and a weighted average is needed. This is not much of a complication. It merely involves starting with the assumption of equal contribution (that is 20% or two out of ten) and then shading up and down, as indicated by Table 6.3. The important point, of course, is that the weightings must add up to ten out of ten.

Table 6.4 gives an example of a completed market complexity assessment. The weightings for each factor are assessed using Table 6.3. In this case, customer complexity is shown as especially important, as is often the case where the subtleties of segmentation are hard for leaders to see. The scores

Table 6.3 *Weightings for market complexity factors.*

Market complexity factor	Increase weighting from 2 when . . .	Decrease weighting from 2 when . . .
Customer complexity	Customer complexity contributes strongly to overall market complexity	Customer complexity contributes only weakly to overall market complexity
Competitor complexity	Competitor complexity contributes strongly to overall market complexity	Competitor complexity contributes only weakly to overall market complexity
Channel complexity	Channel complexity contributes strongly to overall market complexity	Channel complexity contributes only weakly to overall market complexity
Remote environment complexity	Remote environment complexity contributes strongly to overall market complexity	Remote environment complexity contributes only weakly to overall market complexity
Value proposition complexity	Value proposition complexity contributes strongly to overall market complexity	Value proposition complexity contributes only weakly to overall market complexity

Adapted from Smith. Reproduced by permission of Elsevier from *Making Marketing Happen* by Smith, Brian D, 2005. Copyright © 2005 Elsevier

Table 6.4 *Example of a completed market complexity assessment.*

Market complexity factor	Weighting (assessed using Table 6.3)	Marketing complexity factor score (assessed using Table 6.2)
Customer complexity	4	8
Competitor complexity	1	2
Channel complexity	1	3
Remote environment complexity	2	4
Value proposition complexity	2	7
Total	10	59
		i.e.: $(4 \times 8) + (1 \times 2) + (1 \times 3) + (2 \times 4) + (2 \times 7)$

Adapted from Smith. Reproduced by permission of Elsevier from *Making Marketing Happen* by Smith, Brian D, 2005. Copyright © 2005 Elsevier

for each are assessed using Table 6.2. In this example, customer complexity and value proposition complexity are the most complex elements of the market, as is often the case in technical and business to business markets. The overall market complexity score is calculated by simply multiplying each factor score by its weighting and adding them up.

We have now completed the process of assessing the complexity of our market. At first it may appear a laborious process but, in reality, it takes a management team no more than an hour or so. Even given the cost of management team time, this is a small price to pay for the reward. We now understand the complexity of our market and what it is about the market that leads to its complexity. And, as with all management tools, there is at least as much value in the discussion needed to use the tool as there is in the end result.

Application point: What is your assessment of the complexity of your market?

An accurate and objective assessment of the complexity of your market is the first step in developing effective scanning behaviour. What are the market complexity component weightings for your situation, based on Table 6.3? Following the example in Table 6.4, what is your judgement of the complexity of your market, on a scale from 0–100, where 0 is simple and 100 is complex.

Understanding and evaluating market turbulence

The way companies understand and assess market turbulence is very similar to the way they understand and assess market complexity, so this section builds on the last and is correspondingly simpler. When we say market turbulence, we mean change and instability in the market environment that we are trying to understand. It is important to us because rational, systematic scanning seems to cope well *When we say market turbulence, we mean change and instability in the market environment that we are trying to understand.* with market complexity but less well with market turbulence. The turbulence of our market, therefore, determines the balance we need to make between different scanning processes.

As described above in our discussion of market complexity, the market is a complex construct. When we talk about market turbulence, therefore, we mean change and instability in the same five factors and subcomponents we discussed when assessing market complexity. That is:

1. customer turbulence;
2. channel turbulence;
3. competitor turbulence;
4. remote environment turbulence;
5. value proposition turbulence.

These five factors and their subcomponents are summarised in Table 6.5 and in Figure 6.2. Two things will be immediately obvious to the reader. Firstly, we are talking about the same aspects of the market and the similar implications of failing to grasp them as we did in the preceding section on market complexity. Market turbulence is simply change and instability in the same factors; and failing to cope with change in market complexity leads to the same problems as failing to grasp it in the first place. Secondly, we can generalise from our research observations that there is less variation between the turbulence of different markets than between the complexity of markets. Markets are spread over a range from simple to complex with a bias to the complex that is associated with market maturity. By contrast, there seems to

Failing to cope with changes in a market leads to the same problems as failing to understand it in the first place.

be rather less spread of markets from stable to turbulent and a marked bias towards the stable, again associated with market maturity. It is a useful starting point to think of markets as starting simple and turbulent and gradually becoming complex and stable, but the generalisation is not strong enough to depend upon. We need to make the same assessment of the five components of market turbulence as we did for market complexity, along a graduated scale derived from our observations of real companies. We then need to aggregate the scores in a weighted manner, as we did for market complexity.

The gradations in market turbulence are shown in Table 6.6. As before, assessment involves looking along each line and judging which description best fits your market. The assessments for each subcomponent are aggregated simply to create a 'marks out of ten' score for each of the five components of market turbulence. Again, the assessment is best made by a team and

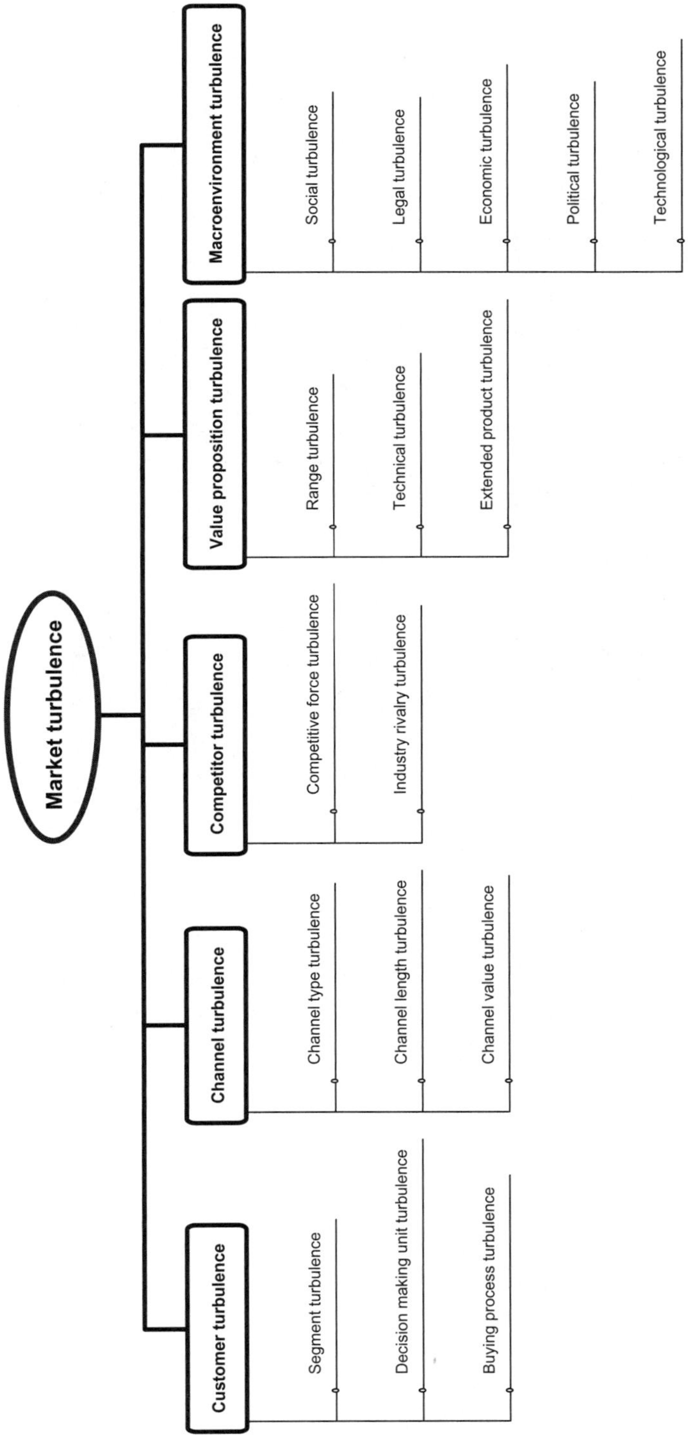

Figure 6.2 *Components of market turbulence.*

Table 6.5 *The nature and implications of market turbulence.*

Subcomponent of market turbulence	Turbulence factors	Typically observed implications of the scanning process failing to cope with this aspect of market turbulence
Customer turbulence	Segment turbulence: change and instability in the number of substantially different market segments	Failure to understand and differentiate between segment needs and especially to identify newly emerging segments
	Decision making unit turbulence: change and instability in the number of significant contributors to the decision making unit	Failure to understand the implications of decision making influence, especially the increased importance of influencers
	Buying process turbulence: change and instability in the length and number of distinct stages in the buying process	Failure to understand the implications of different stages in the decision making process, especially new stages or less obvious stages
Channel turbulence	Channel type turbulence: change and instability in the number of different types of channel to market	Failure to understand the implications of different channel types, especially new channels or new interactions between channels
	Channel length turbulence: change and instability in the number of different tiers in the channel to market	Failure to understand the implications of different levels in the decision making process, especially new intermediaries
	Channel value turbulence: change and instability in the extent to which the channel to market adds to the value proposition	Failure to understand the implications of value adding or destroying activity in the channel, especially new activity
Competitor turbulence	Competitive force turbulence: change and instability in the number of different competitive forces significant in the market	Failure to understand the implications of different competitive forces in the market, especially new or newly strong forces
	Industry rivalry turbulence: change and instability in the number of different strategic sets into which direct competitors may be classified	Failure to understand the implications of newly strong or weakened competitive forces

Remote environment turbulence	Social turbulence: change and instability in the extent to which sociological factors have significant impact on the market	Failure to understand the implications of newly important social factors in the remote environment
	Legal turbulence: change and instability in the extent to which legal factors have significant impact on the market	Failure to understand the implications of newly important legal factors in the remote environment
	Economic turbulence: change and instability in the extent to which macroeconomic factors have significant impact on the market	Failure to understand the implications of newly important economic factors in the remote environment
	Political turbulence: change and instability in the extent to which political factors have significant impact on the market	Failure to understand the implications of newly important political factors in the remote environment
	Technological turbulence: change and instability in the extent to which technological factors have significant impact on the market	Failure to understand the implications of newly important technological factors in the remote environment
Value proposition turbulence	Range turbulence: change and instability in the number of different product components offered to the market.	Failure to understand the implications of changes in the product range, especially interactions within the range
	Technical turbulence: change and instability in the technological turbulence inherent in developing, supplying and selling the value proposition	Failure to understand the implications of changes in technical complexity of the value proposition, especially new technology or gradual erosion of technology
	Extended product turbulence: change and instability in the extent to which the value proposition extends beyond the core product into higher benefits	Failure to understand the implications of changes in the extended product, especially with respect to intangible parts of the extended product

Table 6.6 *Graduated scales of market turbulence.*

Subcomponent of market turbulence	Turbulence factors	Stable (1)	Moderately stable (2)	Median turbulence (3)	Moderately turbulent (4)	Turbulent (5)
Customer turbulence	Segment turbulence: the change and instability in the number of substantially different market segments	There is no noticeable change or instability in the number and relative size of substantially different market segments	There is no noticeable change or instability in the number of substantially different market segments but some slow change or mild instability in their relative size	There is slow change in the number of different market segments and some slow change and mild instability in their relative size	There is slow change in the number of different market segments and quite rapid change and instability in their relative size	There is rapid change or significant instability in the number and relative size of substantially different market segments
	Decision making unit turbulence: the change and instability in the number of significant contributors to the decision making unit	There is no noticeable change in the number of significant contributors to the decision making unit	There is only small and slow change in the number of significant contributors to the decision making unit	There is significant but slow change in the number of significant contributors to the decision making unit	There is significant and constant change in the number of significant contributors to the decision making unit	There is rapid and sudden change in the number and relative size of substantially different market segments
	Buying process turbulence: the change and instability in the length and number of distinct stages in the buying process	There is no noticeable change in the length and number of distinct stages in the buying process	There is only small and slow change in the length and number of distinct stages in the buying process	There is significant but slow change in the length and number of distinct stages in the buying process	There is significant and constant change in the length and number of distinct stages in the buying process	There is rapid and sudden change in the length and number of distinct stages in the buying process

Channel turbulence	Channel type turbulence: the change and instability in the number of different types of channel to market	There is no noticeable change in the number of different types of channel to market	There is only small and slow change in the number of different types of channel to market	There is significant but slow change in the number of different types of channel to market	There is significant and constant change in the number of different types of channel to market	There is rapid and sudden change in the number of different types of channel to market
	Channel length turbulence: the change and instability in the number of different tiers in the channel to market	There is no noticeable change in the number of different tiers in the channel to market	There is only small and slow change in the number of different tiers in the channel to market	There is significant but slow change in the number of different tiers in the channel to market	There is significant and constant change in the number of different tiers in the channel to market	There is rapid and sudden change in the number of different tiers in the channel to market
	Channel value turbulence: the change and instability in the extent to which the channel to market adds to the value proposition	There is no noticeable change in the extent to which the channel to market adds to the value proposition	There is only small and slow change in the extent to which the channel to market adds to the value proposition	There is significant but slow change in the extent to which the channel to market adds to the value proposition	There is significant and constant change in the extent to which the channel to market adds to the value proposition	There is rapid and sudden change in the extent to which the channel to market adds to the value proposition
Competitor turbulence	Competitive force turbulence: the change and instability in the number of different competitive forces significant in the market	There is no noticeable change in the number of different competitive forces significant in the market	There is only small and slow change in the number of different competitive forces significant in the market	There is significant but slow change in the number of different competitive forces significant in the market	There is significant and constant change in the number of different competitive forces significant in the market	There is rapid and sudden change in the number of different competitive forces significant in the market
	Industry rivalry turbulence: the change and instability in the number of different strategic sets into which direct competitors may be classified	There is no noticeable change in the number of different strategic sets into which direct competitors may be classified	There is only small and slow change in the number of different strategic sets into which direct competitors may be classified	There is significant but slow change in the number of different strategic sets into which direct competitors may be classified	There is significant and constant change in the number of different strategic sets into which direct competitors may be classified	There is rapid and sudden change in the number of different strategic sets into which direct competitors may be classified

Table 6.6 (*Continued*)

Subcomponent of market turbulence	Turbulence factors	Stable (1)	Moderately stable (2)	Median turbulence (3)	Moderately turbulent (4)	Turbulent (5)
Remote environment turbulence	Social turbulence: the change and instability in the number of different social factors which impact significantly on the market	There is no noticeable change in the number of different social factors which impact significantly on the market	There is only small and slow change in the number of different social factors which impact significantly on the market	There is significant but slow change in the number of different social factors which impact significantly on the market	There is significant and constant change in the number of different social factors which impact significantly on the market	There is rapid and sudden change in the number of different social factors which impact significantly on the market
	Legal turbulence: the change and instability in the number of different legal factors which impact significantly on the market	There is no noticeable change in the number of different legal factors which impact significantly on the market	There is only small and slow change in the number of different legal factors which impact significantly on the market	There is significant but slow change in the number of different legal factors which impact significantly on the market	There is significant and constant change in the number of different legal factors which impact significantly on the market	There is rapid and sudden change in the number of different legal factors which impact significantly on the market
	Economic turbulence: the change and instability in the number of different macroeconomic factors which impact significantly on the market	There is no noticeable change in the number of different macroeconomic factors which impact significantly on the market	There is only small and slow change in the number of different macroeconomic factors which impact significantly on the market	There is significant but slow change in the number of different macroeconomic factors which impact significantly on the market	There is significant and constant change in the number of different macroeconomic factors which impact significantly on the market	There is rapid and sudden change in the number of different macroeconomic factors which impact significantly on the market
	Political turbulence: the change and instability in the number of different political factors which impact significantly on the market	There is no noticeable change in the number of different political factors which impact significantly on the market	There is only small and slow change in the number of different political factors which impact significantly on the market	There is significant but slow change in the number of different political factors which impact significantly on the market	There is significant and constant change in the number of different political factors which impact significantly on the market	There is rapid and sudden change in the number of different political factors which impact significantly on the market

	There is no noticeable change	There is only small and slow change	There is significant but slow change	There is significant and constant change	There is rapid and sudden change
Value proposition turbulence — Technological turbulence: the change and instability in the number of different technological factors which impact significantly on the market	There is no noticeable change in the number of different technological factors which impact significantly on the market	There is only small and slow change in the number of different technological factors which impact significantly on the market	There is significant but slow change in the number of different technological factors which impact significantly on the market	There is significant and constant change in the number of different technological factors which impact significantly on the market	There is rapid and sudden change in the number of different technological factors which impact significantly on the market
Range turbulence: the change and instability in the number of different product components offered to the market	There is no noticeable change in the number of different product components offered to the market	There is only small and slow change in the number of different product components offered to the market	There is significant but slow change in the number of different product components offered to the market	There is significant and constant change in the number of different product components offered to the market	There is rapid and sudden change in the number of different product components offered to the market
Technical turbulence: the change and instability in the technology inherent in developing, supplying and selling the value proposition	There is no noticeable change in the technology inherent in developing, supplying and selling the value proposition.	There is only small and slow change in the technology inherent in developing, supplying and selling the value proposition	There is significant but slow change in the technology inherent in developing, supplying and selling the value proposition	There is significant and constant change in the technology inherent in developing, supplying and selling the value proposition	There is rapid and sudden change in the technology inherent in developing, supplying and selling the value proposition
Extended product turbulence: the change and instability in the extent to which the value proposition extends beyond the core product into higher benefits	There is no noticeable change in the extent to which the value proposition extends beyond the core product into higher benefits	There is only small and slow change in the extent to which the value proposition extends beyond the core product into higher benefits	There is significant but slow change in the extent to which the value proposition extends beyond the core product into higher benefits	There is significant and constant change in the extent to which the value proposition extends beyond the core product into higher benefits	There is rapid and sudden change in the extent to which the value proposition extends beyond the core product into higher benefits

informed, where possible, by reference to known data or facts. Inevitably, the discussion is as valuable as the score and any errors tend to cancel out, making the net scores more reliable. At the end of the process, the five component scores are used to calculate the overall market turbulence by means of a weighted average calculation.

Again consistent with the assessment of market complexity, the calculation of market turbulence is quite straightforward. A completed example is shown in Table 6.8. In this example, remote environment turbulence was judged to be the most important factor and the overall level of market turbulence assessed as quite low, an important consideration in the choice of the optimum scanning approach.

Application point: What is your assessment of the turbulence of your market?

An accurate and objective assessment of the turbulence of your market is the second step in developing effective scanning behaviour. It is a simple calculation using the weighting assessments and component scores. What are the market turbulence component scores for your market, based on Table 6.6? What are the market turbulence component weightings for your situation, based on Table 6.7? Following the example in Table 6.8, what is your judgement of the turbulence of your market, on a scale from 0–100, where 0 is simple and 100 is complex? How does that assessment differ from the one you made, without these tools, earlier in this chapter?

Combining the assessments of market complexity and market turbulence

By following the methods described in the preceding sections of this chapter, the reader should now have two numbers, one a calculation of market complexity and one a calculation of market turbulence. Each should have a value of between 0 and 100 and, taken together, they give a well-considered judgement of the market conditions. Remember that what we have done here is not a market audit. That analyses the market and draws out opportunities

Table 6.7 *Weightings for market turbulence factors.*

Market turbulence factor	Increase weighting from 2 when . . .	Decrease weighting from 2 when . . .
Customer turbulence	Customer turbulence contributes strongly to overall market turbulence	Customer turbulence contributes only weakly to overall market turbulence
Competitor turbulence	Competitor turbulence contributes strongly to overall market turbulence	Competitor turbulence contributes only weakly to overall market turbulence
Channel turbulence	Channel turbulence contributes strongly to overall market turbulence	Channel turbulence contributes only weakly to overall market turbulence
Remote environment turbulence	Remote environment turbulence contributes strongly to overall market turbulence	Remote environment turbulence contributes only weakly to overall market turbulence
Value proposition turbulence	Value proposition turbulence contributes strongly to overall market turbulence	Value proposition turbulence contributes only weakly to overall market turbulence

Adapted from Smith. Reproduced by permission of Elsevier from *Making Marketing Happen* by Smith, Brian D, 2005. Copyright © 2005 Elsevier

Table 6.8 *Example of a completed market turbulence assessment.*

Market turbulence factor	Weighting (assessed using Table 6.7)	Marketing turbulence factor score (assessed using Table 6.6)
Customer turbulence	4	8
Competitor turbulence	1	2
Channel turbulence	1	3
Remote environment turbulence	2	4
Value proposition turbulence	2	7
Total	10	59 i.e.: $(4 \times 8) + (1 \times 2) + (1 \times 3) + (2 \times 4) + (2 \times 7)$

Adapted from Smith. Reproduced by permission of Elsevier from *Making Marketing Happen* by Smith, Brian D, 2005. Copyright © 2005 Elsevier

and threats. What this chapter has described is an assessment of the nature of the market. The purpose of this assessment is to enable the firm to make a more informed and less subjective judgement about the sort of scanning behaviour most appropriate to the particular context in which it operates. Exactly how this assessment informs the choice of scanning approach is discussed in the following chapters.

Powerpoints

- Market insight is based on effective scanning of the market.
- The first step in achieving effective scanning of the market is to make an objective, realistic assessment of the complexity and turbulence of your market.
- Both market complexity and market turbulence are complex constructs; simplistic approaches are misleading.
- The different components of market complexity and market turbulence can contribute differentially, depending on the market and the company.
- The tools in this chapter allow us to assess both market complexity and market turbulence for our market.

7

What is the best way to understand the business environment?

'There is always a best way of doing everything, if it be to boil an egg.'
Ralph Waldo Emerson

At last, we are now in a position to discuss the best way to understand the business environment. We have covered a number of key ideas in previous chapters that we can build upon to address the core issue of how individuals and organisations can optimise their scanning practices to gain the data and information needed to create market insight.

In Chapter 4 we elaborated on what market insight looks like. In Chapter 5 we learnt what real managers actually do to understand the environment and derived four types of managerial scanning behaviour – Analysts, Categorists, Monitors and Viewers. And in Chapter 6 we outlined how to understand and assess the complexity and turbulence of a market. All of these ideas and learnings can now be brought together to form a framework to help guide you and your organisation's scanning practices.

You will recall in previously setting out the characteristics of successfully understanding and analysing the markets we commented firstly on when a market insight is not an insight. We recounted that only when information is contextualised and synthesised with other information does it become knowledge and only some of that knowledge constitutes insight. We also discussed and illustrated the four criteria for knowledge to be insightful –

valuable, rare, inimitable and organisationally aligned – and appreciated that knowledge that meets these criteria is 'exquisite' (i.e. very uncommon). A further three 'indicators' of market insight were shared, based on our research: namely that market insight is associated with market turbulence, market complexity and 'soft factors'. What also emerged from our research was a taxonomy of market insight being narrow versus broad, continuous versus discontinuous and transient versus lasting. This was very useful to understand in theory what managers should be producing as an output from their scanning efforts. But in order to prescribe what changes managers should undertake, we also need to understand what managers currently do to understand the environment.

Our prior analysis of what real managers do to understand the environment revealed four distinct groups of managers – Analysts, Categorists, Monitors and Viewers – that have dis-

The pros and cons of each group are reflected in their major behavioural traits and how well they achieve scanning goals.

tinctive and differentiable scanning behavioural traits. The traits varied across the four groups in terms of preferred methods of gathering information: degree of structure applied to scanning effort; capacity to process information; and ability to analyse and derive market insight. As you might expect, it is possible to generalise the pros and cons of each scanning group by reflecting on their major behavioural traits and considering how well they contribute to achieving overall scanning goals. For example, let's consider Categorists. This group is very systematic in their approach to scanning and therefore effective in identifying a comprehensive and broad set of relevant information topics. On the other hand, Categorists can be slow, bureaucratic and inflexible in how they gather and manage external information. This example illustrates how we can begin to draw out some general findings on strengths and weaknesses of each group with respect to scanning behaviour. In this chapter, we will begin by assessing the pros and cons for each of the four groups of managers.

Assessing the strengths and weaknesses for each group of managers will provide us with general insights into the effectiveness and consequences of each type of scanning behaviour. We can gauge the effectiveness of scan-

In order to provide more sophisticated guidance on scanning practices, we should consider the impact of different market contexts on scanning effectiveness and consequences.

ning behavioural traits by considering how well they support our scanning goals of gaining genuine insight. But in order to provide more sophisticated guidance on scanning practices, we should consider the impact of different market contexts on scanning effectiveness and consequences. As previously discussed, the two most important underlying dimensions of the market are complexity and turbulence. Hence, a useful starting point is to consider at least four market contexts derived from combinations of two levels of market complexity (low and high) and two levels of market turbulence (low and high). This is represented in a simple two by two matrix table which is elaborated later in this chapter. While considering each of four market contexts, i.e. each quadrant of the market context matrix, we will comment on the effectiveness and consequences of each group of managers in successfully scanning the business environment.

We have learnt that markets can be usefully assessed in terms of their complexity and turbulence, lending itself to a crude typology of at least four market states – low complexity low turbulence, low complexity high turbulence, high complexity low turbulence and high complexity high turbulence. Against each of these four market states we can deduce how it may impact on the effectiveness of different scanning behaviours and outcomes. For example, in a high complexity high turbulence market state the task of comprehensively gathering information is likely to be very difficult and the information by the time it is gathered may be too historic to be useful; hence scanning behavioural characteristics of Categorists are likely be less valuable in these circumstances than those of Analysts.

Markets can be usefully assessed in terms of their complexity and turbulence, which lends itself to a crude typology of at least four market states.

This chapter aims to provide insight into the best way to understand the business environment. As Ralph Waldo Emerson states in the quote that heads this chapter, there is a best way to do everything. While we acknowledge that managerial best practices change over time, we believe that striving for a best way to scan is a worthwhile goal, even if challengeable in theory. We trust that some of our core insights and prescriptions will survive the test of time, as have the basic steps and ingredients to boil an egg! We will begin by understanding the strengths and weaknesses of each major type of managerial scanning behaviour. In a nutshell, these can be distilled down to four general statements:

- Analysts are insightful but can be conventional and incomplete.
- Categorists are comprehensive but often provide data rather than insight.
- Monitors can identify major task environment changes but are unlikely to develop original insights.
- Viewers may identify novelties but are unreliable.

We will elaborate further on these generalisations and their implications later in this chapter. Following on from this analysis of the pros and cons of each major type of managerial scanning behaviour, this chapter then goes on to make the point that scanning effectiveness is impacted by market conditions. Specifically, we explore what impact market complexity and market turbulence may have on scanning effectiveness.

Finally, this chapter concludes by proposing a framework for ensuring effective scanning behaviour of both the task environment and the remote environment. This framework utilises all four major types of managers – Ana-

The best way to understand the business environment, from an organisation's perspective, requires deliberate collaboration among different manager types.

lysts, Categorists, Monitors and Viewers – in an attempt to capitalise on the strengths of each type and compensate for the weaknesses of any one type of manager. We conclude that the best way to understand the business environment, from an organisation's perspective, requires deliberate collaboration among different manager types and also requires changing the mix of managerial scanning types to suit the particular market context.

Strengths and weaknesses of Analysts
Analysts are insightful but can be conventional and incomplete.

In Chapter 5, we described an Analyst as a type of manager who is deliberate in his or her scanning efforts, systematic and structured in approach to gathering and interpreting information, and has higher than average ability to process significant levels of information and effectively interpret that information.

A short set of key terms that reflect Analysts' overall behaviour are systematic, rational, business objective orientated, information hungry, deterministic, knowledgeable of business management techniques, problem solvers, capable information processors and confident and capable in data interpretation.

Keeping in mind the criteria for knowledge to be insightful, we can generalise how well Analysts contribute to gaining genuine market insight. For knowledge to be insightful we concluded that it should be valuable through informing or enabling actions that will increase customer preference or increase the efficiency of serving the customer base. Therefore to identify whether knowledge is valuable

Analysts are well positioned to determine what knowledge is valuable since they are generally conscious and alert to news about their firm's business.

requires an understanding of existing customer preferences and a sense for what would increase customer preferences for a firm's products and services. Alternatively, or additionally, to identify whether knowledge is valuable requires at least a high level understanding of the processes and costs to serve the existing customer base. Analysts claim a sound knowledge of their firm's business models, and are generally very business objective orientated which means that they are conscious and alert to news about their firm's business. Hence, Analysts are well positioned to meet this first test of insight of determining whether knowledge is relatively valuable to their firm.

For knowledge to be insightful we also concluded that it needed to be rare. By rarity we mean knowledge that is somewhat exclusive to you and not known by your competitors. As previously acknowledged, in practice the rarity of a piece of knowledge sits somewhere on a continuum of common knowledge known by almost anyone who is active in the industry, and a truly unique piece of knowledge known exclusively to one party. We also appreciate that the rareness of knowledge is time dependent and it reduces over time, as competitors discover this knowledge for themselves or it leaks out through employee transfer or through the work of researchers or industry commentators. Therefore, knowledge is rare for so long as only one firm has embedded and appreciated that knowledge to a degree significantly greater than other firms in its competitive set.

There are two reasons why Analysts are better than other managers at assessing the rarity of a piece of knowledge. First, Analysts are very orientated to the external business environment. Analysts are outward looking and hungry for information in both the task and remote environments. Hence, they are more likely than other managers to be aware of what other competitors are doing and what they know (often by inference) at any point in time. This awareness of competitors is crucial to assess whether a piece of knowledge in question has the potential to be embedded and appreciated to a degree significantly greater than the other firms in its competitor set. The second reason that Analysts are relatively better at assessing the rarity of a piece of information is because they are continuously paying attention to the external business environment. This continuous attention allows them to assess changes in rarity of knowledge, as exclusive knowledge inevitably becomes known to a broader set of individuals and firms. Hence, Analysts can better recognise the changes in rarity on a continuum and thereby assess the extent to which knowledge is truly insightful.

Being well orientated to and paying continuous attention to the external business environment, makes Analysts well positioned to assess whether knowledge is practically inimitable.

For similar reasons, Analysts are relatively better at assessing the inimitability of a set of knowledge. Inimitability is an important concept as it is our third criterion by which knowledge may be judged to be truly insightful. Of course, we acknowledge that no knowledge can be truly inimitable as a competitor can undertake research to gain the same knowledge as your firm or knowledge can be transferred by poaching key employees. Hence, by inimitability we mean 'practical inimitability' whereby a piece of knowledge could not be imitated within a timescale that mattered or for a cost that was affordable to its competitors. Again, as Analysts are very orientated to the external business environment and as they pay continuous attention to the environment (as opposed to intermittent viewing) they are relatively better positioned and capable of assessing whether knowledge is practically inimitable.

Analysts have above average skills in forecasting and conceiving of future scenarios, making them the front runners to derive market insight.

As discussed in Chapter 4, the fourth criteria for genuine market insight was organisational alignment. We previously proffered that knowledge is organisationally aligned if the firm can act on it within its current situation or a situation that could arise within a foreseeable future and business context. Knowledge is not organisationally aligned if, in order to act on it, the firm would need to change at a cost disproportionate to the benefits of that change. To assess the net benefits of a change requires forecasting into the future and projecting revenue and costs associated with acting on a particular insight. Overall, this task is better performed by Analysts and usually falls to managers with those behavioural traits to complete. Analysts have above average skills in interpreting information, tolerating ambiguity and forecasting the future. It is these skills in forecasting and conceiving of future scenarios that mean that the Analyst is once again the front runner to derive market insight.

From the above discussion we can generalise that the major pro of Analysts is that they are insightful. They are insightful because they are capable of assessing whether knowledge meets the four criteria – valuable, rare, inimitable and organisationally aligned – for it to be market insight. Analysts are relatively more capable at making this assessment because they have a sound knowledge of their firm's business model and are business objective orientated. This makes them more conscious and alert to news about their firm's business and, consequently, highly orientated to the external business environment. By nature they are outward looking and hungry for information in both the task and remote environment, paying continuous attention to the business environment. Having gathered information, they then have above average skills in interpreting it, tolerating ambiguity and forecasting the future.

Another major strength of Analysts is their general confidence and comfort in dealing with large volumes of information. They also claim confidence in their ability to assess the significance of information among the large volumes of information that they are exposed to. Analysts are least likely to complain and stress about information overload. We know that Analysts use a myriad of information sources and will pay attention to a broad range of information topics, even though some information may not be immediately recognised as relevant to a specific business purpose. All told, they are confident in their ability to process or reflect upon large volumes of information with the expectation that they will be able to assess significant items for further investigation.

While it is valuable to process information and assess which items may be significant, it is of further value to consider the implications of such items. Analysts possess above average skills

Analysts have a strong ability to forecast and conceive of multiple future scenarios and to theorise and model the implications for their firm.

in thinking through the implications of information and knowledge upon the business environment at large, the strategic group (made up of a firm and its competitors) and their own firm. Analysts have a strong ability to forecast and conceive of multiple future scenarios and to theorise and model the implications for their firm.

Picking up on an earlier point about organisational alignment reminds us that, unless insight is connected to strategy formulation or decision making, it is effectively moot or 'an academic exercise'. A by-product of Analysts being involved in forecasting and scenario development (i.e. exercises concerning the future of the firm) and their high degree of involvement in firm matters, combined with their implied seniority or access to senior management, means that their outcomes are likely to be debated at senior levels. Analysts, by nature, are better equipped to persuade colleagues and senior management to their point of view. After all, Analysts are pre-armed with information to support their point of view and analytical conclusions. Their confidence in their analytical skills and conclusions is also a positive force to get their views onto the management agenda.

As you'd expect, for all the positives of Analysts outlined above, there are also some negatives to be aware of. One major weakness is the potential slowness in reporting due to the thoroughness of investigation and the complexity of the analysis undertaken. Analysts spend significant time processing and analysing information. You might be forgiven for thinking they actually enjoy it! Their above average abilities to interpret information often lead them down many different avenues of exploration and investigation. On occasions, they may also draw upon specialists or experts to assist with their understanding and analysis,

Analysts aim to substantially understand the complexities of a phenomenon and its implications; this can mean that insight can be slow in coming about.

or task other individuals with specialist tasks. Either way, the process of evidence seeking and analysis can be time consuming. Analysts are likely to investigate a phenomenon to the point where they substantially understand the inherent complexities and have dutifully considered the implications: that is, answers to the 'so what' question. This combination of thoroughness of investigation and need to get behind the complexity can mean that insight can be slow in coming about. The preponderance of IT systems and ease of assessing further data and information can aggravate this weakness.

A further con of an Analyst is his or her propensity to be swayed by expert opinion. Analysts are typically top scorers in standardised tests of mathematical and verbal skills. They are likely to have achieved high grades in traditional school environments, and are likely to be top achievers in higher management education programmes. As such, Analysts are likely to assign credibility to individuals of a similar ilk, or individuals who have institutional credibility (e.g. business school professors, recognised industry commentators, leading researchers, published authors etc.). A potential implication is that Analysts' opinions tend to be heavily influenced by so-called experts. Accordingly, Analysts' opinions, across the community of Analysts, tend to be similar and ultimately reinforce one another's views! The downside is that Analysts' views may simply reflect commonly held and socially acceptable views of the business environment, versus contribute any unique or differentiable insights – a phenomenon that is also referred to as 'groupthink'.

Analysts' views may reflect commonly held and socially acceptable views of the business environment – a phenomenon also known as 'groupthink'.

We are aware that Analysts sense that the vast majority of information they are exposed to is helpful. Typically, Analysts do not reject outright certain types of information; instead they are open minded to the value that disparate types of information may bring. We know that Analysts hold the view that information can be important even though it is not immediately recognised as relevant to a specific business purpose. As a result, Analysts seek out or organise for a broad range of information to be brought to their attention. But ultimately, even Analysts have only limited time and resources to commit to understanding the business environment and deriving insight. At some stage, Analysts need to choose which information topics to further investigate. Analysts' choices of topic may well be driven by what stimulates them, that is often new information topics with some depth or complexity to them, akin to a puzzle to solve! Hence, a risk for Analysts is that they will focus on topics of interest to them and that precludes being able to comprehensively assess topics for strategic significance.

Analysts' choices of topic to research may be driven by what stimulates them – often new information with depth or complexity – sometimes to the exclusion of topics with strategic significance.

As Analysts lead the pack in deriving market insight, they are very valuable to their firms and generally valuable in the market. Therefore, overall Analysts are a relatively expensive resource, albeit highly skilled, and hence can be costly to recruit and retain. Of course, ultimately their market insight should inform decision making and create value or prevent value loss sufficient to justify their cost. However, it is often the case that Analyst resources or activities are perceived to be expensive, especially if not directly connected to decision making and resource allocation.

A summary of the main pros and cons of an Analyst, as discussed above, is provided in Box 7.1. These generalisable strengths and weaknesses should be kept in mind when thinking through developing a firm wide scanning capability, which we'll comment on further later in this chapter.

Application point: How can your firm capitalise on Analyst pros and compensate for Analyst cons?

Reflecting on the above analysis of Analysts, there are clear pros and cons to consider. How can your firm capitalise on Analysts' skills in gaining insight and identifying implications? How can your firm compensate for slowness of reporting and Analysts' groupthink?

Box 7.1 Analyst pros and cons

Analyst pros

- Insightful (can assess whether information is valuable, rare, inimitable and organisationally aligned).
- Confidence that available information has been comprehended.
- Implications are considered.
- Persuasive and will impact on decision making.

Analyst cons

- Can be slow to report due to investigation of complexity.
- Swayed by 'expert opinion'.
- Focus on favourite interest areas at expense of comprehensiveness.
- Expensive discrete resource.

Strengths and weaknesses of Categorists
Categorists are comprehensive but often provide data rather than insight.

You'll recall that a Categorist refers to a type of manager who is very systematic in his or her approach to scanning for key information in the business environment. Categorists are somewhat sceptical about the ability to absorb and effectively interpret significant volumes of business environment information and conservative about their ability to derive genuine market insight.

In brief, Categorists are formal in their information gathering efforts, well organised, mindful of business objectives and capable researchers and synthesisers of information. To recap on further detail of Categorists refer to Chapter 5.

More than any other type of manager, Categorists are well organised and systematic and structured in their approach to scanning the business environment. This is a major differentiator and perhaps the main strength of a Categorist. Categorists are very well organised and competent at data and information capture, storage and retrieval. They usually have in place established processes detailing the specific activities to undertake when scanning the business environment. These processes are often formalised and documented to make clear the work that needs to be done, who should do this work and what is the required output. The documentation could be in the form of process maps, work roles descriptions, an instruction manual, or simply a list of key activities noted in a work schedule or calendar. Regardless of the form of documentation, Categorists will typically have in place a well established process for data capture, storage and retrieval. This includes specifying the type of data and information to gather, the sources (both specific known sources and general information media) and the categorisation scheme by which this information should be stored. The categorisation scheme usually takes the form of a directory of information organised by topic, source and date, similar to directories and categorisation schemes utilised in libraries. The high levels of organisation, combined with formal processes

High levels of organisation, formal processes and a well established categorisation scheme, enable Categorists to efficiently and regularly manage large volumes of information.

and a well established categorisation scheme to manage information, enable Categorists to efficiently and regularly manage large volumes of information.

Categorists set out to comprehensively cover a broad range of topics. The ability to achieve comprehensive coverage of information topics is a further pro of a Categorist. When Categorists, and their directed resources, undertake scanning they set out criteria or a list of information topics to which they should pay attention. For example, a list of local market factors may cover customers, competitors, channels and suppliers, followed by a further set of sub-topic headings. For example, under competitors, a further list of sub-topics could be competitor objectives, competitor successes, competitor failures, competitor threats and emergent competitors. The benefit of this approach is that it incorporates a checklist to make sure that all preconceived areas of importance in the business environment are subject to scanning thereby ensuring comprehensive coverage.

Once Categorists decide what areas of the business environment to pay attention to, they will plan on what information sources to use. A positive characteristic of a Categorist is the deliberate use of many and varied information sources. The act of sys- *Categorists are agnostic when it* tematically planning to get informa- *comes to source usage.* tion on certain topics forces the Categorist to explicitly think through and identify what information sources are best suited to the task. Categorists will select and use all and any sources if they provide the desired information. They are agnostic when it comes to source usage! Our research showed that Categorists frequently use each of the four main information sources: internet sources, including search engines, company websites and email information subscription services; company personnel including senior management, peers and staff; traditional mediums such as television, radio, newspaper and business magazines; and personal networks of individuals outside the company.

A major advantage of using many and varied information sources is that it allows Categorists to triangulate information from different sources to identify significant information types. Triangulation historically means measuring the distance to a fixed point that you cannot reach (e.g. the top of a mountain) by measuring the angle to it from multiple points. If you know the angles and the distance between the measuring points you can work out the distance to the unreachable point. In management research, triangulation means to cross-compare information gained from multiple sources. The ability to triangulate information helps to validate the information in question and so provides the researcher with greater confidence. The ability of Categorists to triangulate sources is a major pro and enables them to confidently identify major events and trends in the external business environment, at least at the topic level.

The Categorist has some major strengths, including being well organised for data capture, storage and retrieval. They also tend to have near comprehensive coverage of information topics through their deliberate and effective use of multiple sources and good triangulation of sources to identify and prioritise topics. However, there are naturally also some weaknesses to be aware of. By far the most significant area in which Categorists fail to succeed concerns their limits in relation to in-depth analysis which would lead to genuine market insight. In our study, Categorists reported themselves to be sceptical about their ability to absorb and effectively interpret volumes of business environment information. Categorists think that the capacity of an individual manager to absorb information via scanning falls far short of the volume of available information and is a definite limiting factor to effective scanning. Linked to this view about lack of capacity, Categorists report feeling uneasy and overwhelmed when attempting to process significant volumes of information. When this

Categorists think an individual manager's capability to absorb information via scanning falls far short of the volume of available information.

feeling of being overwhelmed arises, Categorists deliberately limit their efforts to absorb or process information as a coping mechanism. By limiting their analytical efforts, they are of course limiting their chances of generating unique insights. Categorists acknowledge this limitation, on the basis of a realistic understanding of what an individual manager is cognitively capable of, and report that they are conservative about their ability to effectively interpret and derive insight from all the business environment information they obtain. Categorists find it difficult to assess the significance of new information on subjects with which they are not familiar. All of the above contributes to a general lack of confidence by Categorists to distil insight, and off the back of this insight, make recommendations for change.

This con of Categorists concerning missing out on deriving genuine market insight is understandable when considering the criteria for knowledge to be insightful. We've previously discussed the four criteria necessary for knowledge to be insightful – valuable, rare, inimitable and organisationally aligned – and appreciated that knowledge that meets this criteria is very uncommon. We maintain that for knowledge to be valuable it should inform or enable actions that will increase customer preference or increase the efficiency of serving the customer base. Therefore, to identify whether knowledge is valuable requires an understanding of one or more of the following: existing customer preferences; a sense for what would increase customers' preferences for a firm's products or services; and a high level understanding of the processes and costs to serve the existing customer base. This implies a broad and in-depth knowledge of a firm's business models. Arguably, Categorists will not obtain both a broad and in-depth knowledge of a firm's business model as it implies a degree of information absorption and processing that is beyond their comfort levels. In other words, the volume of information implied to do this would seem overwhelming to the Categorist. Hence, it is unlikely that Categorists would generally pass the first test of determining whether knowledge is relatively valuable to their firm.

In assessing whether knowledge is insightful, we also discussed that it must be rare; that is, knowledge that is somewhat exclusive to you and not known by your competitors. So to assess rarity is to imply being aware of what other competitors are doing and what they know, and to continuously

Although well suited to paying continuous attention to competitors as part of their scanning process, Categorists are less adept than Analysts at assessing competitor information and inferring intentions.

pay due attention to competitors. Categorists are well suited to paying continuous attention to competitors as part of their scanning process, but it is in the area of assessing competitor information and inferring intentions that Categorists are disadvantaged (say compared with Analysts). Hence, arguably Categorists are only partially effective at recognising changes in rarity on a continuum and thereby assessing the extent to which knowledge is truly insightful.

As Categorists are only partially effective at in-depth analysis, they are only partially effective at assessing the inimitability of a set of knowledge, the third criterion by which knowledge may be judged to be insightful. The issue, once again, is not Categorists' orientation to the external business environment, nor their continuous attention to the environment, but instead the quality of assessment of 'practical inimitability'.

To complete our discussion of Categorists' skills in determining market insight, let's consider the fourth criteria for market insight which is organisational alignment. We previously commented that knowledge is organisationally aligned if the firm can act on it within its current situation or

Categorists may lack skills to create sharp market insights because there are limits to their skills in accurately assessing information that is independently and simultaneously valuable, rare and inimitable.

a situation that could arise within a foreseeable future and business context. There are two main challenges to Categorists regarding organisational alignment. The first challenge is in terms of straightforward analytics. In order to act on market insight there needs to be a proposed initiative or action. To develop this proposal requires a degree of analysis and consideration of implications that is generally not exercised by the Categorist. The second challenge is that developing a proposal for future courses of action requires having a future orientation. A proposed business initiative needs to demonstrate that it will deliver positive net benefits. This requires forecasting into the future and projecting revenues and costs associated with acting on a particular insight. This requires skills in interpreting information, conceiving of future scenarios, extrapolating information and tolerating ambiguity.

These skills are not the forte of Categorists and hence are a limiting factor to effective forecasting of the future and ultimately achieving organisational alignment.

Insight comes to Categorists through the reading of new information, combined with some time to reflect on it.

From the above discussion we can generalise that the major con of Categorists is that they may lack skills to create sharp market insights. This is so because there are limits to their skills in accurately assessing information that is independently and simultaneously valuable, rare and inimitable. Further, Categorists may struggle to fully assess the degree of future organisational alignment, which relies on the ability to forecast probable futures. Of course, we need to put these observations into perspective. We are not representing that Categorists never gain market insight, or that all of the market insight they gain is mundane. There will be many instances when insight comes to Categorists through the reading of new information, combined with some time to reflect on the new material they are exposed to. The process of reflection is common to us all and will produce insights in ways that we cannot programme or predict. We have all experienced moments of epiphany or 'ah ha' moments of insight! Categorists too will generate valuable market insights. All we are attempting to do in the above discussion is to make some empirically supportable generalisations about the major features of Categorists' behaviour. Through doing this we can better highlight different aspects of scanning behaviour that will be useful to keep in mind when we discuss optimising the mix of different scanning behavioural types later in this chapter.

For the Categorist, the process of gathering information, categorising it, and storing for retrieval can become an end unto itself.

The Categorists' preference for logic and order often leads to another weakness, namely their bureaucratic tendencies. Left unchecked, Categorists will spend significant amounts of time creating information directories and archives and then further time capturing information to populate these directories. A Categorist's job, much like a librarian's job, is never really done. Sometimes the process of gathering information, categorising it and storing it in a way that is convenient for retrieval, becomes an end unto itself. This sort of dynamic is sometimes seen when corporations set up 'centres of knowledge' whose prime aim is usually loosely described as 'capturing and exploiting knowledge assets'. These centres, as with Categorists, will demonstrate progress through measuring and reporting on the information that is stockpiled through their efforts. Unfortunately, what Categorists often miss is the broader view which requires assessing the merits of gathering

Without a clear view of strategic importance, the Categorist risks producing reports that contain a mass of information but no guidance.

certain types of information, in certain measure, to guide where best to devote their limited resources and effort. Without a clear view of what information is strategically important, the Categorist risks producing reports that seem to be a mass of information with no real guidance for the reader on where to focus and why.

Categorists, as their title suggests, are competent in gathering and categorising information. Perhaps as a by-product of being competent Categorists, they are relatively less competent at deriving insight and, in turn, debating implications and proposing courses of action. They are only moderately equipped to persuade other managers to their view as, although they can reference information, they cannot necessarily confidently build an argument based on insight. In this way, Categorists are somewhat marginalised in getting their view onto a management agenda and being central to management decision making. Just as a librarian's skills are different from those of an author, a Categorist's core skills are not those of a shaper of managerial decisions.

Categorists are somewhat marginalised in getting their view onto the management agenda.

The effort to capture and categorise a broad range of business environment information is substantial. The degree of effort is directly related to comprehensiveness of coverage of the business environment, number of information items and depth of content, and the extent of real-time or continuous scanning required. If Categorists put in place formal systematic scanning processes that aim to comprehensively scan the task and remote environments on a regular basis, then this implies a significant overall resource investment. As implied above, the expense largely results from the volume of work to be undertaken versus the expense of the individual Categorists themselves. Indeed, a scanning process designed by a Categorist is capable of being broken down into its component parts and each part allocated to a low to moderately skilled resource. In this way, through deconstruction and deskilling, the overall individual labour cost per unit can be low to modest. However, because of the sheer volume of work the overall resource costs, including the organisational structures and systematic processes and resources to execute the work, may be significant and another con to be aware of.

A scanning process designed by a Categorist can be broken down so that the overall individual labour cost per unit can be low to modest.

A summary of the major pros and cons of a Categorist is provided in Box 7.2. The net impression is that Categorists are competent in providing

---

Box 7.2 Categorist pros and cons

Categorist pros	*Categorist cons*
• Well organised for data capture, storage and retrieval.	• May miss deriving genuine market insight.
• Near comprehensive coverage of topics.	• Bureaucratic and difficult to decipher.
• Deliberate and effective use of multiple sources.	• Disconnected from decision making.
• Triangulation of information to identify major topics of interest.	• Expensive in total due to volume of work required.

---

comprehensive coverage of significant information topics in the task and remote environments, but less skilled in deriving market insight.

Application point: How can your firm capitalise on Categorist pros and compensate for Categorist cons?

Reflecting on the above analysis of Categorists, there are clear pros and cons to consider. How can your firm capitalise on Categorists' skills in establishing structured processes and systems to capture, store and retrieve key information on business environment matters? How can your firm benefit from a near comprehensive coverage of important topics concerning the business environment? How can your firm compensate for missed insights embedded in the information gathered? How can your firm compensate for the costs and administrative burden associated with Categorists and their approach to scanning?

Strengths and weaknesses of Monitors
Monitors can identify major task environment changes but are unlikely to develop original insights.

By way of recap, we described a Monitor as the type of manager who is moderately systematic but will generally not adhere to a formal business environment scanning process. He or she does not have fine grained screening criteria but will pay attention to information that is brought to his or her attention, generally using a few trusted sources of information.

In short, Monitors are likely to be rigid in their scanning practices; they are reasonably clear on what information seems helpful and how it links to achieving a business purpose. If information becomes overwhelming they limit scanning, but still invest enough effort to obtain a simplified view of the local environment sufficient to identify major changes. For a further detailed description of the scanning behavioural characteristics of Monitors refer back to Chapter 5.

Monitors are unlikely to design or follow a strictly formal business environment scanning process. They are only moderately systematic and formal in how they go about their scanning efforts. This moderately systematic approach manifests itself in creating established ways or routines by which monitors go about their scanning. By routine we mean an unvarying or habitual method or procedure that occurs at fixed times or regular inter-

Monitors adopt a moderately systematic approach to scanning, creating established routines and habits.

vals. The routines that Monitors develop can become established or entrenched over time. Put another way, once these routines are established they become very resistant to change. Even attempts to change behaviour through changes in formal roles and processes have limited chance of success as Monitors are only moderately systematic and therefore will only pay partial attention to such changes. The upside of routines is that they create predictable patterns of behaviour that can then be relied upon to occur. In the case of Monitors, they are likely to develop established routines focused on particular environmental sectors. We learned in our research that Monitors have a view that effective scanning should focus on the local market and adopt a short term to medium term outlook. Hence, we expect Monitors' routines to focus on, at least, the task environment covering key information concerning customers, competitors, channels and

Monitors predictably and reliably monitor select environmental sectors, especially the task environment.

suppliers. Hence, a major pro of Monitors is their predictable and reliable monitoring of select environmental sectors, and the task environment in particular.

A further positive of Monitors, related to their adoption of routines, is their regular use of established sources. Over time, Monitors become familiar with certain sources of information that have proved useful to meet their scanning goals. From our study, we learnt that Monitors tend to scan for information that is relevant to their job and firm as opposed to satisfying personal interests. To the extent that certain information sources help meet these needs, these sources become the preferred sources. These sources can be relied upon, in the eyes of the Monitor, as they have proved successful in the past. Hence, the ongoing use of these tried and tested sources is likely to result in useful information and de-risk the prospect of not identifying important information in the task environment.

Many modern managers have a short term outlook when it comes to developing strategy and doing business planning. This is in part due to the short term performance pressures exerted on managers by stakeholders, shareholders and the financial markets in general. This short term view is also

Monitors focus on information that is immediately relevant.

driven by individual managers who increasingly expect that their tenure in a particular role is short term. This last point is consistent, for example, with the continued fall in average CEO tenure to well under five years. Monitors also focus on the short term outlook and devote most of their scanning activities toward the local market. Part of the reason for Monitors' short term focus is their perception that there is only limited time available to use for external scanning and hence they need to prioritise and focus on local market changes which may demand an immediate response. A further reason for their focus on the short term is that they tend to scan for information that is relevant to their job and firm, as opposed to personal interests. This tight focus means they are once again more likely to pay attention to information in the immediate task environment than the longer term remote environment. So from the viewpoint of the modern manager, a pro of a Monitor is their focus on information that is immediately relevant.

Sometimes it is helpful to have a simplified view of the business environment. After all, a simplified view is better than no view at all! Also, a simplified view may impart clarity of the situation which helps to make decisions with confidence. Arguably, a pro associated with Monitors is that they develop a somewhat simplified view of the business environment. Monitors' view of the business environment is a simplified view for a number of reasons. First, Monitors don't have fine grained screening criteria but will instead pay attention only to information items that come to their attention. Hence, their view of the business

Monitors often develop a simplified view of the business environment, through which they often impart clarity.

environment will not be comprehensive. Second, Monitors use fewer and less varied information sources than other managers which again restricts the range of information to which they are exposed. Third, they perceive there is only limited time available for external scanning, given other job requirements. A limited amount of time translates to a limited view. Fourth, Monitors tend to scan for information that is relevant to their job and firm as opposed to broader interests. On the one hand, it is admirable that Monitors are business focused, yet on the other hand this once again limits the type of information to which they are exposed. Fifth, Monitors will limit their scanning if they perceive they are being overwhelmed by information. Again, the implication is that Monitors will have a partial view of the environment. The net outcome of the above is that a benefit Monitors can bring to the organisation is their simplified but current view of the local business environment.

The above discussion of pros of a Monitor hint at the major con which is lack of comprehensive coverage. Monitors cannot be relied upon to comprehensively cover both the task environment – customer, competitor, channel and supplier – and remote environment – political, economic, social and technological. There are three main reasons for this. First,

Monitors use established routines and limited sources so fail to comprehensively cover the environment.

Monitors do not have clear scanning objectives that explicitly target certain environmental sectors. They do not systematically set out to obtain information that covers the major events and trends in each of the task and remote environments. Nor do they have fine grained screening criteria which would at least indicate which sectors they'll pay attention to, and which sectors would be missed. Instead, Monitors will pay attention to items that are brought to their attention through executing their established routines and use of limited sources. Use of limited sources, along with contributing only limited time to scanning, is the second major reason that Monitors do not comprehensively cover the environment. As Monitors develop their scanning routines they come to use and rely on just a few trusted and tested sources. This reliance on a few sources only is a limiting factor to comprehensive coverage. We also know from our research that Monitors perceive that, in light of their job responsibilities, there is only limited time available to scan. This restricts, once again, achieving comprehensive coverage of the business environment. A third significant reason why Monitors only partially scan the environment is their unease in dealing with large volumes of information. When Monitors sense that the level of information is overwhelming they simply limit their scanning efforts. For them, this is a reasonable response as they don't have clearly held scanning goals in mind which would be threatened by this action. They also view other job roles and responsibilities to be priorities. Hence,

When Monitors become overwhelmed they simply limit their scanning efforts.

in these circumstances, Monitors will limit their scanning activities, contributing to less than comprehensive coverage.

There is one major downside to Monitors, unique to this type of manager. This concerns routines. By routine we mean an unvarying or habitual method or procedure. Over time, managers develop routines or work patterns connected with learning about events and trends in the environment outside their organisation. Ways of gathering external business information, monitoring the environment and making sense of it, eventually become routinised. If these routines are well established and are not readily influenced, then we refer to the routines as 'embedded routines'. Embedded routines are well established work patterns that are not obviously strongly related to changes in extraneous factors. Embedded scanning routines encompass biases or preferences that ultimately reflect the managers' own preferred way of learning about the business environment. Most senior managers, who exhibit Monitor scanning characteristics, will have embedded routines. The consequence is that their scanning practices will not substantially change in different circumstances. As different scanning practices are differentially effective in different market circumstances, Monitors' scanning behaviour will therefore be suboptimal in line with changing market contexts. We will discuss the

Monitors with embedded routines do not substantially change their scanning practices in different circumstances.

link between effective scanning practices and market contexts later in this chapter when we discuss market contexts and the mix of scanning behavioural types.

It's also worth noting that Monitors report themselves as having only limited skills in assessing the strategic significance of information. This is consistent with their view that they rarely receive unhelpful information! A combination of factors serves to limit Monitors' interpretative capabilities. These include lacking clear scanning goals, being only moderately systematic and analytical, absence of criteria to direct attention and satisfaction with obtaining a simplified view of the local market environment. A Monitor's difficulty stems from knowing whether knowledge is insightful. As previously argued, to assess whether knowledge is insightful, it should be tested as to whether it is simultaneously valuable, rare, inimitable and organisationally aligned. Monitors are only moderately capable of accurately making this assessment since they are only moderately alert to news about their firm's business and have limited orientation to the external business environment.

A final con of Monitors to comment on, which we have already alluded to above, is their tendency to limit information if it exceeds comfort levels. The term 'information overload' was coined by Alvin Toffler in his book, *Future Shock*. Toffler's book refers to the state of having too much information to make a decision or remain informed about a topic. Large amounts of historical information to assess, compounded by a high rate of new information being added, contradictions in available information and a low signal-to-noise ratio all contribute to information overload. Tactics to deal with information overload include not delving into too much detail, networking with knowledgeable people to source filtered knowledge and insight, parcelling out responsibilities for knowing certain subject matter among different individuals and simply limiting the amount of information exposed to when they no longer have the capacity to take it on board. The most common tactic for Monitors to deal with information overload is simply that – they limit the amount of information they are exposed to.

A summary of the major pros and cons of a Monitor is provided in Box 7.3. The net impression is that Monitors can identify major task environment changes but are unlikely to develop original insights.

Box 7.3 Monitor pros and cons

Monitor pros	*Monitor cons*
• Predictable and reliable monitoring of select environmental sectors.	• Lack comprehensive coverage.
• Regular use of established sources.	• Attention based on routines which are unlikely to change.
• Focus on information that is immediately relevant.	• Limited skills in assessing business significance.
• Form a simplified but current view of local environment.	• Will limit information if it exceeds comfort level.

Application point: How can your firm capitalise on Monitor pros and compensate for Monitor cons?

Reflecting on the above analysis of Monitors there are clear pros and cons to consider. How can your firm capitalise on Monitors' skills in predictably and reliably monitoring the task environment? How can your firm better utilise current information of key events and trends? How can your firm compensate for lack of comprehensive coverage of the environment and the remote environment in particular? How can your firm compensate for Monitors' limited skills in assessing the significance of gathered information and knowledge?

Strengths and weaknesses of Viewers
Viewers may identify novelties but are unreliable.

A Viewer is a type of manager who approaches scanning the business environment in an ad hoc manner. Viewers are uncertain about their ability to process large volumes of information and assess it for significance. As a result, they tend to spend more time attuned to internal information concerning the organisation's level of effectiveness than to external information.

In short, Viewers are unsystematic scanners, not attuned to the significance of information. They commit limited time and effort to scanning, being mostly inwardly focused. They generally lack clarity about what to scan and how to use the results to progress achieving business purposes.

In light of this description you'd be forgiven for jumping to the conclusion that Viewers are a bit useless when it comes to gaining market insight! However, as with most human attributes, a weakness can be a strength in certain circumstances. Viewers in fact have four significant benefits to an organisation in terms of their scanning behaviour. First, they intermittently scan across a broad range of information. Viewers will intermittently scan for information with no particular business purpose in mind. They consider that data or information by itself can be important even though it is not recognised as relevant to some particular purpose. The upside to this is that Viewers may literally stumble across some valuable information that may not be picked up through traditional systematic scanning processes.

> *Viewers may stumble across valuable information not picked up through traditional systematic scanning processes.*

The somewhat random nature of Viewers' attention means that their view of important events and trends in the business environment is likely to be different to views commonly held by other managers. Therefore, the value of the Viewer is the value of the alternative view. Admittedly, the value of the alternative view is a bit like a lottery ticket. In all probability, it will be worthless. After all, Viewers are not purposeful, they are limited in capacity to absorb and process information, and they are not attuned to the significance of information. The chances of them surfacing valuable information are reasonably low, as they would almost need to stumble across it, and then be just sufficiently alert to recognise it as novel and potentially valuable. An analogy is that of an unconventional gold prospector with pan and sieve in hand. This prospector goes seeking his treasure in creeks and streams that are off the beaten path and not targeted by other prospectors. One day, while wading through a stream, the prospector stubs his toe on something hard and shiny and has the wherewithal to recognise the object as a gold nugget. Admittedly, like the lottery, the odds are long but, nonetheless, incidents like this do happen. Similarly, a Viewer may stumble

> *The value of the Viewer is the value of the alternative view.*

across a piece of knowledge that could transpire to be valuable market insight.

A further pro of Viewers arises from their unpredictable approach to scanning. Specifically, Viewers will not scan in the same way, over and over. Unlike Monitors, they do not develop scanning routines, unvarying or habitual methods or procedures that occur

Viewers change their scanning practices in different circumstances, increasing the chance that they will uncover an elusive and valuable 'nugget' of knowledge.

at regular intervals. There is little chance that Viewers will develop scanning routines or work patterns that become established or entrenched over time. Rather, Viewers will change their scanning practices in different circumstances in ways that generally increase the chance of uncovering those elusive knowledge 'nuggets'. Changing scanning practices in response to changing circumstances is a pro of Viewer scanning behaviour.

A third pro of Viewers is their use of one or more varied information sources when they scan. In our research we looked at the frequency of usage of four major sources of information. The four sources were: external personal networks; internet sources including search engines, company websites and email information subscription services; traditional mediums such as television, radio, newspaper and business magazines; and company personnel such as management, colleagues and staff. Viewers reported using one or more of these sources, in different measures, as part of their scanning activity. This is important and contrasts with Monitors who tend regularly to use a few limited sources. As

Switching use of information sources increases Viewers' chances of discovering uncommon knowledge and market insights.

Viewers aren't purposeful and don't have an upfront rationale for using different sources, it appears as though they simply enjoy the variety of changing scanning practices and use of multiple sources. Switching use of information sources, and switching across a wide range of sources, increases the chances once more of discovering uncommon knowledge and market insights.

Another pro of Viewers is that they attend to more than just current information. Viewers do not insist that information needs to be immediately current for it to be valuable. The result is that, from time to time, Viewers will scan across information that is both current and historic. It is generally well accepted that there is value in obtaining current, up to date information. Traditional and systematic scanning practices focus on obtaining such information. But there can also be value in looking back at historic events and reflecting on implications for future opportunities. For example, considering a past scientific breakthrough such as DNA mapping may prompt ideas about future exploitable potential that has been missed by others. Through identifying historical events of interest, and through processes of reflection, analysis and intuition, it may be possible to generate knowledge that is simultaneously valuable, rare, inimitable and organisationally aligned. If so, then the Viewers' breadth of scanning interest, including covering pertinent historical events, can directly contribute to creating market insight.

We have highlighted above four specific pros of Viewers. In short, these are: intermittent scanning across a broad range of information; changing scanning practices in different circumstances; use of one or more of many varied sources when they scan; and attendance to more than just current information. This is useful to note and helpful to ultimately understand what Viewers can contribute to the mix of other types of scanning behaviour. Later in this chapter we discuss how to utilise a mix of scanning behavioural types. This shows how Viewers' strengths can be complementary to the strengths and weaknesses of other management types in respect to scanning.

However, when Viewers are considered in isolation, it is clear that on average, the cons outweigh the pros. The net profile of a Viewer that emerges is that of an ad hoc hapless scanner!

As standalone scanners, Viewers are not sufficiently skilled or well equipped to reliably and effectively scan the business environment.

The first major difficulty with Viewers is the ad hoc nature of their scanning which leads to variable outcomes at unpredictable times. Viewers' approach to scanning the business environment is the least systematic of all types of manager. They do not have established criteria to discern what information they need in the first place, nor do they have a structured process, explicit or implicit, to gather information. As a result, Viewers can neither be relied upon to identify knowledge nor to create insight. They may sometimes make a positive contribution to the overall mix of scanning behavioural types but, as standalone scanners, Viewers are not sufficiently skilled or well equipped to reliably and effectively scan the business environment.

Of course, to be an effective scanner of the business environment it helps to be orientated to the external environment. Alas, Viewers are the least outwardly orientated of all manager types. Viewers tend to spend more of their time attuned to internal information concerning their organisation's level of effectiveness than to external information. This may be due in part to their perception that there is a lack of reward or penalty associated with their scanning behaviour and outcomes. Whatever the reason, the result is clearly a downside to Viewers' scanning behaviour. The less exposure that Viewers have to the business environment, the less likely it is that they will identify and discern market insight.

Even if Viewers were more externally orientated, they would still be significantly disadvantaged in terms of creating market insight. This is due to their limited ability to discern what information is strategically significant, a further failing of Viewers. Viewers consider that their capacity to absorb information falls far short of the volume of information available about the business environment. They also think that, even if information in the business environment were effectively filtered down to just significant information, it would still be too voluminous to process. The perception of limited processing capacity is a limiting factor to effective scanning, as it dissuades Viewers from attempting to assess external information for strategic significance in the first place. Viewers contend that scanning for relevant strategic information in the business environment will always be an incomplete and imperfect process. Therefore, they understandably find it hard to get motivated about scanning the business environment.

The perception of limited processing capacity dissuades Viewers from attempting to assess external information for strategic significance.

A final con to comment on is the limited time that Viewers commit to scanning. Viewers commit less time to scanning than any other manager type. As discussed, this is partly due to lack of motivation to scan which seems destined to fail due to lack of ability and capacity to effectively assess information for strategic significance. Another factor is that Viewers tend to spend more of their time attuned to internal information concerning the organisation's level of effectiveness than to external information. Again, this reflects focusing on areas and activities in which Viewers think they can be effective. It also reflects their view that there is a lack of reward or penalty associated with their scanning behaviour. This issue of linkage

---

Box 7.4 Viewer pros and cons

Viewer pros

- Intermittently scan across a broad range of information.
- Scanning practices change in different circumstances.
- Use of one or more of many varied sources when scanning.
- Attend to more than just current information.

Viewer cons

- Ad hoc scanning manner is unreliable.
- More inward than outward focused.
- Limited discernment of what is significant information.
- Commit only limited time to scanning.

---

between scanning behaviour and reward is an interesting one. Our research agreed with Viewers in one respect as we found that it was rare that scanning activities were explicitly built into senior managers' perfor-

Although it is rare for it to be an explicit performance target, effective scanning is often implied in senior managers' performance goals.

mance goals. However, in another respect, our research disagreed with Viewers as many senior managers pointed out that effective scanning was implied in many of their performance goals. These senior managers considered that effective scanning was a necessary condition to meeting many of their goals which were connected to achieving success in the marketplace.

A summary of the major pros and cons of Viewers is provided in Box 7.4. The net impression is that Viewers may identify novelties in the business environment but are individually unreliable as effective scanners.

Application point: How can your firm capitalise on Viewer pros and compensate for Viewer cons?

Reflecting on the above analysis of Viewers, there are clear pros and cons to consider. How can your firm capitalise on Viewers' intermittent scanning that may reveal novel and valuable knowledge? How can your firm capitalise on Viewers' tendency to use a wide variety of information sources? How can your firm compensate for the ad hoc nature of Viewers' scanning behaviour? How can your firm compensate for Viewers' internal focus and general lack of skills in assessing the significance of external information?

The best way depends on the market

With all this knowledge we have gained from our research, the practical question remains: what is the best way to understand the business environment? The answer is something that we have alluded to several times already. The best way to understand the environment is to utilise a mix of scanning types and refine the approach to scanning, based on market context. In the remainder of this chapter we discuss how to do this.

Mix of scanning behavioural types

In Chapter 4 we made clear the characteristics of successfully understanding and analysing markets. In other words, we previously described what the outcome would look like if you were able to execute the best way to understand the business environment. We concluded that, for knowledge to be considered insight it needs to meet four criteria – valuable, rare, inimitable and organisationally aligned. We also discussed three 'indicators' of market insight being market turbulence, market complexity and soft factors. But let's put market context to one side for the moment; we will comment on this later in this chapter when we discuss market contexts and the mix of scanning behavioural types. The overarching point here is that, in order to assess the pros and cons of scanning behaviour of managers, it is helpful to begin with the end in mind.

To this end, it was helpful to understand and dissect scanning behaviour, as we did in Chapter 5. In that chapter, we shared a key research finding: we found that managers can be broadly categorised into one of four groups – Analysts, Categorists, Monitors and Viewers – and that each group has distinctive and differentiable scanning behavioural traits. We uncovered and described how each group varied in

Managers will find that no single scanning behavioural group exactly matches their scanning behaviour, but they will likely relate to one group more than the others.

terms of preferred methods of gathering information, the degree of structure applied to the scanning effort, their capacity to process information, and their analytical abilities. Of course, the four groups we described are representative of clusters of behaviour. No one manager will find that a single scanning behavioural group exactly matches his or her scanning behaviour. However, managers will likely be able to relate to one group more than the others. They will likely recognise major aspects of their own scanning behaviour in one of the groups. Uncovering the four groups enabled us to undertake a more refined analysis of scanning behaviour. Rather than generalising about what is effective and ineffective scanning behaviour as a whole, we were able to do detailed analysis and draw specific conclusions for each group of Analysts, Categorists, Monitors and Viewers.

In this chapter so far, we have concerned ourselves with assessing the pros and cons of each scanning behavioural group. We learnt that Analysts are insightful but can be conventional and incomplete; Categorists are comprehensive but often provide data rather than insight; Monitors can identify major task environment changes but are unlikely to develop original insights; and Viewers may identify novelties but are unreliable. For each group we identified and elaborated on the top four pros and cons. These strengths and weaknesses were identified by thinking through what attributes worked for and against identifying key events and trends helpful to developing strong strategy and gaining genuine market insight.

Based on our analysis of each scanning group, we can conclude that no one scanning group is optimal. Each scanning group has clear pros, but also has definite cons. We have seen that Analysts' key strength lies in their ability to be insightful through assessing whether information is valuable,

No one scanning group is optimal. Scanning effectiveness requires using various scanning types in complementary ways.

rare, inimitable and organisationally aligned. However, we also know that Analysts can end up regurgitating conventional wisdom such as a commonly held view about the business environment that is endorsed by expert analysts and industry commentators. While Categorists are highly competent at gathering a broad range of information and so achieving near comprehensive coverage of the business environment, they falter in other areas. For example, Categorists lack the interpretative skills to consistently derive market insight from the information they have gathered. A strength of

Monitors emerged as predictably and reliably monitoring select environmental sectors. For certain environmental sectors, Monitors can be relied upon to identify major events and trends of strategic significance. However, the downside is that Monitors are blind to sectors that they don't routinely monitor, and they lack the awareness to change focus regardless of changes in market context and circumstances. Viewers intermittently scan the environment in unpredictable ways that may occasionally unearth novel and valuable information. However, their ad hoc scanning manner is essentially ineffective and unreliable to provide required market insight. So it is clear that no one scanning type is optimal. No one scanning type – Analyst, Categorist, Monitor or Viewer – is sufficient to meet stated scanning goals and derive needed market insight. This suggests that it is worth thinking about scanning effectiveness from an organisational perspective that could involve various scanning types in complementary ways.

From an organisational perspective, it is imperative to understand the business environment. If an organisation fails to notice changes that turn out to be important, or does not correctly interpret changes in the environment, it may not make needed adjustments to an organisation's strategy or structure. A lack of fit between the environment and an organisation's

The strong strategy needed for success relies on competent scanning that covers the task and the remote environment.

strategy may result in performance decline. As discussed in Chapter 1, success usually has its roots in strong strategy, and strong strategy is underpinned by a sound understanding of the market. To achieve a sound understanding of the market, an organisation needs a competent scanning capability. Our research findings suggest that an organisation's scanning capability should be based around individual managers rather than systems or practices. This is because our research uncovered that there are no obvious and reliable determinants of managerial scanning behaviour per se. We found that scanning behaviour of individual managers is essentially embedded as part of their work routines. Therefore, scanning practices and systems should account for and be based on established behavioural biases.

A competent organisational scanning capability should result in a high

Scanning practices and systems should account for and be based on established behavioural biases.

degree of organisational alertness. Organisational alertness implies an ability to identify significant events and trends in both the immediate task environment and the remote environment. This is reflected in Figure 7.1, in which the x-axis represents the business environment, divided into the task environment (covering factors of customer, competitor, channel and supplier) and the remote environment (covering broader factors of political, economic, social and technological). The y-axis reflects the level of capability to identify significant events, trends and changes. Although the task and remote environments are presented in this figure as discrete and mutually exclusive, this is of course a simplification. As you use this model and tailor it to your own circumstances, it may be useful to conceptualise the task and remote environments on a continuum of scanning perspective. The narrowest perspective is the task environment, comprising internal information concerning the organisation's effectiveness, and the broadest perspective is the remote environment comprising distant events with no obvious and immediate impact on an organisation's performance.

As illustrated in Figure 7.1, an organisation needs to develop a high capability in scanning, across both the task and remote environments, in order to achieve organisational alertness. So the challenge then becomes how to build a highly competent organisational scanning capability through the involvement of different managerial scanning types. We know

Analysts, with their strength in effectively analysing business environment information, have a core role to play across the spectrum of scanning activity.

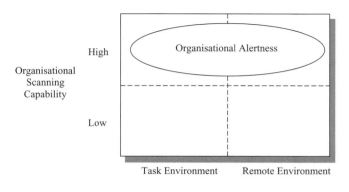

Figure 7.1 *Organisational alertness.*

that scanning capability should be developed first and foremost around senior managers in order to work with and not against embedded scanning behaviour. We also know that a competent scanning capability will result from a mix of scanning types, in order to capitalise on various known strengths and mitigate known weaknesses of any one scanning type. So let us consider the ways in which different scanning types can contribute to an organisation's scanning capability. We know that a critical skill for effective scanning is the ability to analyse information and discern which information is strategically significant and could provide genuine insight leading to competitive advantage. This ability was most obvious in the Analyst. The Analyst is therefore a key part of an organisation's scanning capability. Whether the organisation is focused on the task environment or remote environment or both, it is essential to competently analyse information from these sectors. This implies that Analysts have a core role to play across the spectrum of scanning activity. The Analyst's ability to effectively analyse the business environment information can be thought of as a dynamic capability which assists organisations to recognise and adapt to external changes.

The Categorist also has a significant role to play in achieving organisational alertness. Categorists contribute a highly structured and thorough information gathering effort directly relevant to stated business objectives. Provided that an organisation can clearly articulate its business objectives, Categorists can develop systematic and structured processes to capture, categorise and present relevant information. Categorists can play a key role in comprehensively gathering information across the task and remote environments. They can also play a useful interpretative role. Categorists' interpretative abilities are not as well developed as Analysts', but they can still be contributory. Categorists can be very effective at interpreting which information topics are generally regarded as strategically significant. These topics can then at least be brought to the attention of other managers, especially Analysts, for further interpretation.

Categorists play a key role by developing systematic and structured processes to capture, categorise and present relevant information.

Monitors also have a role to play in contributing to a competent organisational scanning capability. You'll recall that Monitors have a reasonably narrow and short term focus on external information and often focus on information directly related to business purposes. Monitors make consistent use of information sources and methods to effectively monitor for the presence of abnormal items or major changes in the environmental sectors upon which they are focused. So, in terms of our model of organisational alertness, Monitors may play a significant and effective role in scanning the task environment, and a less obvious role in scanning the remote environment. Once Monitors have identified significant changes or other strategically valuable information in the task environment, they can then share this with Analysts and Categorists, who both have better analytical and interpretative skills.

Monitors play an effective role in scanning the task environment, making consistent use of information sources and methods to monitor for the presence of abnormal items or major changes.

If an organisation was restricted to using just three scanning types to form its Organisational Scanning Capability it should undoubtedly choose Analysts, Categorists and Monitors. Two of these types, Analysts and Categorists, are necessary to create a highly competent scanning capability; Analysts are needed for their interpretative skills and Categorists for their comprehensive coverage. Monitors, while not strictly necessary to create a highly competent organisational scanning capability, are helpful as they can perform some of the scanning functions very effectively (i.e. scanning for major changes in the task environment), and quite possibly at the lowest cost and in a more timely manner. That leaves Viewers as somewhat surplus to requirements, although not entirely without value. Viewers undertake periodic informal reviews of information items of intuitive interest using alternative sources and methods. The greatest possibility for a Viewer to make a complementary contribution is to detect some novel

Viewers might make a complementary contribution by detecting a novel event or trend in the remote environment that may be strategically significant.

event or trend in the remote environment that may be strategically significant. A Viewer would then need to bring these novel items to the attention of an Analyst for interpretation.

In summary, each scanning behavioural type – Analyst, Categorist, Monitor and Viewer – can play a contributory role in achieving organisational alertness. Analysts are essential to competently interpret significant

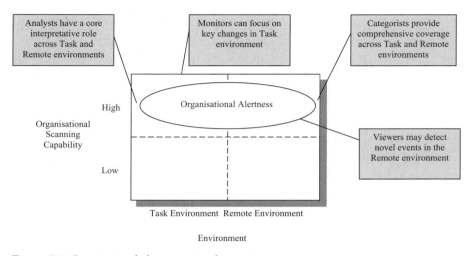

Figure 7.2 *Organisational alertness: mix of scanning types.*

events and trend information across both task and remote environments. Categorists are necessary to comprehensively gather information and identify key topics across the task and remote environments. Monitors can be set up to identify significant changes or strategically valuable information in the task environment. And Viewers, as an optional extra, can potentially detect some novel events or trends in the remote environment that may be strategically significant. Figure 7.2 illustrates where and how each of the different scanning types may effectively contribute to organisational alertness.

If an organisation wants to develop a high capability to effectively scan the business environment, it should leverage the strengths of Analysts, Categorists, Monitors and Viewers. Through utilising all scanning types, *An organisation requires enough Analysts to complete the interpretative role, being careful not to fall into the trap of 'analysis paralysis'.*

in the specific areas and ways discussed above, an organisation can optimise its scanning capability. In terms of the mix of scanning types to utilise, some guidelines are as follows. Analysts are a necessary part of the mix. Without Analysts in the fray, an organisation's interpretative ability will be impaired and the quality of any outcome will be in question. We know that quality Analysts are rare and that they are an expensive resource. Therefore they should be carefully sourced and used judiciously. An organisation should involve as many Analysts as required to complete the crucial interpretative role, while being careful not to fall into the trap of 'analysis paralysis'. The number of Analysts will therefore be a function of the amount of information they need to analyse and interpret. If possible, the information provided to Analysts should be pre-filtered through an initial assessment for significance. This initial assessment and filtering activity can be competently undertaken by Categorists.

The number of Categorists needed is largely a function of the targeted breadth of coverage and depth of information to obtain. Generally

The number of Categorists needed depends on market context and content complexity.

speaking, we'd expect the number of Categorists to be greater than the number of Analysts, although this can differ based on market context and complexity of content which we'll discuss in the next section of this chapter. As Categorists are less rare and expensive than Analysts, it pays to increase the Categorist to Analyst ratio. This is on the basis that Categorists can effectively assess and pre-filter information for strategic significance.

We have seen that Monitors can be effective in identifying significant changes or strategically valuable information in the task environment. We also know that Monitors do this

Monitors can reduce the work effort of expensive Analysts and Categorists.

through established work routines. Hence, it is desirable to capitalise on their work routines as much as possible. By leveraging the scanning work that Monitors are already doing we avoid having to add further resources and incur further costs. Also, by explicitly understanding the scanning work that Monitors are doing, we can reduce accordingly the work effort of Analysts and Categorists. This helps once again to reduce overall costs of an Organisation Scanning Capability.

Similar to Monitors, Viewers are already undertaking their particular scanning activities and hence it's useful to leverage that work. However, unlike Monitors, it is not possible to rely on Viewers' output as a substitute for work done by Categorists in iden-

Viewer output needs to be passed to Categorists to be assessed and filtered for significance.

tifying key events and trends in the remote environment. Instead, Viewer output needs to be fed into Categorists who can initially assess and pre-filter

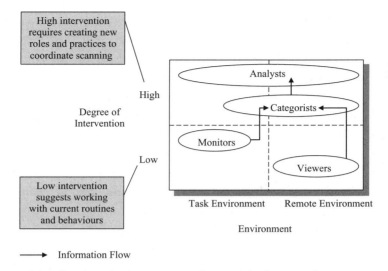

Figure 7.3 *Mix of scanning types: environmental cover and information flows.*

for significance and possible forwarding to Analysts. Again, Viewers are an optional extra. It is worth including them in the mix of scanning types; however, it is not sufficient to achieve a competent organisational scanning capability.

Some of the key relationships discussed above are illustrated in Figure 7.3. On the x-axis we have reflected the task environment and the remote environment. On the y-axis we have indicated the degree of intervention needed to guide scanning behaviour. At the low end, the degree of intervention required for both Monitors and Viewers is merely to pass on the outcomes of their scanning activities to Categorists for initial assessment. At the high end, a greater degree of design and intervention is required to ensure that Analysts' and Categorists' activities are coordinated and mutually supportive. In Figure 7.3, we have also illustrated the suggested degree of environmental coverage for each scanning type. Analysts should cover all of the task and remote environments. Categorists should cover some of the task environment (i.e. that part not already covered by Monitors) and the entire remote environment. Monitors should cover the part of task envi-

Monitors and Viewers need to pass on the outcomes of their scanning activities to Categorists for initial assessment. Analysts' and Categorists' activities need to be coordinated and mutually supportive.

ronment that they can comprehensively cover and adequately interpret. And Viewer activity should be encouraged in the remote environment. We have also illustrated information flow to highlight that Monitors and Viewers should pass their findings to Categorists. Categorists should, in turn, undertake an initial assessment and categorisation of all information and then forward it to Analysts as appropriate.

The above discussion and Figure 7.3 highlight that a mix of all scanning types can be helpful to achieve a highly competent organisational scanning capability. We have pointed out which scanning types are necessary for effective scanning; which combination of scanning types are necessary and sufficient for effective scanning; and which combinations provide the best set up for effective scanning. We have also offered guidelines for determining the right number of scanning types and, in some cases, the right relative ratio of scanning types. These recommendations hold true in the vast majority of cases. However, sometimes in different market contexts it is advantageous to alter these recommendations and the mix of scanning types employed. Suggested refinements to the mix of scanning types based on different market contexts is the subject of the next section in this chapter.

Application point: What is the best mix of scanning types to develop a competent organisational scanning capability?

In light of the above discussion, what is the right mix of scanning types to establish a highly competent organisational scanning capability in your organisation? What mix of Analysts should your firm utilise to complete the crucial interpretative role while being careful not to fall into the trap of 'analysis paralysis'? What mix of Categorists is required given your firm's coverage and depth of information required? What scanning routines are being undertaken by Monitors that could be leveraged as part of the scanning mix? In your circumstances, is it helpful to include Viewers in the mix to identify additional needed assets?

Market contexts and mix of scanning behavioural types

We've previously argued that gaining market insight is increasingly difficult with the growing complexity and turbulence of markets. We've pointed out that market complexity is increasingly due to increases in the number of significant market factors, the increasing significance of those market factors on business performance and the intertwining of those market factors. This, combined with increased turbulence (i.e. increases in the rate of changes in market factors) in both the remote and task environments, is adding to the difficulty of understanding the business environment.

However, this difficulty in understanding the business environment can also be an opportunity for organisations with superior scanning capability. You'll recall from Chapter 2 that our research identified three 'indicators' of market insight: namely that market insight is associated with market turbulence, market complexity and soft factors. A relevant Chinese proverb comes to mind concerning crisis as opportunity. The meaning is that, in chaos, opportunities will present them-selves if you are ready to take advan-tage of them. An organisation that invests in developing superior scan-ning capabilities will be better posi-tioned to recognise and take advantage of the opportunities that exist in complex and turbulent markets.

An organisation that develops superior scanning capabilities is better positioned to take advantage of opportunities in complex and turbulent markets.

Understanding market context is crucial for three reasons. First, market context is an indicator of the presence of potential market insight. Where there are high levels of complexity and turbulence there are greater oppor-tunities to gain unique market insight. Second, different market contexts impact on the effectiveness of scanning behaviours. For example, in a high complexity and high turbulence market state, the task of comprehensively gathering information is likely to be very difficult and, by the time informa-tion is gathered, categorised and ready for analysis, it may be too historic to be useful. Hence, in these circumstances, the scanning behavioural charac-teristics of Categorists are likely to be less valuable than Analysts. Third, a particular market context suggests what mix of scanning behaviours is likely to be effective. If we understand

Market context suggests the mix of scanning behaviours likely to be effective.

the current market context, we can proactively alter the mix of scanning types to optimise our scanning process and outcomes. We will elaborate on this link between market context and scanning mix shortly.

In understanding market context, the key dimensions to understand are market complexity and market turbulence. Market complexity, as perceived by practising managers, can be a difficult concept to pin down. Most managers, when asked whether their market is complex, will reply affirmatively. As most managers are immersed

Most managers perceive their market to be complex, whether or not it is.

in the detail of their business and markets, it undoubtedly seems complex. But it is also possible to test whether their perceptions are borne out by objective analysis. As a starting point, our working definition of market complexity is a measure of the number of implications that a market has for the business. Put another way, the greater the number of implications the environment holds for a business, the more complex it is. Hence, market complexity is increasing if any of the following are true: the number of significant market factors we have to consider is increasing; the implications of each of those market factors is increasing; and market factors are combining differently to create more implications for the business. By market factors, we mean the components of the task and remote environments.

It is also worth recapping briefly on the meaning of market turbulence as the other key dimension underlying market context. Market turbulence is defined as the rate of change of the market factors that contribute to complexity. More specifically, we define turbulence as the rate of change in the implications of the remote and task environments. Turbulence can arise from changes in three areas of implications: implications due to new factors; new implications of existing factors; and implications that arise from combinations of factors. (For further detail on the growing complexity of markets and the increasing turbulence they exhibit, refer back to Chapter 2.)

For the two dimensions of market turbulence and market complexity, it is important to understand the concepts and also very useful to be able to quantifiably measure complexity and turbulence. This is important to

Objective assessment enables a more accurate diagnosis of the complexity and turbulence of the market.

provide a more objective assessment of each dimension. After all, we are aware that managers' perceptions are often distorted; the majority of managers perceive the environment to be more complex and more turbulent than it really is. This more objective assessment will in turn enable a more accurate diagnosis of the state of your market.

In Chapter 6 we set out how to more objectively assess market complexity and turbulence in an evidence-based way. Although no market assessment can ever be completely accurate or objective, we proposed an approximate solution to a problem that is not completely solvable. Our solution involves dividing up the market into several component parts and then assessing the complexity and turbulence of each component. Specifically, we proposed assessing five component areas for complexity: customer complexity; channel complexity; competitor complexity; remote environment complexity; and value proposition complexity. This serves as a checklist to make sure that important factors contributing to market complexity are taken into account when assessing the market. We also developed scales of market complexity for each of the above five component areas. These modes help assess various subcomponents of market complexity on a 1 (simple) to 5 (complex) scale. Our approach also involves weighting each of the components resulting in an overall average weighted score of market complexity. Similarly, self assessment checklists and scales were developed to help assess market turbulence. The net result is that we have a standardised approach and set of diagnostics that more accurately and objectively measures market complexity and market turbulence.

Accepting that the two most important underlying dimensions of the market are complexity and turbulence, and appreciating that we have a process and tools to assess levels of complexity and turbulence, it is possible to derive at least four market contexts from combinations of two levels of market complexity (low and high) and two levels of market turbulence (low and high). For ease of reference we have attached labels to each market context as follows: Market Context 1 is 'Gusty'; Market Context 2 is 'Storm'; Market Context 3 is 'Calm'; and Market Context 4 is 'Fluky'. As you will probably recognise, these are common labels used to describe different weather and wind conditions. The meaning behind labels Storm and Calm is self evident. The label Gusty reflects dramatic changes in wind strength, such as light air followed by a gust of strong wind, whereby the direction of the wind is reasonably constant. In this way, it seems an apt reflection of

It is possible to derive at least four market contexts from combined levels of complexity and turbulence.

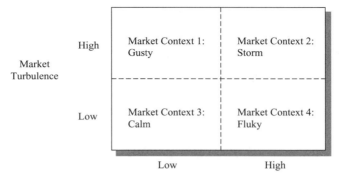

Figure 7.4 *Four market contexts.*

high turbulence (i.e. changes in the force of wind) but low complexity (i.e. generally no change in the direction of the wind). The label Fluky may not be so well known to non-sailors. Fluky reflects conditions in which the wind changes direction in unpredictable ways, although the wind strength is generally light to moderate. Fluky wind conditions are difficult or complex conditions in which to sail. The four market contexts, and their labels, are represented in a simple two-by-two table in Figure 7.4.

Using the process and tools in Chapter 6, you can assess which of the four market contexts described in Figure 7.4 best reflects your situation. Once you have done this, it is possible to deduce the impact of any one market context on the effectiveness of individual scanning types.

Let us look at one example to illustrate this point. Let us suppose that your market context is 'Market Context 2: Storm'. This is a market context comprising high complexity and high turbulence. For this market context we can consider whether it makes each of Analysts, Categorists, Monitors and Viewers more or less valuable than average in terms of scanning effectiveness and gaining insight. In this case, for Market Context 2: Storm, we argue that Analysts become more valuable because interpretative and analytical skills are in greater need to gain insight. It is important to quickly comprehend information and learn lessons; and there is less likelihood of being swayed by commonly socialised 'expert opinion', as it won't have time to form. As for Categorists, we argue that they would be less valuable than average in Market Context 2: Storm. This is because there is limited historic information available to capture. Comprehensive coverage may be too slow and achievable only at the expense of honing in on key areas. In this context, too, it will be more difficult for Categorists to do the initial discernment of strategically significant topics and information. Monitors, on the other hand, are more valuable in Market Context 2: Storm. This is so because it is more important to have a constant focus on the business environment and especially important to focus on the task environment and short term changes and implications. A real-time, albeit simplified, view of the task environment is useful in a highly complex and turbulent situation. In contrast, Viewers are less valuable. Although they may still detect novel events, there are many more novel and significant events that will likely be missed. Rather than independent and intermittent scanning, more scanning activity is needed and, in this market context where the external environment is more significant, more seasoned externally orientated managerial talent is needed. Hence, in Market Context 2: Storm, an organisation's scanning capability can be optimised by changing the mix of scanning behaviour types in favour of more Analysts and Monitors, and fewer Categorists and Viewers.

In Table 7.1 below, we have indicated the impact of four market contexts on the scanning effectiveness of each of the four scanning types of Analysts, Categorists, Monitors and Viewers. An upward arrow indicates where a scanning type is more valuable in a certain context; a downward arrow indicates less value in that context. We have also set out key points that support our net assessment of the change in value for each scanning type. This table should be referenced to guide decisions about the mix of scanning types in different contexts, with the aim being to optimise an organisation's overall scanning capability.

Application point: How should you alter the mix of scanning behaviour types to optimise your scanning capability in your market context?

As discussed above, market context impacts on scanning effectiveness. Consider the four market contexts above and assess which best reflects your own market. For your market context, which of Analysts, Categorists, Monitors and Viewers are relatively more valuable than average? For your market context, which are relatively less valuable on average? What changes to mix of scanning behaviour types are therefore required?

Table 7.1 *Changes in mix of scanning types by market context.*

	Analyst	Categorist	Monitor	Viewer
Market Context 1:	⬇ Reasons:	⬆ Reasons:	⬆ Reasons:	⬇ Reasons:
Gusty Low Complexity and High Turbulence	• Less difficult to secure exclusive insight due to low complexity • In-depth considerations of implications is not required • Analysts are expensive resource if main use is to keep up to date with non-complex, albeit fast paced change	• Sufficient interpretative skills to identify strategically significant information and derive insight • Context suits a structured process to quickly gather and update information banks • Use of multiple sources and triangulation is helpful to speed of update of information and ensures comprehensive view is obtained	• Reliable and regular monitoring of the environment is helpful to keep track of fast paced changes • Focus on task environment in turbulent times is helpful to identify short term impacts and address short term implications • A current but simplified view of local environment is sufficient for scanning purposes, given low complexity	• Intermittent frequency of scanning is disadvantage in fast paced environment as many changes will likely be missed • Most important information is current and not historic • Fast pace of change will further frustrate efforts at accurate discernment of significant information

Table 7.1 (*Continued*)

	Analyst	Categorist	Monitor	Viewer
Market Context 2:	⬆	⬇	⬆	⬇
	Reasons:	Reasons:	Reasons:	Reasons:
Storm High Complexity and High Turbulence	• Difficult to get insight, therefore need more Analyst skills • Need to quickly comprehend information, so need quick learners • Less likely to be swayed by commonly accepted 'expert' opinion as it will not have time to form	• Limited historic information available to capture • Comprehensive cover may be too slow, and at expense of honing in on key areas • More difficult to do initial discernment of strategically significant topics and information	• More important to have constant focus on environmental sectors • Especially important to focus on task environment and short term impacts • At least generates a current, real-time view, even if a bit simplified	• Although may still detect novel events, there are now many more novel and significant events in the market that will likely be missed • Rather than infrequent, intermittent scanning, more scanning is now needed • Given the environment is now more significant with greater implications on performance, need seasoned externally orientated managers

Table 7.1 (*Continued*)

	Analyst	Categorist	Monitor	Viewer
Market Context 3:	⬇ Reasons:	⬆ Reasons:	⬇ Reasons:	⬆ Reasons:
Calm Low Complexity and Low Turbulence	• Less need for interpretative skills as market context is straightforward • Less complexity in general which may be dealt with more cost effectively with lesser skilled resources • More likelihood to be hobbyist and focus on favourite interest areas at organisation's expense	• Well suited to competently interpret given low level of complexity • Sufficient time available to do structured scanning approach • Can de-skill process into discrete tasks and reduce cost to execute	• Changes detected in task environment are likely to already be picked up by Categorist • Less need to focus on immediately relevant information as rate of change is slow • Simplified view is less valuable as it should be possible to develop a comprehensive view	• May add to stock of market insights which are difficult to come by in this market context • Limited time commitment to scan is OK as increased time doesn't greatly increase chances of finding insight in this context • Focus on more than just current information is helpful as new information is slow to emerge

Table 7.1 (*Continued*)

	Analyst	Categorist	Monitor	Viewer
Market Context 4:	⬆	⬆	⬇	⬇
	Reasons:	Reasons:	Reasons:	Reasons:
Fluky High Complexity and Low Turbulence	• High complexity places a premium on interpretative and analytical skills • Low turbulence helps to provide time and space to thoroughly investigate events and implications • Can effectively utilise expensive Analyst resource through focus on complex areas, rather than keeping abreast of large volume of information as in turbulent environments	• Greater need to ensure right information to investigate complexity • Triangulation of sources is particularly helpful to test validity of information • Complementary interpretative abilities are useful in complex environment, and more likely to be incorporated in state of low turbulence	• Value of constant attention on environmental sectors is less valuable as there are fewer changes occurring • Focus on short term is less important as slow moving environment allows time to react to changes and implications • Simplified view is second best given highly complex environment	• An increase in complexity further challenges ability to discern strategic information • Broad brush and infrequent scanning is unlikely to help grapple with complexity • Low turbulence does not essentially change ad hoc and ultimately ineffectual nature of scanning

Powerpoints

- Analysts are insightful but can be conventional and incomplete.
- Categorists are comprehensive but often provide data rather than insight.
- Monitors can identify major task environment changes but are unlikely to develop original insights.
- Viewers may identify novelties but are unreliable.
- The best way to understand the environment is to utilise a mix of scanning types.
- The right mix of scanning types can result in high organisational alertness across the task and remote environments.
- Scanning effectiveness is impacted by market context.
- At least four market contexts should be considered – derived from two levels of market complexity (low and high) and two levels of market turbulence (low and high).
- Each of the four market contexts impacts on the relative value of Analysts, Categorists, Monitors and Viewers.
- A self assessment of market context, and application of research learnings, can lead to changes in mix of scanning types to optimise a firm's scanning capability.

8

Putting it together – how firms create insight

*'Once you understand the foundations of cooking you really
don't need a cookbook anymore'*
Thomas Keller

We're probably on safe ground if we assert, even without evidence, that
more management books are bought than read. We think it is also quite
likely that more management books are read than applied in practice. And
of those precious few examples of applied management books, we think a
fair proportion of the attempted applications probably fail, ending in frustra-
tion, wasted time and opportunity cost. Why this is may be attributable
to a million reasons, but our combined experience of writing, reading and
applying more management texts than we care to remember suggests at least
one plausible explanation. Many management books, we argue, lack foundation. Either the authors had no basis,
other than opinion, for what they
wrote or they failed to communicate
what underpinned their ideas to the
reader. An incomplete understanding of management ideas, we believe,
condemns them to failure when the concepts meet the stern test of practice.
It is for that reason that we have tried to give this work strong foundations
in the preceding chapters. The prescriptions of this penultimate chapter are
built on the foundation ideas discussed so far in this book.

*The prescriptions of this chapter
are built on the foundation ideas
discussed so far in this book.*

In Chapter 1, we identified market insight as a near essential antecedent of strong strategy and organisational success. Some organisations, it is true, get lucky and exist in market contexts where favourable circumstances and weak competitors combine to create success without insight, but we and they would be foolish to depend on that situation occurring or continuing.

In Chapter 2, we examined how difficult it is to make market insight and be successful, as evidenced by a failure rate of firms that is the same as that for biologically driven species. We also described the false promise of analytics and the vain hope that data crunching alone would lead to market insight. Instead, we found that analytics is just one element of the 'data-to-value' process captured in Smith's Wheel model.

In Chapter 3, we invited the reader to be self critical and examine his or her own scanning behaviour. This involved understanding dimensions of scanning such as formality, breadth, incompleteness and what might be called 'personalness'. In most circumstances, this dissection of scanning and self examination leads to an increased self awareness of one's weaknesses and one's potential.

In Chapter 4, we applied the maxim 'begin with the end in mind' to explore what market insight looks like. Defined as knowledge about the market that meets the VRIO criteria, we developed research based but practical definitions of each of these four criteria. Further, we developed a taxonomy based on breadth, continuousness and transience. We also identified that market insight usually has its roots in complexity, turbulence and intangible factors.

In Chapter 5, we explored the results of our research into how firms scan their environment. We found scanning to be embedded in behaviour and consequently hard to manage. It is also frequently neglected and under-resourced as a business process. Importantly, we found that managers' actual behaviour clustered into four general types or groups, which we labelled Analysts, Categorists, Monitors and Viewers.

In each of Chapters 1 to 5, market complexity and market turbulence recurred as moderators of scanning and insight creation processes. Hence Chapter 6 looked at market complexity and turbulence, defined them and uncovered the problem of subjectivity in assessing them. Accordingly, the bulk of Chapter 6 developed approaches for the objective assessment of both complexity and turbulence.

In Chapter 7, we began to knit together the ideas that insight is fed by scanning behaviour and that different types of scanning behaviour exist. Critically, we examined the pros and cons of each different scanning behaviour. This led us toward the conclusion that no single behaviour is ideal and that a balance of behaviours is needed. The ideal nature of that balance, however, depended on the complexity and turbulence of the market.

In this chapter, Chapter 8, we will build on the foundations of Chapters 1 to 7 and prescribe a process for making market insight. This is described in two parts. Firstly, developing an effective scanning behaviour that makes sense of the business environment in which you operate. Secondly, using the data and information that comes from the scanning process to create knowledge and find market insight amongst that knowledge. Hence, by the end of this chapter, the reader should not only know what to do but why they should be doing it, making it much more likely that this book, already bought and read, will be applied with success in practice. As the quote from Thomas Keller at the head of this chapter implies, we seek to make you not need this book ever again.

Developing scanning capability to make sense of the business environment

In our experience, developing an effective scanning capability can be broken down into a few critical steps. Based on our research, these steps represent the minimum necessary activities to develop an effective and competent scanning capability.

Step 1: Allocate scanning capability responsibility

A precedent to undertaking these steps is allocating the responsibility to someone, ideally one person, for planning how to achieve scanning effectiveness. This person should be formally responsible for designing the scanning capability and developing the scanning process. The person needs to be skilled and experienced in a number of areas to be successful in this endeavour. First, they need to be knowledgeable of the firm's strategy. This is important in order to develop and articulate key scanning goals in light of the current or emergent strategy. Knowledge of the firm's strategy will help in prioritising which environment sectors to pay the greatest attention to. Second, they should be skilled in assessing individual managers and their scanning behaviours. In order for the prescriptions in this book to be acted upon, it is helpful to broadly classify managers into one of four scanning behaviour types – Analysts, Categorists, Monitors or Viewers (as described in Chapter 5). If this proves too difficult then it is suggested to ascertain which pros and cons of scanning behaviour (as described in Chapter 7) are exhibited by each of the management team and senior associates who may contribute to scanning activities. And if this proves too difficult, it should at least be possible to assess managers' scanning behaviour on four key dimensions of formality, personalness, completeness and breadth (as explained in Chapter 3). The point here is that the person designing the scanning capability and scanning processes needs to be capable of accurately assessing the scanning strengths and weaknesses of fellow managers and associates. Third, the lead candidate needs to be able to objectively assess the market context,

The person designing the scanning capability and processes needs to accurately assess the scanning strengths and weaknesses of fellow managers and associates.

and not fall into the trap of assuming that the local market is overly complex or turbulent, as discussed in Chapter 6.

We would expect this person to be directly allocated scanning design and process responsibility by the CEO, given the critical nature of the activity. We would also expect that this person will be a member of the senior management team. It is desirable to have a senior person in this position, as their organisational authority can be helpful to ensure cooperative behaviour among senior managers, and to ensure that scanning activities are afforded due importance and priority. For ease of reference throughout the rest of this chapter, we will refer to this person as the Scanning Capability Manager.

Application point: Who is best qualified to design your organisation's scanning capability?

In light of the preferred criteria set out above, who is the best candidate in your organisation to be responsible for achieving firm-wide scanning effectiveness? Are they knowledgeable on the firm's strategy? Are they skilled in assessing individual managers and their scanning behaviours? Are they equipped to accurately assess market context?

Step 2: Reflect on strategy

One of the initial steps for the Scanning Capability Manager is to reflect on the firm's current strategy, whether explicitly documented, espoused or emergent. In Chapter 1 we discussed that, for the most part, success flows from strong strategy and that strategy is best understood as a set of managerial decisions by which effort and resources are allocated. By reflecting on a firm's strategy, it is possible to identify key underlying assumptions (there will always be assumptions as strategy relates to a future state which is unknowable for certain) that connect

A firm's strategy is based on underlying assumptions, as it relates to a future state which is unknowable.

to certain environmental sectors, events or trends which therefore require prioritised scanning attention.

We also previously explored the connection between strong strategy and market understanding as follows: success comes from strong strategy, which is the result of effective strategy making processes, which is a function of matching that process to market conditions, and hence success is underpinned by an understanding of the market. Gaining an understanding of the market does not necessarily mean the analysis would be led by the marketing department, although in many firms the primary responsibility for assessing where the market is going lies with marketers. It is therefore instructive to consider what the key characteristics of strong marketing strategy are, as these characteristics can highlight core items to pay attention to in the market place. For example, we know that strong strategy should define real segments, tailor the offer, be unique, anticipate the future and be SWOT aligned. This implies that scanning should cover certain items, at a minimum, such as customer needs and motivational drivers; knowledge of the 'marketing mix' – i.e. product or service, promotion, price, place, people, process and physical evidence – for your own firm and competitors; information on competitor offerings for analysis to identify how to distinguish your offerings; output that informs development of viable future market scenarios; and a profile of competitor strengths and weaknesses to permit SWOT analysis.

Reflect on the strategy to highlight sectors and factors that have the most significant impact on your firm's ability to gain and sustain competitive advantage and, therefore, warrant the most scanning attention.

As well as the specific items described above, it is useful to generally identify which sectors of the environment are most important and deserve prioritised attention. A starting point is simply to consider where to pay attention across the task and remote environments, and to determine the ranking of importance among the factors of customer, competitor, channel, suppliers, political, economic, social and technology. Reflecting on the strategy should highlight which sectors and factors are most important to scan. It is those factors that have the most significant impact on your firm's ability to grow market share, and gain and sustain competitive advantage, that warrant the most scanning attention.

Application point: What does your strategy imply in terms of where to prioritise your scanning attention?

What is the status of each of the following items and which items are a high priority for ongoing scanning attention: customer needs and motivations? marketing mix? competitor or substitute offerings? future market scenarios? competitor strengths and weaknesses?

Step 3: State scanning goals

In Chapter 3 we commented extensively on our puzzlement at the lack of formal systematic scanning systems, practices and processes. We concluded, consistent with numerous prior studies, that scanning behaviour among senior managers was fundamentally ad hoc, informal and unsystematic. Our study highlighted that ad hoc scanning behaviour is characterised by an upfront lack of clarity on what data and information are being sought and why. In other words, what was noticeably missing were scanning goals.

By scanning goals we mean explicit aims for each of the three main components or areas of scanning. To recap, *Ad hoc scanning behaviour noticeably lacks scanning goals.* those components were: how managers gather external information; what external business information managers pay attention to; and where managers source external business information from. The Scanning Capability Manager should create goals for each of these three areas and factor in the characteristics of individual scanning behavioural types before parcelling out individual responsibilities.

Scanning goals, like other managerial goals, are useful to inform us about what we are striving to achieve. In clearly setting out our aims, it is easier for managers to determine what needs to be done and what resources and effort are needed to enable these activities.

Scanning goals should connect to strategy. As a result of reflecting on your strategy, it should be possible to identify which aspects of your strategy are particularly reliant on or sensitive to market insight. A well developed strategy should show the link between market insight and organisational performance. For those areas where market insight is fundamental to performance (i.e. if market insight is wrong then performance may immediately and dramatically suffer), specific scanning goals should be developed to update understanding of the business environment in those relevant areas. Further, in those areas where we expect market insight to be short-lived (for example, in business environments with high complexity and high turbulence), specific scanning goals should be established to ensure frequent scanning leading to frequent updates to market insight.

A review of the strategy may also highlight significant issues (measured in terms of long-term return on investment) and urgent issues (those which constitute an immediate problem). If an issue has informational needs that are clearly definable, then these should be translated into clear scanning goals.

Scanning goals should take into account the adequacy of existing information, the availability of additional information or data and the predictability with which information may appear. Scanning goals should also sensibly be moderated by the time and effort that senior managers and associates can devote to scanning; the number and nature of important issues competing for attention and the type of managerial scanning types (i.e. Analyst, Categorists, Monitors and Viewers).

Once scanning goals have been set, they should be re-enforced through reward and recognition policies. All scanning types – Analysts, Categorists, Monitors and Viewers – should be expressly rewarded or penalised based on their scanning behaviour, in accordance with expectations set out by the Scanning Capability Manager.

Application point: What are your organisation's scanning goals?

Setting scanning goals is particularly important given the endemic state of scanning as ad hoc, informal and unsystematic. What are your goals in terms of: how managers gather external information? what external business information managers pay attention to? where managers source business information from? how goals connect to your strategy? specific goals for Analysts, Categorists, Monitors and Viewers?

Step 4: Prioritise environment sectors for attention

An important part of effective scanning is directing scanning attention to the right areas of the environment. The right areas are largely a function of strategy, potential for market insight

An important part of effective scanning is directing scanning attention to the right areas of the environment.

and market context. In certain circumstances, it will be clear which business environment sectors to focus on and for how long. In other circumstances, it will be less clear where to prioritise attention and determinations about prioritisation may need to be regularly reviewed. Let us consider further the key drivers of prioritising attention.

The first major driver is strategy. As discussed in Step 2: Reflect on strategy, scanning should cover certain items as a minimum as part of developing strong strategy. These items include customer needs and motivational drivers, knowledge of the 'marketing mix' for your own and competitor firms; information on competitor offerings and customer perceived value; and competitor SWOT (strengths, weakness, opportunities and threats) analysis. This implies a focus on the task environment, with general prioritisation given to customer factors and competitor factors, over channel and supplier factors. But this could change depending on a firm's specific strategy. For example, if a strategy hinged on tying up exclusive arrangements with key suppliers then supplier factors would take on additional importance. Reflecting on the specifics of a strategy should highlight which sectors and factors are most important to scan. Issues that directly relate to gaining and sustaining competitive advantage and achieving growth targets should be prioritised along with accordant scanning attention.

Issues that directly relate to gaining and sustaining competitive advantage, and achieving growth targets, should be prioritised along with accordant scanning attention.

The second major driver of which business environment sectors to focus on is potential for market insight. As discussed in Chapter 4, only when information is contextualised and synthesised with other information does it become knowledge and only some of that knowledge constitutes insight. We also learnt that a critical first step towards gaining insight is to filter knowledge through the VRIO criteria (i.e. valuable, rare, inimitable and organisationally aligned criteria). Therefore, scanning attention should be directed to knowledge that has the greater potential to simultaneously meet with VRIO criteria. Of course, it may be difficult to intuit upfront which knowledge has a high likelihood of simultaneously meeting the VRIO criteria and hence guiding scanning effort. Nonetheless, the VRIO criteria are helpful to keep in mind because, if some knowledge under consideration does not meet one of the initial criteria (e.g. valuable), then scanning attention could be re-directed away from that item.

The sectors to pay attention to should also be driven by market context. We're aware that true market insight, whereby knowledge simultaneously meets all VRIO criteria, is exquisite. We also know that the first two indicators of where exquisite knowledge may be found are market turbulence and market complexity. All markets have some degree of turbulence or change going on and it's in these pockets of turbulence that market insight is often found. The second indicator is market complexity. Where there is complexity, there is greater potential to derive insight. In Chapter 7 we derived four market contexts from combinations of two levels of complexity (low and high), and two levels of turbulence (low and high). We then attached labels to each of the four market contexts as follows: Market Context 1: Gusty (low complexity, high turbulence); Market Context 2: Storm (high complexity, high turbulence); Market Context 3: Calm (low complexity, low turbulence); and Market Context 4: Fluky (high complexity, low turbulence). An assessment of the market contexts in which your firm operates can be valuable as a predictor of market insight. Prime facie, market contexts labelled Storm and Fluky are the most likely contexts to house insights. A ranking of contexts from most to least potential for market insight is: Storm, Fluky, Gusty, Calm. This provides some further guidance on where to pay attention.

We recommend that you also think about prioritisation at the level of task and remote environments. Consider whether one of these environments is more important in terms of strategic significance and impact on performance. Next, consider the factors within the task and remote environments and rank them in terms of importance. For each ranked factor, articulate the rationale for importance and think through appropriate tactics to scan each of these sectors.

Application point: What is the ranking of importance of environment sectors to attend to?

In light of the discussion above, what does your strategy suggest you should pay attention to? what knowledge is likely to meet the VRIO criteria and therefore warrants attention? and what does your current market context imply about where to prioritise attention?

Step 5: Assess barriers to insight

Our research, along with many prior studies, confirmed that obtaining market insight is rare and difficult. This is due, in part, to the presence of many typical barriers to insight. Devel-oping an effective scanning capability requires being aware of the major barriers and developing tactics to overcome them as much as possible. Some typical major barriers to be aware of are as follows.

Developing effective scanning capability requires being aware of the major barriers and developing tactics to overcome them.

A well known cognitive limitation is the concept of 'bounded rationality'. This is an assertion that the decision making process will proceed in steps and at no time will be concerned with the 'whole' problem in all its complexity, but always with parts of the problem. Relating the principle to scanning presents a difficult problem, a barrier to insight, because it suggests that managers cannot comprehensively understand the environment because it is so vast and complex. A number of implications of 'bounded rationality' on scanning behaviour have been theorised, such as: 'average performance' will re-enforce 'limited search'; scanning will be directed toward the familiar, the convenient and the inexpensive; managers will scan according to their perceptions of the necessity for infor-mation; managers will narrow their scanning to areas they think they know how to act upon; and managers will converge on a common way of viewing the environment.

A number of implications of 'bounded rationality' on scanning behaviour have been theorised.

As well as 'bounded rationality' there are a number of other types of perceptual biases to be aware of. These are many and can briefly be summarised as follows. Prior hypothesis bias means that evidence may be ignored and gaps not perceived. Adjustment and anchoring is the bias which results in evidence being under-used and gaps not perceived. Escalating commitment means the significance of gaps may be minimised and strategy not revised. Reasoning by analogy results in problems being misdefined, possibly oversimplified, resulting in inappropriate strategy revision. A single outcome calculation restricts alternatives to a single one. Inference of impossibility is the premature rejection of alternatives. Denying value trade-offs is the biased use of evaluation criteria. Problem sets bias means that alternatives are restricted. Representativeness bias is the insensitivity to predictability and sample size, leading to illusion of validity. Illusion of control is the bias which leads to an inaccurate assessment of the risks associated with alternatives. Finally, devaluation of partially described alternatives is the rejection of strong but poorly presented alternatives.

On the theme of cognitive limitations, it's worth keeping in mind that most managers have a low degree of self awareness of their scanning behaviour. We are aware that managers spend very little time explicitly considering their scanning behaviour, the scanning process and the related issues associated with market insight and the link to organisational performance. We know that, although scanning and interpretation may be among the most important functions that senior managers perform, the process is so familiar that it is almost taken for granted. This lack of awareness is a barrier to insight as it obscures knowledge of current practices and assessment of implications and requirements for change.

The rarity of market insight is related to the current means by which managers scan the business environment. Currently, managerial scanning is ad hoc, informal and unsystematic. We have learnt that, despite the opportunity for management to put in place formal scanning practices, invest in supporting systems and technologies, and commit significant resources to gain business environment insights, most knowledge at top levels is gained through informal personal sources. Ad hoc scanning is evidenced through the many instances of an upfront lack of clarity on what data and information are being sought and why. Most managers are likely to learn of new business environment information through corridor conversations, coffee room remarks, work breaks and social functions than through meetings, reports and business forums. Our premise is that improvements through the deliberate design of a scanning capability and improvements in scanning processes will lead to more frequent and higher quality market insights.

Another major barrier is the embedded nature of scanning. We observed a lack of significant associations between a myriad of independent variables (covering areas of individual perceptions, objective environmental characteristics, individual job characteristics and organisational characteristics) and scanning behaviour. We reasoned that scanning is sufficiently complex to avoid being dependent on a few exogenous variables, and that managers developed individualised routines. The more senior the managers, the more likely they are to have developed their own routines. These routines reflect personal biases or preferences concerning how to enquire into and learn about the business environment. These established routines are also referred to as embedded behaviour. Once behaviour is embedded, it is all the more difficult to change, and hence it should be made explicit and analysed for its potential to act as a barrier to gaining market insight.

A final major barrier to bring to the fore is the extent of under-resourcing of scanning activities. We observed that there is rarely a separate position, role or unit set up to analyse the environment. It is rare for there to be a separate budget dedicated to gathering information and intelligence about the business environment. And despite many advances in IT and business reporting and intelligence systems, we noted a lack of dedicated systems to support business environment information gathering and analysis. The point here is that the degree of under-resourcing and under-investment in scanning practices, system and process represents a further barrier to gaining insight.

Application point: What are your barriers to insight and how might they be overcome?

As discussed above, there are some typical barriers to insight to be aware of. These barriers included bounded rationality; perceptual biases; lack of self awareness of scanning behaviour; ad hoc, informal and unsystematic nature of scanning; embedded nature of scanning behaviour; and under-resourcing and under-investment in scanning activities. For each of these barriers, how significant are they in your organisation? What can be done to overcome them or to lessen their impact?

Step 6: Determine scanning mix

Our prior analysis unearthed four major scanning behavioural types – Analysts, Categorists, Monitors and Viewers – that each have distinctive and differentiable scanning behavioural traits. For each group we identified pros and cons with respect to effective scanning and gaining market insight. We concluded that no one scanning behavioural type is optimal. For example, we learnt that Analysts are insightful but can be conventional and incomplete; Categorists are comprehensive but often provide data rather than insight; Monitors can identify major task environment changes but are unlikely to develop original insights; and Viewers may identify novelties but are unreliable. This led us to think about an optimal mix of scanning behavioural types to help meet scanning goals.

A mix of scanning behaviour types has the potential to capitalise on known strengths and mitigate known weaknesses of any one scanning type. In this way, it is possible to build to highly competent scanning capability through the involvement of different managerial scanning types. We know that building capability around managerial scanning behaviour is particularly important in order to work with and not against embedded scanning behaviour.

A mix of scanning behaviour types can capitalise on known strengths and mitigate known weaknesses of any one scanning type.

Some summary guidelines in terms of the mix of scanning types to involve are as follows. An organisation should involve as many Analysts as required to complete the crucial interpretative role, while being careful not to fall into the trap of over analysis for little incremental benefit. The mix of Analysts is a function of the amount of information they need to analyse and interpret. The mix of Categorists is a function of the targeted breadth of coverage and depth of information to obtain. Categorists can play a useful role of pre-filtering information for significance and subsequent passing on to Analysts. Based on this, we'd expect the mix of Categorists to be greater than the mix of Analysts, although this can differ, based on market context and complexity of content. Monitors are useful in the mix as a way of leveraging the scanning work routines they are already doing. Through involving Monitors, we can accordingly reduce some of the work effort of Analysts and Categorists. The mix of Monitors is a function of how many exist within an organisation and whose work routines can therefore be leveraged, and the extent to which their work routines can substitute for certain Analyst and Categorist activities. Viewers are not able to reliably substitute for activities of any of the other scanning behavioural types. Viewers' contribution comes from identifying novel events, particularly in the remote environment. The mix of Viewers is at the discretion of the Scanning Capability Manager. Viewers are an optional extra. The extent to which Viewers can detect valuable novel events in the remote environment, traded off against the management effort to direct their efforts and consolidate their findings, will dictate the appropriate mix of Viewers to involve in establishing an effective scanning capability.

Application point: What should be your scanning mix (i.e. mix of Analyst, Categorist, Monitor and Viewer scanning types)?

===

Step 6 is based on our finding that no one scanning behaviour type is optimal. For each scanning type – Analyst, Categorist, Monitor and Viewer – how can you capitalise on strengths and mitigate weaknesses? For your situation, what is the best mix given the level of interpretative skills required and the desired breadth and depth of scanning coverage?

Step 7: Assess market context

Assessing market context is important as market context is an indicator of the presence of market insight. Different market contexts impact on the effectiveness of individual scanning behaviour; and market contexts have implications for the mix of scanning behaviours that are likely to be effective.

Market context is an indicator of the presence of market insight and has implications for the best mix of scanning behaviours.

In assessing market contexts, the key dimensions to understand are market complexity and market turbulence. Our working summary of market complexity is a measure of the number of implications that a market has for a business. Put another way, the greater the number of implications the environment holds for a business, the more complex it is. Market complexity is increasing if any of the following are true: the number of significant market factors we have to consider is increasing; the implications of each of those market factors are increasing; and market factors are combining differently to create more implications for the business. Market turbulence is the rate of change of the market factors (in both the task and remote environments) that contributes to complexity. Turbulence can arise in three areas of implications: implications due to new factors; new implications of existing factors; and implications that arise from combinations of factors.

The first step to assessing market context is to assess and quantifiably measure the dimensions of market complexity and market turbulence. Although no assessment of market complexity and market turbulence can ever be completely objective or accurate, we proposed an approximate solution to a problem that is not completely solvable. Our solution involves dividing up the market into five component parts – customer complexity, channel complexity, competitor complexity, remote environment complexity and value complexity – and then assessing the complexity and turbulence of each component. You'll recall that we developed an assessment scheme using a 1 (simple) to 5 (complex) point scale, combined with an importance weighting, to produce an overall weighted score of market complexity. Self assessment checklists and scales were also developed to help assess market turbulence. Use these standardised approaches and diagnostics to more objectively and accurately assess market complexity and market turbulence. Refer to Chapter 6 for full details.

As discussed in Chapter 7, it is possible to derive at least four market contexts from combinations of two levels of market complexity (low and high) and two levels of market turbulence (low and high). You'll recall that we attached labels to four market contexts for ease of reference, as follows: Market Context 1: Gusty (low complexity, high turbulence); Market Context 2: Storm (high complexity, high turbulence); Market Context 3: Calm (low complexity, low turbulence); and Market Context 4: Fluky (high complexity, low turbulence). Using the diagnostic tools in Chapter 6, you can assess the level of market complexity and market turbulence and so determine which of the four market contexts best reflects your circumstances.

Application point: What is your market context?

As discussed above, understanding market context is important as it is an indicator of the presence of market insight and has implications for scanning mix and scanning processes. How turbulent is your market? How complex is your market? Which of the four market contexts described above best fits your circumstances?

Step 8: Refine scanning mix

Given your assessment of market context, the next step is to refine the scanning mix. We know that any one market context impacts on the effectiveness of individual scanning behaviour. Therefore, you need to consider the impact of market context on each of the scanning types – Analysts, Categorists, Monitors and Viewers – and deduce whether, in your circumstances, each type is more or less valuable than average in terms of scanning effectiveness and gaining market insight. If a particular scanning type is relatively more valuable in a given market context, this suggests altering the mix in favour of this type. Conversely, we suggest reducing the scale and nature of a relatively less valuable scanning type in a given context. In this way, it is possible to refine the scanning mix to optimise your organisation's scanning capability.

Considering the impact of market context, you can deduce which scanning types are more or less valuable in your circumstances.

We have drawn some general conclusions about which scanning types are relatively more or less valuable than average in each of our four market contexts. These general conclusions were presented in Chapter 7. Some highlights and extracts of our analysis now follow. In Market Context 1: Gusty, we consider Analysts to be relatively less valuable due to it being more difficult for them to secure exclusive insights in a low complexity environment. Categorists, on the other hand, are relatively more valuable as they have sufficient interpretative skills to identify strategically significant information and derive insight in this market context. Monitors are also relatively more valuable in this context, as their regular and reliable monitoring of the environment is particularly helpful at detecting changes in this fast-paced market context. Viewers lose out in this market context; their intermittent scanning means that many more significant events may go unnoticed than noticed. These general conclusions can be used to refine the scanning mix and optimise your firm's scanning capability.

In Market Context 2: Storm, as you'd expect, the relative value of each scanning type changes yet again. Our analysis suggests that Analysts are relatively more valuable in this context as they have the best chance of gaining insight in this exceptionally difficult and complex market context. Because of the complexity and fast pace of change, Categorists are relatively less valuable than average, as their output tends to be too limited or historic to hone in on current issues. Monitors are relatively more valuable as they develop a current view, even if a bit simplified, that can be acted upon. Not surprisingly, Viewers are out of their depth in this market context and, rather than infrequent intermittent scanning, more frequent and considered scanning is required.

Market Context 3: Calm, suggests a different set of refinements to the scanning mix is required. The straightforward context means there is less need for interpretative skills; consequently, Analyst skills are required relatively less than average in the mix of scanning types. In this more straightforward context, Categorists are particularly well suited as they have sufficient time to execute a structured scanning approach and have sufficient interpretative skills. While Categorists are more valuable in the mix, Monitors are less so. This is because the role that Monitors perform is likely to duplicate that already performed by Categorists. This leaves open the opportunity for Viewers to play a particularly complementary role to Categorists. As Viewers may add to the stock of market insights which are difficult to come by in this market context, they are relatively more valuable in the scanning mix.

Finally, Market Context 4: Fluky, favours both Analysts and Categorists. In a highly complex environment, a premium is placed on interpretative and analytical skills, which increases the relative value of Analysts. The market context also necessitates identifying and gathering the right information to investigate the complexities. In this slower-paced context, Categorists can effectively do this and, hence, are highly valued. The slower pace of change means that Monitors are relatively less valuable and there is time to react to changes. In this market context, Viewers once again struggle with the inherent market complexities and the ability to discern strategic information.

Application point: What is your refined scanning mix, appreciating your market context?

As discussed above, market context impacts on the effectiveness of individual scanning behaviour. For your market context, which scanning types are relatively more valuable than average? less valuable than average? What does this suggest in terms of optimal mix?

The above steps are the major activities required to develop an effective scanning capability. In summary, these steps are as follows:

- allocate scanning capability responsibility;
- reflect on strategy;
- state scanning goals;
- prioritise sectors;
- assess barriers to insight;
- determine scanning mix;
- assess market complexity and turbulence;
- refine scanning mix;
- scan ongoing.

The above steps combine to create an effective scanning capability that, at least, provides high quality market information and is conducive to deriving market insight. Of course, the critical step in all of the above is translating information into insight. Further discussion and guidance on how to do this is provided in the next section.

From information to insight

This and the remainder of our book builds on the preceding discussion. We assume that the scanning behaviour of the business in question has been assessed and then adapted to fit the context of the business and the market environment. Effective scanning behaviour is a foundation of creating insight and value and, without it, it is unlikely that a firm will be able to create strong insight. This echoes the point we made earlier that insight can't be achieved by simply throwing money at gathering data and buying computing power. No amount of number crunching will, our work suggests, draw value out of data that has been hobbled by an ineffective scanning process.

This section also begins from another assumption, one that is necessary for a book that is not an information systems textbook. We assume that the firm has in place a reasonably effective information system. By that we mean that the firm already collects data on its costs, sales and other outcomes in sufficient detail to meet most of the firm's current operational needs. Typically, an effective information system allows a firm to know what it is selling to whom, through what channels and at what prices. In addition, the internal side of the information system can tell the firm's leaders what everything costs to make and deliver (including indirect costs, such as marketing communications). Finally, we assume that the firm has at least a rudimentary system of measuring outcomes beyond sales and profit, such as customer satisfaction, complaints etc. In assuming a reasonably effective information system, however, we don't assume a hugely expensive, integrated enterprise resource planning (ERP) and customer relationship management (CRM) system, although increasingly even small firms have systems that would have been unimaginable a decade ago. Nor do we assume the sort of extensive market research systems that a large consumer goods company might have. We simply assume a system includes pretty average quantitative and qualitative information gathering – one that can, with some tweaking, develop to meet needs identified by the firm as it works towards an effective insight creating process.

Based on the assumptions that we're scanning well, and using a reasonably effective information system, this second section of this chapter considers how firms turn the information provided by the system into insight and thence into value. What we will describe is what emerged from research and, to some extent, our application of the research in our work with clients. It should be remembered, however, that what we describe is not typical practice. The way most firms handle information is mostly about operational needs and insight creation is, if anything, an afterthought.

Taking a 'helicopter view' of how firms make the journey from information to value via insight, our research taught us that this happens in three connected, interlocking, overlapping phases:

- Firstly, contextualising the information into knowledge.
- Secondly, selecting market insight from that knowledge and drawing out the actions implications of that insight.

- Finally, translating those implications into value creating actions, a stage which also involves reflecting and feeding back into the information pool.

This reductionist approach is useful, in that it allows us to dismantle and understand the complex and often implicit activities that firms engage in. That understanding is what we then use to create our own insight. These three phases form the structure of the rest of the book. The first phase, contextualising the information into knowledge and selecting insight from that knowledge is covered in the remainder of this chapter. Drawing out the implications of the insight and acting upon it, together with implementation considerations, form Chapter 9.

Contextualising information into knowledge

In our context, the central challenge in creating knowledge is not, of course, shortage of information. Since Alvin Toffler, in his 1970 book *Future Shock*,[1] coined the phrase 'information overload', managers have understood that they face a needle-in-a-haystack situation. An embarrassment of riches makes it costly to find information which is useful to creating insight and also makes it hard to see critical gaps in what information we have. That is the central challenge facing managers in organisations and was at the core of our research.

The process of turning information into knowledge is something human beings do so easily that, in many instances, it is unconscious. If you have information that the road is wet, traffic is heavy, you're 60 miles from your destination and your appointment starts 10 minutes from now, your brain synthesises those things into the knowledge that you will be late. No 'thinking' is needed. This autonomic process is both a help and a hindrance. It allows us to process the huge amounts of less important information we receive continuously into the basic knowledge we need to operate in our daily lives. On the other hand, the

Firms augment rather than replace human instinct by making it explicit, visible and therefore shared.

unconscious subroutines of our mind are opaque to us and they are more than capable of reaching the wrong conclusion, especially when we are dealing with the complex situations that our businesses usually involve. In researching how firms coped with this conundrum – how to contextualise large volumes of complex information efficiently *and* effectively – we observed that they augmented, rather than replaced, human instinct by making it explicit, visible and therefore shared. Three stages of contextualising were visible when watching firms create insight, stages which mimic what goes on when an individual works out, say, that they are going to be late for a meeting. Essentially, these three stages can be summarised as three questions:

- What information do we have?
- How do those bits of information interrelate?
- How does that interrelated information fit with my context?

At each of these three stages, we were able to observe good and bad practice in the firms we studied. By 'good' and 'bad', we don't mean with reference to some arbitrary academic standard. We mean practice that the firms in question found worked well for them or didn't. The following three subsections try to capture those experiences. We should stress, however, that even in good practice, it was rare to see these stages made explicit and they were never referred to in the terms we use. What follows is an explication of often subconscious management behaviour given labels for the sake of clarity. For clarity, this is summarised in Figure 8.1.

What information do we have? Good and bad practice in assembling the available information

Assembling the information available is a common weak link in the process of market insight creation. When, in our research, we asked 'what information relevant to the market do you have?' the answer was usually long but rarely complete. Typically, managers can recite long lists of information sources but, when prompted, can then recall many more sources which they had 'forgotten' or which they 'never really thought of as an information source, but do now it is mentioned'. Whilst unsurprising, this weakness has

Bad practice at information assembly is a little like building Lego™ in the dark.

clear and negative implications for the subsequent use of the information; unless otherwise corrected, managers are quite likely to neglect some of the information they have and not notice important gaps in their information

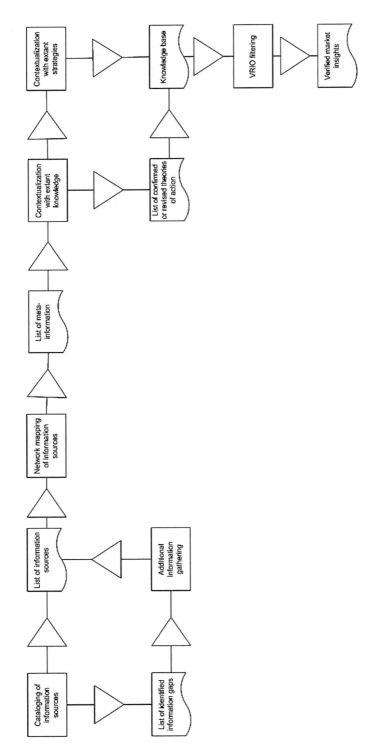

Figure 8.1 A summary of the *information to insight process.*

resources. In other words, bad practice at information assembly is a little like building Lego™ in the dark.

There seem to be two explanations for this failure by managers to catalogue effectively what information they have at their disposal. The first is psychological; there is little motivation for a manager to invest time in this arduous task. It will never be complete and the rewards, although potentially large, will accrue to the organisation and rarely to the individual. Under such circumstances, motivations theories like Expectancy Theory[2] predict the observed outcome. The second is structural; the sources of information that are relevant to creating market insight lie in many functional silos from operations to finance to marketing. Again, this outcome is predicted by theory, as it is a particular example of cognitive bias.[3] Few individuals have the knowledge, authority and network to pull this Diaspora together. Hence, typical bad practice in this area was for firms to be able to list large but incomplete lists of their information sources that were biased strongly towards the functional role of the person questioned. By contrast, best practice in assembling information resulted in a much larger list of sources that was well-balanced across functional areas and usually included the clear designation of possible gaps in the firm's information.

Why and how were some firms better at marshalling their information resources than others? We found that firms that showed good practice differed from their weaker comparison companies in two ways, one a critical role, the other a critical process. These roles and processes effectively overcame the structural and psychological constraints mentioned above.

In terms of a critical role, the best practice companies had seemingly overcome the psychological and structural barriers by means of a de facto 'Chief Information Officer', whose role involved cataloguing all the useful sources of information available to the firm. This person, by way of his or her role and personal interests, made a point of assembling complete and balanced catalogues of the firm's information resources and needs.

However, we use the term 'de facto' advisedly. We found that the presence of a person with such a title was a poor indicator of the actual role played. So, for instance, some firms with no such official position had in fact filled the role with someone with an unrelated title, such as a Marketing Manager. Similarly, we found role labels such as

What matters is that someone takes responsibility for cataloguing the firm's sources of information.

'Chief Information Officer' or 'Business Intelligence Manager' were often filled with IT or marketing specialists respectively. In such cases, the information cataloguing was often incomplete and predictably biased to the functional background of the role occupant. More than title, what seems to matter is that an individual (or a small group) takes responsibility for cataloguing the firm's sources of information, regardless of that person's title and not considering the functional source of the information. That person or group, note, was responsible for cataloguing the information, not creating or managing it, although they often played a key role in that latter process too.

In addition to the key role played by a de facto 'Chief Information Officer', more accurately described as 'Information Source Cataloguer', the second feature of best practice was some form of 'framing' practice. By this, we mean a deliberate attempt to define what information was needed and available. At a detailed level, this varied between firms, but in all cases could be seen to be needs led rather than source led. By this we mean that, in good practice, firms created a framework of the sort of information they needed, and populated that with their information sources or designated gaps where they existed. This compared with simply listing all of the sources of information the firm knew they had.

In Tables 8.1 and 8.2, we have created a simplified, stereotypical example of this framing approach, synthesized from numerous case studies but simplified and generalised. As these tables show, our observations were that comprehensive catalogues of information sources covered the whole breadth of activity. Wittingly or otherwise, firms divided up their activity according to the value chain in which they operated and asked what they knew about each stage. Then, within each stage, they considered internal and external factors of the environment. In this they mimicked the way academics structure the environment into the remote and task environment and the value proposition. Table 8.1 indicates the sort of questions firms asked themselves (i.e. the information needs they had) whilst Table 8.2 represents examples of information sources which answered those questions and addressed those needs. Of course, in any one case, each box of this grid contained several, sometimes many, needs or sources that were very specific to the context of the company. Also, a firm might typically not be able to identify an information source for some of the questions, which would lead to the designation of an information gap. Typically, the most well-supplied information needs related to internal information about tangible factors (e.g. sales figures)

Table 8.1 *Simplified framing chart for organisational information needs.*

Value chain stage / What information needs do we have relating to . . .	Inventing, acquiring and developing products and services	Operations and logistics	Understanding and communicating with customers
Social, legal, economic, political and technological factors that influence our market	How are SLEPT factors influencing our capability to acquire, invent, develop and protect new products and services?	What do SLEPT factors imply for our capability to deliver our product or service?	What do SLEPT factors imply for our capability to understand and communicate with the market?
Customer, channel, competitor and supplier factors	How are task environment factors influencing our capability to acquire, invent, develop and protect new products and services?	How are task environment factors influencing our capability to deliver our product or service?	How are task environment factors influencing our capability to understand and communicate with the market?
Value proposition factors	What are our relative capabilities and what are the relative outcomes of our new product and service development processes?	What are our relative capabilities and what are the relative outcomes of our operational and supply chain management processes?	What are our relative capabilities and what are the relative outcomes of our strategic management and marketing processes?

Table 8.2 *Stereotypical populated framing chart for organisational information needs.*

What information needs do we have relating to . . . \ Value chain stage	Inventing, acquiring and developing products and services	Operations and logistics	Understanding and communicating with customers
Social, legal, economic, political and technological factors that influence our market	Scanning outcomes about SLEPT factors relevant to innovation. Outcomes of formal SLEPT analyses by R&D or other functions.	Scanning outcomes about SLEPT factors relevant to operations and logistics. Outcomes of formal SLEPT analyses by operations or other functions.	Scanning outcomes about SLEPT factors relevant to strategic management and marketing processes. Outcomes of formal SLEPT analyses by marketing or other functions.
Customer, channel, competitor and supplier factors	Scanning outcomes about competitor and supplier activity. Results of market research into customer needs and channel roles.	Scanning outcomes about competitor activity. Results of market research into customer needs. Results of internal assessments of supplier, our own and channel value chains.	Scanning outcomes about task environment factors relevant to strategic management and marketing processes. Outcomes of formal analyses by marketing or other functions.
Value proposition factors	Benchmarking and scanning outcomes about the relative capabilities and results of our new product and service development activities.	Scanning outcomes about competitor activity. Results of benchmarking activity against competitor activity. Results of internal assessments of supplier, our own and channel value chains.	Scanning outcomes about competitor activity. Results of benchmarking activity against competitor activity. Results of internal assessments of strategic management and marketing processes and outcomes.

whilst the least adequate information related to external information about intangible factors (e.g. customer motivations or competitor capabilities). Whatever the outcome, however, the act of creating and populating these frameworks in a detailed manner that was relevant to the firm was a critical, basic process that enabled effective information assembly.

Application point: What does your information catalogue look like?

Use Figures 8.2 and 8.3 as guides to construct information source catalogues for your firm or organisation. Make it as tailored and comprehensive as possible. What sources have you identified that you might not otherwise have listed? What information source gaps have you identified?

How does our information interrelate? Good and bad practice in structuring the available information

Assembling and cataloguing the sources of information held by the firm, and any designated gaps, results in a large and varied collection of sources that, at this stage, has no real structure. Until it is in some way aggregated and structured, it may be of operational use but of little use in creating insight. Eventually, this panoply of information will be contextualised into knowledge but good and bad practice in this respect vary in an important way; good practice involves an intermediate step between assembling and contextualising. This intermediate step involves the processing of the information from a random collection of sources to a network of connectivity between sources.

This is a complex and important step, so it is worthwhile explaining in a little more depth. Weak practice in structuring information will be most familiar to readers: managers structure information sources into groups and classes. At a superficial level, this is according to source or functional use. So managers would talk of various 'buckets' of information that might be labelled 'sales numbers', 'market research information', 'marketing effectiveness metrics' and so on. Such categorisation could be seen in all firms we studied, whether they reported themselves happy with their outcomes or not. The difference between good and bad practice lay in the more effective firms going further to draw out connectivity between information sources.

In firms that reported good results about the way they structured their information, we observed an additional and different way of 'grouping' information sources. Partly, this derived from the framing process used as the information was assembled (see above). However, it is clear that effective structuring of information sources also involves understanding connectivity between different sources. Managers spoke of how information from different 'buckets' connected to give better understanding. For example 'sales numbers' and 'market research' connected to give an understanding of how the value proposition appealed to different market segments. Similarly, marketing metrics data about direct responses, trial usage and repeat usage connected with customer satisfaction information to give an understanding of what drove or hindered loyalty.

Just as we used the framing process in Tables 8.1 and 8.2 to explicate the often implicit information-assembling behaviour of good practice firms, then Figure 8.2 explicates their implicit information-connecting behaviour.

In this example, in which the thickness of the arrows indicates the strength of connection between sources, three 'network hubs' emerge. In this greatly simplified map, we can see the information resources grouping around these hubs to provide knowledge about three interrelated aspects of the business:

- How sales are doing.
- What the customers think of the product.
- What problems have occurred in manufacturing.

In turn, these three hubs connect and begin to explain sales variances related to quality issues. This simplified example shows one important but small area of the firm's business. In practice, the map for a whole business unit can include dozens or hundreds of information sources and the clusters of information (that is, the concentration of strong links between information hubs) inform not only sales variances but every aspect of the business, from how channels add value, to how customers choose, to how our products dissatisfy our customers.

From the processes of assembling and interrelating the information that

Meta-information is information that has changed in some way but is not yet fully-fledged knowledge.

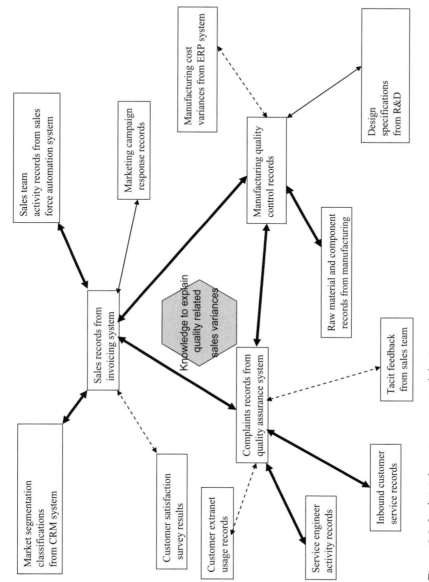

Figure 8.2 *Implicit information-connecting behaviour.*

we have and identifying gaps, there emerges something that is 'neither fish nor fowl'. The catalogued and interrelated information captured in the network map is now beginning to show some of the attributes of knowledge, as the simple example in Figure 8.2 shows. This semi-contextualised information may be called 'meta-information' in that it represents information that has been changed in some way, but is not yet fully fledged knowledge.

Application point: How does your information interrelate?

Using the outputs from the previous application point, construct a network map that includes all of the sources of information you have identified, including ones you do not currently have. Estimate the connectivity of these as strong, medium and weak links and arrange into network hubs and spokes. What meta-information emerges from this for your organisation?

How does our information fit our context? Good and bad practice in contextualising the available information

From the cataloguing and network mapping of our information sources comes the raw material for contextualising that information into knowledge. By this stage, we have a reasonably complete and unbiased catalogue of information sources. In addition, we've structured those sources not only according to their functional buckets but also according to their connectivity. As a result of the network mapping, our information has begun to transform into meta-information that speaks directly to particular concerns at every stage in the value chain. What we don't have yet, however, is knowledge and insight.

To complete the process of transmutation from information into knowledge, we need to complete the contextualisation of our information sources. Context, however, means more than the other information that connects to any one information source. It also refers to the 'other knowledge' context in which the information will be used and the 'strategy context' within which the firm will use any knowledge it holds. Thus, there are two complementary perspectives on contextualising information:

• How does what we know, or think we know, change the meaning of the information we have and vice versa?

- How do our current and future strategies change the value of the information we have, and vice versa?

In contextualising the available information, the difference between good and bad practice was visible from both these perspectives. Simply put, good *Good information contextualisation considers current knowledge and strategy.* information contextualisation considers both factors, bad knowledge contextualisation does neither. To understand good practice, therefore, we need to explore what we know about each kind of contextualisation.

Existing knowledge as a context of our information

New, or newly considered, information interacts with the existing knowledge through a process of organisational learning. In doing so it changes the existing knowledge by refuting it, confirming it, extending it or modifying it in some way. At the same time, the new information is itself contextualised and therefore becomes part of our knowledge environment. A couple of simple examples, selected from our own experience, help to illustrate the point.

Part of a medical diagnostics firm's existing knowledge explained limited penetration of a new product as the result of some inadequacy in the product performance and its pricing. As a result of this view, the firm was about to reduce its pricing levels. Prior to this move, however, penetration of the product was examined across the twelve sales regions. In this case, the customers, product and pricing were identical across all regions and all that varied was the approach of the local sales manager. This examination revealed huge variations in penetration between regions, for which no customer, product, pricing or other explanation could be found. This new information therefore modified the firm's understanding of (i.e. knowledge about) the firm's overall penetration. At the same time, the regional variation data became part of the firm's knowledge set.

An agrochemical firm's existing knowledge about the decision making process of the market was largely built on tacit knowledge fed to the firm's sales team through their distributor contacts. Central to this knowledge was the tenet that the distributor representative directed farmer buying behaviour strongly, to such a degree that farmers' preferences played little part in the decision. As a result, promotional resources were focused mostly on distributor incentives and away from farmer-directed advertising. When a new entrant to the market reversed this strategy with a campaign that focused on farmers and neglected distributors, the new rival was hugely successful, despite having no strong product, price or other advantages. This new information was used to challenge accepted wisdom and revise the incumbent's marketing communications strategy. In doing so, information about competitor marketing strategies and shares became part of the firm's knowledge base.

These two small examples merely illustrate a general phenomenon that we observed in our research and which is well recorded and explained in the organisational learning literature. Although there are several schools of thought about how organisations learn, there is a common thread between them. This is that organisational learning works when a firm explicates its current thinking, then tests it against new information, then revises or confirms its thinking. This concept is, for example, at the core of Chris Argyris's ideas of 'double loop learning'[4] in which current thinking is defined as the firm's 'theory in action'. Such current thinking directs current activity and is often implicit and therefore hard to challenge. In practice, the most direct way to surface the current thinking is to deduce it from current or planned actions. This is illustrated by the way we can deconstruct our two simple examples, above, as follows:

1. Medical diagnostics example:
   - Planned action: reduce the average selling price of the product.
   - Theory in action = sales penetration is limited by poor product performance/price value.
   - New information = variation in penetration across regions with identical product performance/price value.
   - Revised theory in action = variation in penetration related to variation in sales process between regions.
2. Agrochemicals example:
   - Current action: focus promotion resources on distributor representatives.
   - Theory in action = purchase decision largely made by distributor representative.
   - New information = outcomes of farmer-oriented strategy by new competitor.

   – Revised theory in action = purchase decision made by farmer even if influenced by distributor representative.

These two examples and the idea of organisational learning represent the first of two ways in which firms translate information into knowledge. The second, which runs parallel to organisational learning, concerns placing the new information in the context of the firm's strategy.

Application point: How does your existing knowledge contextualise and transform information into new knowledge?

Based on the discussion above, identify two or three important planned or current actions (i.e. allocation of some resources). Deduce from those what you believe to be your firm's theories of actions underpinning those actions. Then, using any relevant information and meta-information captured in your information network map (see above), test those theories. Are the theories confirmed, modified, or refuted by the information? What does this imply for future or planned actions? How does this add to your knowledge?

Strategy as a context for our information

Strategy, to refer back to Chapter 1, is a sustained pattern of resource allocation. This pattern of where we plan to put our money, time and other resources forms an important part of the context into which we place information. To illustrate this, consider the same piece of information in two different contexts. For example, a manufacturer of heavy commercial trucks and one of sports utility vehicles each gathers information about rising fuel prices and increasing environmental concerns. The relevance for the latter is large, competing as they do against less thirsty and polluting vehicles with a brand image as 'gas guzzlers'. For the former, selling to perennially cost-conscious fleet operators and competing against similar products, the relevance is much less. The contextualisation of new or newly considered information therefore involves considering it in the context of the firm's strategy. The challenge, however, is that strategy (that is, the allocation of resources) occurs at different levels in an organisation.[5] For our purposes, this is best expressed as:

- generic strategy;
- growth strategy;
- marketing strategy.

Consideration of the information we have in the context of each of these three levels of strategy completes the process of transforming information into knowledge.

Information in the context of generic strategy

Generic strategy is a concept developed by Porter[6] and elaborated on by Treacey and Wiersema,[7] whose work some of the terminology used here comes from. It is that set of decisions about which part of the value chain you choose to compete with. In simple terms, we can compete in one of three ways:

- Product excellence: we compete by having the best products (that is, competing with our new product or service development capability).
- Operational excellence: by having the lowest costs (that is, by competing with our operations and supply chain management).
- Customer intimacy: by having the closest match to customer needs (that is, by competing with our market understanding and customer relationship capabilities).

Readers unfamiliar with this concept may find it worthwhile reading the references given above, but it is worth remembering that any of these approaches still requires adequacy in the rest of the value chain. Frequently used examples of these generic strategies include Intel (product excellence), Wal-Mart (cost leadership) and Amazon (customer intimacy).

The relevance of generic strategy to insight creation is that it dictates what information is most valuable. In doing so, it begins to tell us where to look for insight. For example, Intel's product excellence strategy indicates that the most important information will be about product performance, the customers who want those prod-

The relevance of generic strategy to insight creation is that it dictates what information is most valuable. In doing so, it begins to tell us where to look for insight.

ucts and the channels to reach those customers. By contrast, Wal-Mart's strategy rests on information about costs, whilst Amazon's business model depends on information about what customers want. Again, it is worth stressing that this model shouldn't be caricatured. Intel doesn't ignore cost information, Wal-Mart care about customers and Amazon care about products. The generic strategy of a firm, however, is an important context for the information a firm uses.

Application point: What's your generic strategy and what does that imply?

Whilst all firms manage the whole value chain, most successful firms emphasise one part of it in the form of a generic strategy. Which of Treacey and Wiersema's three strategies do you think best characterises your firm? What does that imply for what information sources are most likely to yield valuable knowledge and thence insight?

Information in the context of growth strategy

Growth strategy is that set of decisions about which markets to serve and what products or services to sell. It will be familiar to most readers in the form of Ansoff's matrix,[8] in which the growth opportunities for growth are defined in four categories:

- Market penetration: Winning market share from competitors in currently served markets with currently sold products or services, or some variation on them.
- New product development: Selling to currently served customers a product or service not currently sold.
- Market development: Selling a product or service currently sold to customers that are not currently served.
- Diversification: Selling a new product or service to customers who are not currently served.

For most firms, market penetration is the thrust of their strategy. However, in mature markets the other options might represent the best opportunity

Valuable knowledge and therefore insight is likely to be found in information about markets and products identified in the growth strategy.

for growth and their growth strategy could be a mixture of Ansoff's options. As with generic strategy, the relevance of growth strategy is that it dictates what information is most valuable. Valuable knowledge and therefore insight is likely to be found in information about markets and products identified in the growth strategy.

Application point: What is your growth strategy and what does it imply?

Which of Ansoff's options represents the future growth of your company? What markets and products or services does that refer to? What does that imply for what information sources are most likely to yield valuable knowledge and thence insight?

Information in the context of marketing strategy

Marketing strategy is that set of decisions about what market segments to serve and what offers to make to each segment.[9] It 'nests' within generic and growth strategies and also should not be confused with marketing communications strategy. The latter is that set of decisions regarding audiences, media, messages etc. and it is not the same as marketing strategy.

As with the higher levels of strategy, marketing strategy is an important context for information. Clearly, information about market segmentation is valuable, especially as it pertains to differentiating between the needs and motivational drivers of

Nuances in the information about target market segments are often the source of market insight.

different segments. Nuances in the information about target market segments are often the source of market insight. Similarly, information about our offer to target segments and the offers made to them by competitors is also valuable. By contrast, information that is not directly relevant to the marketing strategy is rarely as valuable. McKinsey don't value information about the millions of one-man management consultancies with which they share market space but do not compete. BMW don't cloud their view of the executive car market with irrelevant detail about less important segments of the car market.

The importance of marketing strategy to contextualising information is, in practice, often hindered by poor definition of marketing strategy. It is not atypical for a firm to define its marketing strategy weakly as a customer category and a product type. In our research, one firm exemplified this as:

> Our marketing strategy is to target large firms with the most advanced telecoms solutions.

Given this strategy definition, almost all market information was equally valuable. When we probed, however, we discovered that a more accurate strategy definition was:

> Our strategy is to target large, geographically dispersed firms with complex telecoms needs and who have an innovative attitude to the value that telecoms systems can add. To these customers, we offer an extended value proposition, built around our systems but including evaluation of their needs, design of the system and continual adaptation to their changing needs.

This may seem like a semantic distinction, but our experience was that a clear and strong definition of marketing strategy was one of the most important antecedents of creating market insight. Marketing strategies may of course include multiple target segments and offers, but strong ones meet the tests of a strong strategy described in Chapter 1.

Application point: What is your marketing strategy and what does it imply?

Considering the example above and the tests in Chapter 1, define your marketing strategy. What are your target segments and offers? What does that imply for what information sources are most likely to yield valuable knowledge and thence insight?

What knowledge do we have?

It is now appropriate to do a small recap of where we are in the process of creating insight. Having assessed and revised our scanning process, we are now able to gather more information, more relevantly and more effectively than before. With the information available, we have now performed a

number of processing tasks that together characterise good practice in transforming information into knowledge:

- Cataloguing the information sources available to the organisation. By
  using a framework, the resultant catalogue is both more complete and less
  biased than a simple listing.
- Network mapping the information sources according to their connectivity. By noting the strong connections between 'hubs,' meta-information
  that informs various parts of the business process emerges.
- Using the meta-information to test the 'theories of action' that underpin
  current and planned activity. By placing new and newly considered information in the context of these theories, the information becomes
  knowledge.
- Placing the meta-information in the context of the firm's generic,
  growth and marketing strategies. By doing so, the relative value of information is assessed and it becomes more robust knowledge.

When carried out with a rigour proportionate to the complexity and importance of the task, these steps yield a body of knowledge, valuable in its own right, from which insight can be filtered.

When carried out with a rigour proportionate to the complexity and importance of the task, these steps yield a body of knowledge, valuable in its own
right, from which insight can be filtered. If the reader cannot yet see the
beginnings of such a body of knowledge, then he or she is not alone. Many
of the companies observed described themselves as 'struggling to find anything new in what we know'. This was usually explained as the result of
their mindset. In other words, managers working in a familiar environment
with a lot of information that is, in large part, familiar to them, will trigger
their mental heuristics, or rules of thumb, to cope with the mental work. A
side effect of this is to put the information into patterns and 'boxes' that are
already defined and which fail to reveal any new connectivity or context.
In part, the tools described in this section are counter measures against this
natural habit. However, managers with the most deeply embedded heuristics
(often those most familiar with the market) may need to 'break' that thinking. In practice, this is best done by changing environment and invoking
challenges to existing thinking. Hence out-of-office days facilitated by
someone external to the organisation were often described as the occasions
on which new knowledge and insight were created.

Application point: What knowledge do you have?

Review the stages above. Write down the aspects of market environment and business process about which you have knowledge. Consider,
given the testing of theories of action, what knowledge is new. Consider which of that new knowledge is, given your strategy, likely to be
valuable and therefore rich in insight.

Selecting market insight from knowledge

Given rigour of approach and the diminution of ingrained thinking patterns,
a body of knowledge should now exist, all of which is valuable to some
degree and much of which may be new, or newly interpreted. The only
remaining challenge is to distil from it those pieces of knowledge which can
truly be called insight.

The ideas behind this have already been described in Chapter 4. True
market insight is that knowledge which has the characteristics of an organisational strength. These were defined by the VRIO acronym and the accom-
panying working definitions.

Valuable:

Knowledge is valuable if it informs or enables actions that will either increase
customer preference or increase the efficiency of serving the customer base.
Knowledge is useful if it informs or enables the execution of existing
activity.

Rare:

Knowledge is rare for so long as only one firm has embedded and appreciated
that knowledge to a degree significantly greater than the other firms in its
competitive set. Knowledge is common if it is already embedded and appreciated by firms in the same competitive set.

Inimitable:

Knowledge is inimitable if, to recreate it, a competitive firm would need to
invest resources that would not generate a positive return within the normal
planning cycle of the industry. Knowledge is imitable if it can be recreated,
copied or acquired by an investment that would generate a positive return
within the normal planning cycle of the industry.

Organisationally aligned:

Knowledge is organisationally aligned if the firm can act on it within its current situation or a development of that situation that seems realistic within the foreseeable business context. Knowledge is not organisationally aligned if, in order to act on it, the firm would need to change its current strategy or structure at a cost disproportionate to the benefits of that change.

Given this understanding of what constitutes insight, distilling it from the firm's body of knowledge may be so straightforward as to be obvious. In *Each piece of knowledge may vary from 'not at all' to 'very' on each of the VRIO criteria.* such cases, the cataloguing, mapping and contextualising of information sources may reveal knowledge that is obviously insightful without any detailed testing. Where such a happy circumstance does not occur, however, or where the firm is likely to risk large assets on the basis of the insight, it is only diligent to assess each piece of knowledge. Where this is done, it must be remembered that the assessment is not a 'binary' one. Each piece of knowledge may vary from 'not at all' to 'very' on each of the VRIO criteria. In practice, the filtering of knowledge to distil insight is a judgement call. This is illustrated in Table 8.3, based on the authors' assessment of the erectile dysfunction market, in which Lilly Icos successfully competed against Pfizer's Viagra despite Viagra's entrenched position.

By the end of this VRIO filtering process, it is typical that much of the knowledge generated from information in the previous stages has fallen out of the assessment by failing one or more of the VRIO tests. This doesn't mean the information is useless, of course. It may well still be of vital operational importance. But the knowledge that has survived the VRIO filtering, often only one or two pieces of meta-information, is the competitively important market insight with which we now concern ourselves. In Chapter 9, we look at how firms create value from insight.

Application point: What insights do you have?

Considering the full process discussed in the second section of this chapter, what insights do you think your firm may have? If none are apparent, what part of the process do you think may require more rigour in execution?

Table 8.3 *VRIO filtering of knowledge to assess insight.*
Insight: There is a segment in the erectile dysfunction market that is driven by the need for intimacy rather than simple satisfaction

Criterion	Consideration	Conclusion
Valuable to us?	This segment would be a valuable entry point into a market dominated by the incumbent (Viagra™).	This insight is very valuable.
Rare?	To the best of our knowledge, no other player in the market is acting in such a way as to indicate they are aware of this segment.	This insight is rare within our competitive group, but not within other markets such as contraceptives.
Inimitable?	This segment is not discernable through the generally held quantitative data in the market and only emerged through laborious qualitative research.	This insight is not totally inimitable, but it would take some time and the imitability is countered by the organisational alignment factors.
Organisationally aligned?	The performance profile of our product allows us to target this market well and our new entrant status allows us to define our position.	Within this market, we are uniquely aligned to exploit this insight.

Powerpoints

- To build effective scanning capability, begin by allocating responsibility.
- Key steps to achieving scanning effectiveness are to reflect on strategic imperatives, set scanning goals and prioritise attention.
- The most important step to scanning effectiveness is to optimise the mix of managerial scanning types to fit with market context.
- Using information begins with cataloguing information sources.
- Network mapping of information sources reveals meta-information.
- Using information to test 'theories of action' contextualises information within extant knowledge.
- Generic, growth and marketing strategies form the context and highlight the value of information and meta-information.
- Information in the context of extant knowledge and strategies is knowledge.
- Knowledge which meets the criteria of VRIO is market insight.

9

From insight to value

'The point is not merely to understand the world, but to change it.'
Karl Marx

This final chapter differs from those preceding it in two very important ways. Firstly, it is not about creating market insight, it is about using it. Secondly, whereas all of the preceding chapters recommended activity that consumed time and money, this chapter is about making money. Or, for non profits, achieving whatever constitutes success for your organisation. Those task oriented readers who have skipped to this part of the book are warned, however: implementing this chapter will be near to impossible without an understanding of its antecedents.

Since this chapter is about the journey from insight to value, we will begin by considering the starting point for this part of our journey; the sort of insights that typically emerge from an effective process for scanning and making sense of the market. We will then go on to describe what our research taught us about the three major stages of the journey from insight to value. As might be expected with the broad range of firms we studied, these differ in detail, case by case; but the wider lesson is that firms make the journey from insight to value not in a single leap, but in something more like a triple jump. Notwithstanding overlaps between steps and the often

> **Firms make the journey from insight to value not in a single leap, but in something more like a triple jump.**

iterative nature of these steps in reality, companies for whom this process worked did three things:

- Drew out the actions that were implied by the insight for the firm.
- Executed a 'sense check' before acting on the insight.
- Anticipated and pre-empted the barriers to change inherent in acting on insight.

Of course, these three steps were followed and accompanied by the changes in resource allocation and activity indicated by the strategy. It is only at that stage, when the organisation actually does something, that Marx's dictum (above) is upheld.

Starting point: what market insight do we have?

Following the process described in Chapter 8 and outlined in Figure 8.1, the information firms have clusters into 'meta-information' about certain aspects of the business process. This meta-information is contextualised with the organisation's existing knowledge to test and hopefully improve the 'theories of action' on which current and planned strategy is predicated. In doing so, the meta-information is itself contextualised into new knowledge. This new knowledge may then be assessed using the VRIO criteria. That which passes the assessment can be called market insight, although that which does not may still be valuable and operationally important knowledge.

Market insight is inherently diverse. It can pertain to almost any part of the market environment or business process. In Chapter 4, we described a taxonomy of insights and described how they could be broad or narrow, continuous or discontinuous, transient or lasting. Given such diversity, it is hard to generalise about how to act upon the insights we may have. However, there is a common attribute in most market insight that allows us to understand and improve the way insight is acted upon. That attribute is that most market insight informs the match between the organisation and its environment. To use a metaphor that emerged in one of our discussions with a senior executive, an insight is the blade of a key that we use to unlock the market.

Each of the insights described in Chapter 4 is different from the others, but all are about better matching the firm to its market. Numico's insight into clinical food and MGA's insight into how little girls' attitudes are changing may vary in breadth, but they both inform the way each company addresses the market. The building firm's insight into customisation and CPF's insight into the 'lawyer and pony' segment involved continuous and discontinuous changes to each firm's respective strategy, but both drove the way those firms designed their customer-facing processes. Pearson's insight into how lesson planning and assessment are integrating needs will serve them only if they act quickly, whilst Nintendo's understanding of the gaming market's shift from geeks to families will underpin their strategy for many years. Despite the transient and lasting nature of these insights, however, both have led to changes in what each company offers its market.

The value of this common feature of market insight is to inform how we act on such insight. If market insight is about matching to the market, then we can use existing models and concepts about that matching process to help us draw out the implications of our market insight. This may seem common sense but, to paraphrase Voltaire again, common sense is not so common. We observed in our research examples of weak market insight being acted upon irrespective of what made sense for the firm (as in the Iceland case) and of good insight being ignored because of some aspect of the firm's culture (as in the case of the firm that did not act on its 'inflection point' insight in Chapter 4). The following section then, about drawing implications of insight, uses this common theme of 'insight as a match maker' to illustrate how firms successfully act on insight.

Application point: What market insight do you have?

Since the following sections concern the application of market insight, you will find it useful at this point to take a moment to reflect on what market insight you think you have. Where does it fit in the taxonomy? How strong do you think it is, in terms of the VRIO tests? Take a moment to write this down before reading further.

What does our market insight imply?

Readers will reach this point of the book at different stages in the development of their own market insight, ranging from the fully developed back to

Box 9.1 von Möltke errors

Helmuth von Möltke was chief of the German General Staff at the outbreak of the First World War in 1914. The Germans' plan, to knock out the French and British forces in the west, then turn on the Russians in the east, had been devised by Schlieffen in 1905. It depended on a powerful swing through Belgium and Luxembourg, capturing Paris and defeating the huge French army before it could fully mobilise. When von Möltke succeeded Schlieffen in 1906, he modified the plan, reducing the strength of the swing in order to strengthen other operations. The plan failed, Paris was never captured and Europe descended into four years of trench warfare that ended with Germany's defeat. Military historians still argue about why the plan failed, but many see von Möltke's amendments as an important cause. In our work with firms trying to apply market insight, von Möltke became shorthand for 'a good plan botched by not putting in enough effort in the critical spots'.

those in the very first stages of working out how to scan the business environment. Ironically, it is those with the most advanced market insight that risk skimming this part of the book and making a mistake we often observed in firms, one that became known to us as the von Möltke error. This refers to an error made when a good plan is modified into a weaker one (see Box 9.1).

The relevance of the von Möltke example for the application of market insight is that it is very easy for firms to do the same. Indeed, it is far easier and more likely for a firm to 'do a von Möltke' than it is to act effectively on market insight. The reasons for this are not hard for anyone with experience of management to see. Resources are always short and there are always other demands. Added to this, the

Indeed, it is far easier and more likely for a firm to 'do a von Möltke' than it is to act effectively on market insight.

typical plan approval procedure is predisposed to plan weakening. Time and again, we heard managers talk of an original plan presented to senior management and challenged along the lines of 'can you do a bit more with a bit less?' Inevitably, the burden of proof in such cases falls on the presenters of the plan and, failing to prove beyond all doubt they need all their resources, the outcome is a weakened and often overstretched plan. The irony lies in the fact that it is the most obvious, clear and well defined market insights that are most prone to this error. Two examples demonstrate the point:

- When, shortly before their takeover by Roche, Boehringer Mannheim (BM) developed market insight into the laboratory diagnostics market, it seemed to be clear cut. The future of that market lay in the segment, labelled 'the tomorrow people', in which the firm's various types of blood analyser were sought as an integrated package with consultancy, laboratory design etc. To subsequently re-orientate BM's marketing strategy to capitalise on this insight required two main sets of actions. The first, relatively superficial, involved a repositioning of the company's promotional material away from the 'best providers of analysers' to a 'pathology business services partner'. The second, altogether more costly, operation involved a substantial revision of its recruitment and training and a restructuring of customer contact teams in sales, service and support. In a slow growth market it was very much harder to justify this more expensive second phase than it was to simply re-assign existing expenditure for the repositioning. Prudence triumphed over planning and only the cosmetic repositioning, without a genuine change in the offer, was attempted. The strategy failed and Roche took over Boehringer Mannheim. This is a fine example of 'doing a von Möltke'.
- By contrast, the Automobile Association, a UK based motoring organisation that provides breakdown, financial and other services to motorists, gained an insight into what drove members to lapse or renew. Its former 'theory of action' explained membership renewal as the outcome of customer satisfaction, a knowledge set that directed the AA's investment towards training its many thousands of roadside rescue mechanics in customer service skills. This was costly, especially as it involved high investment for marginal improvements of already good service levels. When the AA found that lapsing was only weakly related to the customer experience but strongly related to each customer's fear of breakdown, they revised their theory of action. If, as the data supported, it was perception of breakdown risk that drove renewal, then they needed a more balanced strategy that provided good customer service and increased the perception of breakdown risk, as well as shifting the AA's positioning to that

of a 'rescuer'. To their credit, the AA combined some additional training of mechanics with a heavily supported media campaign based on the theme of 'The 4th Emergency Service'. They eschewed the obvious cost savings of reducing training budgets and accepted the hard-to-justify costs of a major media campaign. In doing so, they form a radical contrast to the Boehringer Mannheim case.

These two contrasting examples illustrate the importance of drawing out the full implications of an insight or set of insights and reveal that the easy mistake to make is not usually the 'do nothing' or 'do the wrong thing' strategy, but the 'do the right thing partially' strategy. This error is compounded in practice because, whilst an erroneous strategy quickly reveals itself as such, a 'von Möltke' strategy only reveals its flaws slowly. What is needed, therefore, is a way of drawing out the full implications of an insight so that it can be acted on fully, powerfully and completely. This task has two components – drawing out customer needs and engineering the offer to meet them – which are the subject of the next sections of this chapter.

Application point: Have you witnessed a von Möltke strategy?

Most experienced managers have experienced, directly or indirectly, a von Möltke type strategy, in which a good strategy is weakened and overstretched by tweaking, thus reducing its efficacy and chances of success. What is your experience of this? What were the critical changes to the original concept? What would you do differently in a similar situation?

How insight informs our understanding of customer needs

If our goal is to draw out the full implications for action created by our market insight, the observation that insight is largely about matching our offer to customer needs is fundamentally important. From that observation flows the truism that, if we can understand the insight in terms of customer needs and the design of our offer, we can design a strong match. It is, of course, a fundamental axiom of all

The observation that insight is largely about matching our offer to customer needs is fundamentally important.

marketing theory that, in a competitive market, the strength of customer preference is a function of the strength of that match. Hence it was an important finding of our work when we observed a common phenomenon amongst those firms that were effective in using market insight.

In our research, we observed repeatedly that design of the offer, when effective, considered the needs of the customer not just in an obvious and functional way, but in respect of higher, non-functional, emotional needs too. This was not surprising in market sectors that were essentially consumer oriented. Markets for luxury or fashion items might be expected to be driven by such needs. We saw those expectations upheld in other mature markets too, such as in cars or personal financial services. What surprised us was the extent to which such needs drove markets that might be expected to be more rational and less emotionally driven, such as corporate IT, pharmaceuticals and business services. From this, we drew the lesson that effective acting on insight involves drawing out the full range of customer needs implied by the insight, whilst weaker practice is based on the delusion that all that matters are functional needs. To readers who are sceptical on this point, we need to be clear about what we mean and do not mean. We do not mean that high-involvement business purchases are based on ephemeral fashion. Doctors don't care much about the colour of a pill and the aesthetics of servers don't drive the IT business. What we do mean is that purchasers of even high-end business products are human beings. As well as very carefully thought out specifications, their decisions are also influenced by how they feel about the firm and the people they are buying from. Often, the importance of the purchase elevates personal needs for, say, reassurance and security from criticism, to a very high level.

The unravelling of customer needs is made more difficult, of course, by corporate personas, the image that we choose to present of being rational and not influenced at all by emotional needs. To get around this problem, we found a piece of work by Uditha Liyanage to be a powerful description of reality and a useful tool in practice.[1] As Figure 9.1 shows, Liyanage developed a model of how brands appeal to customers. For our purposes, however, Liyanage's work can be thought of as applying to the entire offer we make to the customer. The model, as readers will see, owes something to the famous Maslow hierarchy of needs,[2] but advances Maslow's thinking and, importantly, applies it to the context of customer preference. In recognising that customers see value for themselves and then the value of themselves

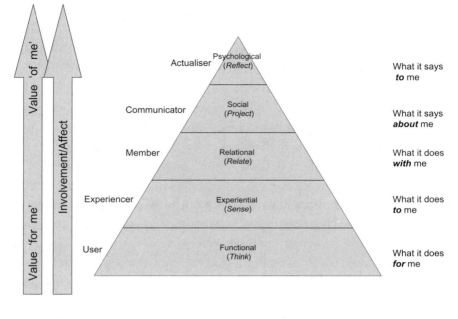

After Liyanage 2005

Figure 9.1 *Liyanage's pyramid of customer needs.*

in the offer, Liyanage's model explains why many purchase decisions are not driven by purely functional needs. Further, the questions that typify the customer at each level (what it does for me, what it says to me etc.) are valuable diagnostic questions in unravelling the needs of a customer.

In our research and working with firms, we observe a frequency distribution in the way in which firms think about matching their offer to customer needs, A large number of firms, perhaps the majority, consider functional needs. A smaller number consider experiential needs. This trend continues up Liyanage's pyramid until very few firms consider the implications of customer's psychological needs, such as when they are concerned about self actualisation. This means, of course, that many firms practically neglect needs that drive customer purchase behaviour when they design their offer to the customer. They are, in effect, blinkered to any needs much beyond functional needs. It is in improving this functionally blinkered approach that market insight connects with customer needs and improves the matching process. What effective firms do, consciously or otherwise, is use their insight to gain better understanding of the higher needs of the customer. When Carpigiani (see Chapter 4) gained insight into the ice-cream making market, its understanding moved up Liyanage's pyramid from

What effective firms do, consciously or otherwise, is use their insight to gain better understanding of the higher needs of the customer.

functional needs to experiential and relational needs. Toyota's success with the Prius has been based on its understanding of self actualisation needs as well as functional needs.

So, a first step in drawing out the implications of one or more pieces of market insight is to think through the Liyanage pyramid for your target customers and, especially, how that insight informs your understanding of the higher needs of those customers. And, as our observations suggest, this is especially important in markets that are superficially rational. Such markets, pharmaceuticals, business services and IT for example, are the markets in which technical complexity and surface rationality mean we are mostly likely to neglect the important higher needs that actually drive customer preference.

Application point: What are your customer's higher needs?

Construct and populate a Liyanage pyramid for the customers in one of your target market segments. At each level, ask and answer the questions on the right of the figure and populate each level with the functional and higher needs of the customer. To what extent do any market insights you have inform your understanding? If you can see gaps in your understanding of customer needs, can these be used to suggest where you need to look for insight?

How insight improves our offer to the market

The rigorous application of the Liyanage model allows firms to emulate part of what effective users of insight do, namely to understand the needs that drive customer behaviour and preference. The second stage of emulating good practice is the engineering of the offer to the customer so that it matches those needs more closely than the competition's. As with the first stage of elucidating needs, we observed that good practice, whilst often

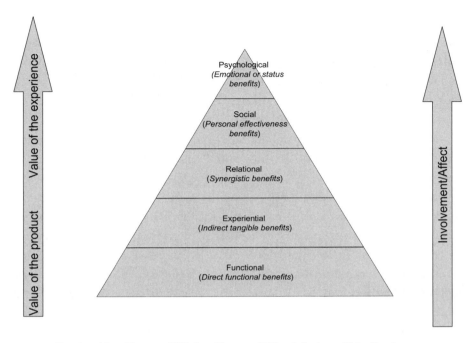

Developed from Liyanage 2005, from Liyanage Uditha, *A Customer Value Typology:
Beyond the Functional – Emotional Dichotomy*, Sri Lankan Journal of Management,
© Postgraduate Institute of Management, July-Dec 2005, Columbo, Vol 8, pp147-171

Figure 9.2 *The customer offer pyramid.*

implicit or unconscious, involved looking beyond the functional benefits of
the product or service to the higher benefits of the offer to the customer. By
contrast, weak practice in this respect involved a strong orientation toward
the core product or service functionality. Unsurprisingly, we observed this
focus on functionality more in firms whose products were technical and
complex and whose customers were businesses rather than consumers.

To facilitate good practice, we found that firms built on the idea of
Liyanage's model to create an internally-oriented version of it, as shown in
Figure 9.2. What this model makes explicit is that the corollary of multi-
layered customer needs is that there are equivalent, multi-layered product
or service benefits. Or, to be more accurate, the offer to the customer could
potentially include such benefits. It is perhaps tautological, given the discussion above, that the more closely the multi-layered benefits of the offer can
be made to match the multi-layered needs of the target customer, the stronger the resultant customer preference.

Although the concepts behind Liyanage's model and our adaptation of it may seem theoretical, the practical application of it is quite straightforward and practical. In short, what firms do to translate insight into an actionable plan involves three steps:

1. Use market insight and other knowledge to populate a pyramid of customer needs at all five levels. The more extensive, thoughtful and focused on the target customer segment, the more effective this will be.
2. Mirror the populated needs pyramid in an equivalent pyramid of product or service benefits that your offer to the customer might make. The more closely related to the needs the benefits are, the better.
3. Use the populated pyramid of benefits to infer the design of the product or service, especially highlighting changes from the current offer. The more the changes to the offer provide the benefits required and meet the needs identified, the better.

An example of this, created for a management consultancy and then made anonymous at their request, is shown in Figure 9.3. In this case, the

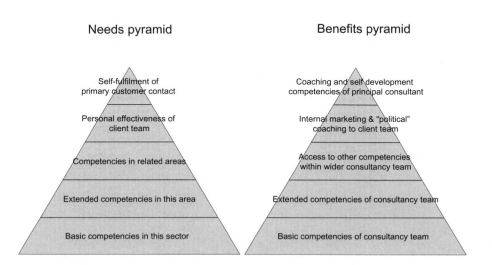

Figure 9.3 *Needs versus offer – consultancy example.*

consulting firm had been attempting to compete on its competencies in its main expertise area. Whilst these were strong, the market was mature and both functional and experiential needs of the target customers could be well met by many other firms. In such circumstances, even the consultancy market can become commoditised and the only strategic alternatives are to go for the low cost route or to somehow differentiate on higher needs.

The market insight available to this firm was obtained by synthesising meta-information about client retention and loss and about the differences between long-term successful client relationships and other, less successful, relationships. This revealed the insight that clients, especially the principal, had personal as well as organisational needs. In short, making the client feel good was at least as important as making the client firm successful. In terms of changes to the offer, this meant two things. Firstly, the consultancy team had to have the skills to help the client team promote their success internally and to manage the politics around that. Secondly, the principal consultant had to have the mentoring skills to help the client principal meet his own self fulfilment needs. Given that the consultants were recruited for their technical skills and sales abilities, this was not a straightforward change for the company. However, they rightly saw it as critical to their success with this target segment and acted accordingly. If this seems obvious, then it is worth comparing this firm's actions with those of its main competitor. The competitor emphasised its technical prowess, thus simply offering to over-fulfil needs that were already well met and, therefore, no longer driving customer preference. The competitor's failure was demonstrated when, shortly afterwards, it adopted a low price strategy that not only failed but also conflicted with its 'expert' positioning in the market.

By this stage in the application of market insight, therefore, we have moved from information, via meta-information, to insight and thence to customer needs, offer design and implied actions. There remain only two more lessons to be learned from our observation of good practice.

Application point: What are your implications for action?

Considering the above for your target segment, follow the three steps of using market insight to populate the needs pyramid, mirroring it in a benefits pyramid, then drawing out the changes to your offer that matching the two pyramids would imply. What does your market insight imply for actions to be taken?

Does it make sense to act on our insight?

It is easy, in the real world, to swing from one extreme to another. Having highlighted the danger of 'doing a von Möltke' and blunting the impact of an insightful strategy, there is a similar but opposite risk of over-enthusiasm. It is quite understandable, if not forgivable, if a market insight with obvious and exciting implications leads a pressured manager to act in haste. It is the corporate equivalent of the fight or flight response that animals exhibit when faced with some external stimulus. We observed, however, that good practice seems to involve avoiding this instinctive response by inserting a 'stimulus response gap' between gaining the insight and acting on it. In simple terms, effective behaviour when acting on insight involves pausing for thought before spending time and money. More accurately, effective behaviour involves an appropriate sense check between drawing out the implications of insight and acting upon them.

We use the word 'appropriate' carefully. In fact, we observed two broad categories of sense checking; what we called 'pause for thought' and 'Marketing Due Diligence', the former taking hours of thought, the latter some days of effort. Interestingly, firms decided on the appropriate amount of sense check-

There are two categories of sense-checking: 'pause for thought' and 'due diligence'.

ing in a non-intuitive way. We expected firms to do less checking when they were sure of the insight and more when they were less certain of the insight. Indeed, we saw that in weaker firms, but not in the firms that were happy with their outcomes. That is to say, in weak practice sense checking was absent or, if present, was done according to the 'intuitiveness' of the insight and actions. So, something that seemed obvious was checked less than something that did not. By contrast, firms satisfied with their outcomes chose between a pause for thought and Marketing Due Diligence not on intuitiveness, but on the size of the assets at risk. That is, if acting on insight was a small bet, a pause for thought was sufficient. If it involved large investment and put a large brand or reputation at risk, due diligence was called for.

The difference between a pause for thought and a due diligence approach is important for two reasons. Not only is it important to sense check well before making an investment, it is important not to over analyse investment decisions and so lose an opportunity. It is important therefore to understand what each approach involves.

The components of a pause for thought

A pause for thought sense check is the appropriate action when:

- acting on insight involves only a small investment and puts only limited assets at risk; and
- the action has to be taken very quickly, such as when the insight is transient.

Of course, both these measures are relative and matters of judgement. A £100,000 investment can be huge for an SME and near negligible for a large multinational. Speed of action is relative to how quickly the firm can act, so even a pause for thought can take months for a slow firm, hidebound by regulation, and hours for a fast firm with perhaps a simple proposition.

At a detailed level, exactly what a pause for thought entails varies between firms but always seems to involve a core process of answering four critical questions.

Am I making this offer to the right segment?

A frequent error when trying to act on insight is to 'gild the lily', making the offer far better than is needed to compete effectively. The typical cause of this is that the offer is aimed at a segment that doesn't really care about (that is, values) the improved offer. In theory, this shouldn't happen because of the Value test in the VRIO assessment. In practice, this does happen, especially when over-enthusiastic technical people or sales people allow their enthusiasm to get the better of them. For firms with a technical- or sales-led culture, this is, therefore, an important part of the sense check.

What's this going to cost?

A not uncommon error, especially in firms with weak or siloed management accounting, is to spend rather more on the offer than the increased customer preference is worth. Again, this shouldn't happen in theory, but does in practice. It is particularly likely if the costs associated with the improved offer are implicit or opportunity costs, such as added levels of customer service or shifting resources away from another part of the strategy. For firms in which the offer is hard to cost accurately, or who don't integrate management accountants into their planning, this is an important part of the sense check.

Will any advantage be sustainable?

The competitive advantage and increased customer preference that flows from an insightful change to the offer almost always has a limited duration. With luck, slow competitors and some way of protecting the offer (e.g. patent protection) an advantage can last some time. Frequently, however, the advantage can be short-lived either because a competitor copies or the market evolves. In this case, the firm has a difficult choice to make. It not only has to assess whether a short life makes the investment worthwhile, it also has to consider if the improved offer will be necessary in any case, just to stay competitive. For firms that operate in fast-moving markets, this is a very necessary part of the sense check.

Does this complement or conflict?

Any change in the offer is likely to interact with other parts of the firm's strategy in some way (see Box 1.3 The concept of complementarity in Chapter 1). It may complement or conflict with another part of the marketing strategy by interacting with other market segments. It may complement or conflict with part of the strategy in other parts of the firm's value chain, such as product and service development or operations. In such cases, the net outcome of these interactions has to be factored in to considerations of targeting, cost and sustainability as discussed above. In firms with complex strategies (that is, those that target more than one segment and make more than one offer), this is an important part of the sense check.

In these four parts of the pause for thought, the reader will see echoes of the Cranfield work (see Box 2.6 The ten commandments of value creation in Chapter 2). They provide a simple and relatively quick way of thinking through the decision to act on an insight when that involves low investment and needs high speed decisions. When this is not the case and a high invest-ment is made or a large asset, such as the corporate brand, is at stake, an altogether more rigorous approach is needed, as discussed next.

Application point: What does a pause for thought tell you?

Consider a limited recent, current or planned investment for your firm. Attempt to answer the four critical questions involved in a pause for thought. What do the answers tell you? Does asking these questions reveal any gaps in your information or your knowledge?

The components of Marketing Due Diligence

Clearly, a binary approach to sense checking an insight-based investment is simplistic. In reality, a pause for thought can be made very rigorous whilst even the most complex Marketing Due Diligence processes can be done in a rough and ready manner. Between the extremes of 'quick and dirty' and 'analysis paralysis' lie all possible shades of grey. That said, our work uncov-ered a fundamental differentiator in the ways firms assess an investment based on market insight. In simple terms, this was between a pause for thought approach that was concerned with 'will this make or lose money?' versus a Marketing Due Diligence approach concerned with 'will this create or destroy shareholder value' (or value for whoever else might own the business).

This Marketing Due Diligence approach should not be confused however with financial due diligence, which primarily involves checking that the numbers are true and that

Marketing Due Diligence assesses the probability that the plan will deliver what it promises.

they add up. In the case of sense checking insight-based investments, we are referring to Marketing Due Diligence, a process first explored and codi-fied in one of our earlier books.[3] In contrast to financial due diligence, Marketing Due Diligence concerns itself with assessing the probability that the numbers projected in the business plan will be delivered. For a full explanation of this process, readers should refer to that earlier book, but an overview is appropriate here.

As discussed, Marketing Due Diligence, when applied to an investment based on market insight, addresses the question: 'Will the investment we plan in order to act on this insight create or destroy value for those who own the business assets?' Because this is more laborious and time consuming than a pause for thought, it is only an appropriate process when the assets employed are large. This is much more common than is realised by many marketers. Very few investments start with a clean sheet of paper, and those that don't inevitably employ some of the firm's existing assets, whether they are the corporate brand, physical assets or intellectual property. Consider the financial services industry, for example. Although new 'products' may have a brand name, they trade mostly on the firm's corporate brand. In consumer goods, line extensions often form the major part of a firm's growth plans. And in many technology markets, apparently new products consist of intellectual property previously developed and patented and sold, in part, under the corporate brand. There is nothing wrong with this, of course, and such incremental product development is often a strong strategy. But some companies make the mistake, when calculating the cost of the investment, of only counting the new or incremental investment involved. In doing so, they ignore the proportion of current assets they are using as if they were free. A responsible approach would assess the assets employed to include both new spending and an appropriate share of shared existing assets. When this is done, the typical cost of an insight-based investment is typically much higher than it first appears. The higher real investment often makes it worthy of the more rigorous Marketing Due Diligence approach.

The basic principle of Marketing Due Diligence is that value is created when the returns exceed the cost of capital. This is not a new concept. However, the returns used to calculate value creation should not be simply those asserted in the business plan. They are, after all, simply assertions. Instead, value creation should be calculated based on a risk adjusted return – that is, the business plan assertions, adjusted for the probability that the plan will deliver its promises. At the core of Marketing Due Diligence, therefore, is a probability assessment process that is, in essence, quite simple.

The probability that a business plan will deliver its promises is multifactorial. In other words, it is the product of the probabilities of the component assertions in the plan. Most business plans are based on three assertions:

- The market is of a certain size.
- Our strategy will deliver a certain share of that market.
- That share will deliver a certain profit.

Clearly, these assertions can be anything from very solid to pure guesses. That is, they each contain an inherent level of risk, which McDonald and his co-authors called Market Risk, Share Risk and Profit Risk respectively. To the extent that these assertions are less than 100% certain and these risks exist, the promises of the business plan should be adjusted before calculating the return on investment. In simple terms, if a high risk plan and a low risk plan both offer the same return on the same investment, the low risk plan offers a better deal.

In the research work that underpins Marketing Due Diligence, McDonald, Smith and Ward found that good practice involves disaggregating each of these three risks into five (that is, a total of fifteen) subcomponent risks, as shown in Figure 9.4. These subcomponent risks range from the probability that the forecasts will meet promise, that pricing will be as expected, and that competitors will respond in the way we expect. The rigour of Marketing Due Diligence lies not only in this disaggregating of business risk, but also in the objective assessment of each individual risk. Hence the business risk associated with any insight-based investment can be calculated by assessing and aggregating its 15 subcomponents. The detail of this process is too much to cover in this book and the reader is referred to our earlier work.[3]

Interestingly, the practice of Marketing Due Diligence results in one of three types of outcome. The first is to find that the plan is robust and that the promised returns have a high probability of being delivered. In such cases, assuming the plan numbers create value, it is worth acting on insight. In other cases, the plan is so risky that the plan numbers have to be risk adjusted to an extent that they represent shareholder value destruction. In such cases, it is not worth acting on insight. The third category of outcome, however, is the most common. In these cases, the outcome can be paraphrased as: 'We've no idea. We've never thought about risk that way before.' In such cases, it is necessary to review the plan so that the risk is better understood. All three outcomes of Marketing Due Diligence are good. The first confirms the plan; the second prevents value destruction; the third is a valuable piece of organisational learning. The only bad outcome is if a firm goes ahead with a large investment, even putting core assets at risk, without thinking about the probability of it delivering a positive return.

When capitalising on market insight involves heavy investment and puts large assets at risk, anything other than a Marketing Due Diligence approach is naïve.

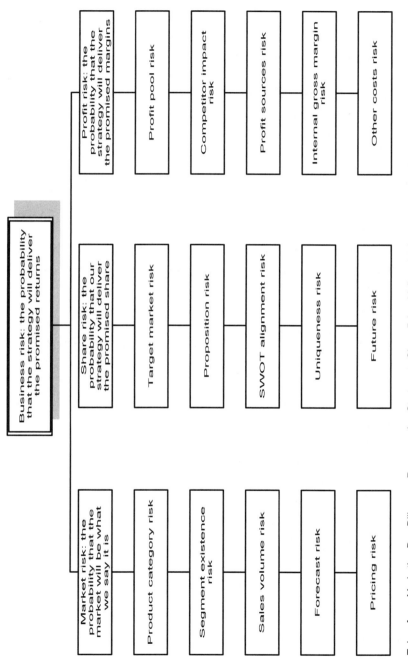

Taken from: Marketing Due Diligence: Reconnecting Strategy to Share Price. McDonald, Smith and Ward, © Elsevier 2005

Figure 9.4 *The components of business risk.*

Even an overview of the Marketing Due Diligence process makes clear that it is a non-trivial process. It is impractical to follow this process for a small investment that has to be acted on quickly. Hence, the division we observed between the assessment of small investments and large investments when acting on insight. We stress, however, that when capitalising on market insight involves heavy investment and puts large assets at risk, anything other than a Marketing Due Diligence approach is naïve.

Application point: What does Marketing Due Diligence tell you?

Consider a large recent, current or planned investment for your firm. Did your firm apply rigour in assessing the probability that it would create value? Did you consider the shared assets at risk, such as brands? How might a Marketing Due Diligence approach make your investment assessment more useful?

How can we ensure that our market insight is acted upon?

By this stage in the process of applying insight, we have drawn out the actions implied by our insight and sense checked our decision to act on that insight in a manner appropriate to the size of the decision. To an inexperienced reader, all that is left is to get on with it. However, it will come as no surprise to more seasoned readers that creating and planning an insight is only a fraction of the task. In this section of the book we will describe some of the lessons of implementation drawn from our research into insight and other areas of strategy.

Defining the implementation problem

Implementation of the actions that flow from an insight-based strategy is problematic in two ways; first in defining what we mean and then improving practice. This section grounds the problem by defining what we mean, and don't mean, by implementation.

As summarised in Figure 9.5, strategy is simply a set of resource allocation decisions, in our case built upon market insight. When these decisions are

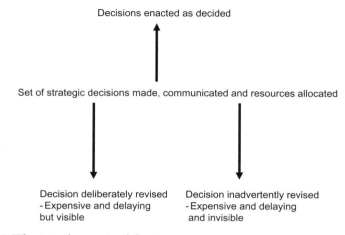

Decisions enacted as decided

Set of strategic decisions made, communicated and resources allocated

Decision deliberately revised
- Expensive and delaying
  but visible

Decision inadvertently revised
- Expensive and delaying
  and invisible

Figure 9.5 *What is implementation failure?*

allocated to the relevant parts of the firm to enact, there are three broad categories of outcome:

- The decisions are enacted exactly as decided. This is relatively rare.
- The decisions are deliberately and consciously modified during execution in the light of new developments or new knowledge. This is common and often appropriate, although less efficient than perfect enactment.
- The decisions are modified by the implementers, sometimes to the point of completely contradicting the original intention of the decision makers. This is extremely common, costly and usually inappropriate.

This section does not concern itself with the second point, which might be considered a form of incremental strategy making. Instead, it focuses on the causes and remedies of the third point, which we label inadvertent non-implementation, or INI.

Application point: Implementation in your firm

Consider recent strategic initiatives that required changes in resource allocation within your firm. To what extent were they implemented exactly as decided? To the degree that these decisions were not implemented as decided, how much of this non-implementation was deliberate (i.e. incrementalism) and how much of it was inadvertent non-implementation?

The causes of non-implementation

The extent and importance of INI has led to a measurement fad amongst senior managers. This school of thought tries to improve implementation by measuring every action that flows from the strategy and correcting any inaction. Prominent among this is the work of Kaplan and Norton,[4,5] who have developed their metrics systems into tools that enable better implementation. If executed rigorously, this approach works to an extent but it is laborious and has its limits, especially in knowledge-based firms in which implementation is critically reliant on intangible factors such as attitude and behaviour. To understand these limitations, we need a small diversion into occupational psychology.

Modern work, as distinct from low-knowledge, manual labour, involves broadly two kinds of tasks, discretionary and non-discretionary.[6] The latter can be observed and measured, so an employee has little choice in executing them. Discretionary tasks, by contrast, are intangible and their execution depends on the employees' commitment. Think for example of executing a sales plan. The basic tasks are non-discretionary and will be judged in terms of sales calls made etc. Many of the component tasks, however, are discretionary. No system can measure an employee's attitude or pre-call preparation, at least not infallibly. Measurement systems such as the Balanced Scorecard can be seen as ways of making as much as possible of the workload into non-discretionary, measured work. These approaches are an

People can usually outsmart measurement systems so we need to convince the implementers, not simply control them.

important part of any implementation approach but they don't cope well with residual discretionary tasks. And such tasks tend to be critical, especially in knowledge-based sectors and in functions such as marketing or sales. In short, when it comes to implementation, people can usually outsmart measurement systems so we need to convince the implementers, rather than simply control them.

The problem, in other words, is to reduce the INI of discretionary tasks that flow from our insight-based strategy. Part of our research has focused on understanding the root causes of this widespread and costly phenomenon.[7] Our research here suggested that INI has three root causes: communication, culture and motivation. INI is almost always the result of some combination of these underlying factors, each of which is complex and requires its own solutions.

Communication is the most straightforward issue. It's long been known that communication involves encoding and decoding a message and both noise and channel effectiveness are critical issues.[8] Often, it seems, managers try to communicate complex strategies through inadequate channels and the message gets scrambled. Thirty minutes at a sales conference and an unread handout just isn't enough, and terse, poorly expressed emails seem positively counterproductive in communicating strategy.

Culture is more complex. Whilst we talk of a single company culture, the reality is a hotchpotch of departmental sub-cultures, each with different values and assumptions.[9] One cause of INI is when a strategy, developed in one culture, dictates actions that the implementing sub-culture rejects. Just consider the different ways that strategy, marketing, sales and legal view the world and it is amazing that a complex idea, for instance a brand positioning, is ever implemented. Factor in national cultures on top of departmental ethos and the problem becomes worse.

Motivation is perhaps the most insidious component of INI. The theory is complex, but in essence we all act according to our own self interest.[10] If the strategy seems to go against that, implementers are at best demotivated and at worst can actively sabotage the strategy. The complicating factor is that motivation is not just about money, but also status, social fulfilment and many other factors. If, for example, our insight suggests a new strategy involving the redirection of the sales team, it can mean (for that team) loss of autonomy and reduced social rewards as well as potentially lower short term earnings. For strategies that depend on the implementers' commitment, this is the critical issue.

What this, albeit simplified, review of the research tells us is that INI has multiple causes, each of which is just the sort of messy problem that doesn't yield to simple solutions. Communica-

Incremental non-implementation has multiple causes, each of which is just the sort of messy problem that doesn't yield to simple solutions.

tion is not improved much by just doing more of it, just as shouting doesn't help when speaking to a foreigner. We need to understand encoding and decoding and the role of channels and noise. Culture is not overcome by cross-functional meetings or rearranging the desks, just as a mixed marriage doesn't dissolve family differences. We need to understand cultural differences better. Motivation is not improved by financial incentives alone, just as bribing our children to behave well isn't a good long-term plan. We need to untangle how the strategy impacts on the implementers' self interest. The problem of strategy implementation doesn't have a quick-fix answer. Hence, the next phase of our research explored what happens when it goes right.

Application point: What are the causes of INI in your firm?

Bearing in mind the three-cause explanation of INI, which of these factors do you see at play in your organisation? Is there a dominant factor, or are they evenly balanced? What do the likely causes of INI in your firm imply for actions you might take to improve implementation?

Resolving inadvertent non-implementation

We observed that the extent of INI varied greatly between the firms we studied. The common factor that divides those that have addressed INI and those that have not is diagnosis. When asked how they solved the problem, successful companies begin with 'Well, the root of the problem was . . .' By contrast, other firms mumble a list of detailed excuses that have no explanatory power. So step one for firms wishing to improve strategy implementation is to diagnose which of the three causes contribute most to their particular INI problem. In most cases, one of the three is dominant and the others are secondary. Sometimes, the mixture of causes is obvious but often it is hard for managers to see the wood for the trees. In any case, it is necessary to elucidate the problem, to analyse the mixture of factors involved, in order to direct the firm to where their corrective efforts would produce the biggest, fastest results.

Once understood, curing INI requires a different therapy depending on whether culture, motivation or communication is the primary cause.

In good firms, curing INI is analogous to medicine versus quackery; it is based on understanding the underlying theory that explains how organisations work.

In good firms, curing INI is analogous to medicine versus quackery; it is based on understanding the underlying theory that explains how organisations work. If the problem is that the implementers didn't understand, then the answer lies in communication theory. If they simply didn't agree, the answer lies in culture theory. And if they understood and agreed but it didn't suit them, we have to look to motivation theory.

Using communication theory, the firm can analyse every stage of the message's journey from sender to receiver. We can observe how the message is encoded, how it travels through channels and intermediaries and how it is decoded by the recipient. In between, we can understand the problems caused by 'semantic noise', which changes the message meaning along its journey. In practical terms, this tells us how to change our communication to make it work. For example, one firm we studied found that the 'marketing speak' they used was a big part of the problem and that formal channels were less powerful than informal channels, the so called 'water cooler chat'.

Cultural theory allows the firm to see beneath the surface 'cultural artefacts' of behaviour, systems and processes to the values and assumptions that lie beneath. This is important because culture is persistent and pervasive. No amount of tinkering will create lasting change. In practical terms, applying a cultural analysis identifies the cross-functional cultural differences that are hindering implementation. These can then be addressed in a meaningful, non-superficial way. For example, one firm we worked with changed its leader's annual awards and planning system as powerful symbols to communicate the values of the firm. Another recognised that many of its existing cultural artefacts, such as titles and hierarchies, were hindering the kind of cross-functional working it sought to achieve.

Motivation theory digs beneath superficial explanations of why we do things and reveals the more powerful underlying drivers of behaviour. This is especially important where the strategic change is dependent on the commitment of the implementers. Despite the complexity of motivation theory, it is remarkably practical and produces fast and useful outcomes. This can include better modelling of incentives, but also often involves 'reframing' the strategy for the implementers, to help them see it in terms of their self interest. The most common result of a motivation theory analysis is to find powerful but implicit self interest, such as personal status and control, as blockers of the new strategy.

The detailed examination of strategy implementation problems and resolutions is beyond the scope of this book but, despite that, our current understanding of what causes INI is helpful in improving the effectiveness of the way in which we act on market insight.

Bearing in mind the factors that might lead to INI within your firm, how might you resolve these? How might you improve communication? How might you reduce cultural conflict? How might you align self interest and organisational interests?

Closing the loop

With the understanding and pre-emption of implementation barriers like culture, communication and motivation, we effectively complete the findings of our research and working with companies. All that is left is to implement the actions identified whilst managing any potential barriers. Well, almost all that is left.

In trying to present this work as a series of linear steps we have, of course, distorted the truth. The reality of all practical work is that it involves steps forward, steps back and reiterations of each stage in the process. The process is anything but linear. Ultimately, the whole process of creating and using insight is a continuous feedback loop. The lessons learned are fed back into near the beginning of the process to

The outcome of a well-designed and implemented strategy is not just success, but also new learning.

create still more powerful insight. This closing of the loop is especially important and often neglected, especially in the context of short term tenures, outsourcing and organisational restructuring.

The best practice we observed in this area was to be fastidious about this closing of the loop, to be a little obsessive that the outcome of a well-designed and implemented strategy was not just success, but also new learning. As with many of the other aspects of best practice, this effective behaviour was often implicit, but it can be thought of as three critical techniques for creating a virtuous circle in insight creation:

- **Probe outcomes for knowledge.** Effective firms ask what lessons can be learned from their outcomes, be they positive or (perhaps especially) negative.
- **Challenge assumptions.** Effective firms are uncompromising in surfacing their existing 'theories of action' and using the information and knowledge derived from new outcomes to challenge their own mind set.
- **Displace concepts.** Effective firms encourage the transfer of lessons and ideas from between different parts of the business and from outside the business.

And, lest these three points be thought of as statements of the obvious, compare them with what we observed in other firms. In those firms, success is taken to mean that current knowledge does not need to be questioned, whilst failure evokes blame rather than learning. Challenging assumptions in less effective firms is hindered by politics and power. Again, Voltaire said it well with 'It is dangerous to be right in matters on which the established authorities are wrong'. Finally, one of the most characteristic features of ineffective firms is their response to externally originated ideas, which are often dismissed as 'irrelevant in our context'.

Application point: Do you close the loop?

Consider the outcomes of your most recent business plan. To what extent did you probe those outcomes for new knowledge? Did you then use that new knowledge to test your extant 'theories of action'? To what extent, if any, do you seek to displace concepts within or into your organisation?

The end of the journey

The consideration of implementation of insight-based actions brings us to the end of this book. It has been a long journey that began with the nature of success and the role of insight in success. We have covered the difficulty of creating insight and explored the nature of scanning processes that feed insight creation. Central to this was an understanding of how market complexity and turbulence determine the optimal nature of scanning behaviour for an organisation. In the last two chapters of the book we shifted from descriptive mode, describing our findings, to prescriptive mode, making recommendations based upon the good practice we have observed. Our hope is that the journey encapsulated in this book was and will be of real value to the practising managers for whom it was written.

Powerpoints

- In implementing insightful strategy, the risk is not to do the wrong thing but to do the right thing weakly.
- Acting on insight begins with elucidating the higher needs of the customer.
- Before acting on insight, an appropriate level of sense check is needed.
- Inadvertent non-implementation has its roots in culture, communication and self interest.
- Effective firms 'close the loop' by learning from the outcomes of their strategy.

References

Chapter 1

(1) Neely, A. (1999) The Performance Measurement Revolution: Why Now and What Next. *International Journal of Operations and Production Management*, 19(2), 205–28.

(2) McDonald, M.H.B., Smith, B.D. and Ward, K.R. (2005) *Marketing Due Diligence: Reconnecting Strategy to Share Price*, Elsevier, Oxford.

(3) Kaplan, R.S. and Norton, D.P. (1992) The Balanced Scorecard – Measures that Drive Performance. *Harvard Business Review*, 70(1), 71–9.

(4) Ward, K.R. and Smith, B.D. (2007) Sat Nav Systems. *Pharmaceutical Marketing Europe*. Ref Type: Magazine Article.

(5) Neely, A. and Al Najjar, M. (2006) Management Learning Not Management Control: The True Role of Performance Measurement. *California Management Review*, 48(3), 99–114.

(6) Hodgkinson, G.P. (2002) *The Competent Organisation*, 1st ed., Open University Press.

(7) Alchian, A.A. (1950) Uncertainty, Evolution and Economic Theory. *Journal of Political Economy*, 58, 211–22.

(8) Mintzberg, H. (1996) Musings on Management. *Harvard Business Review*, 74(4), 61–5.

(9) Smith, B.D. (2005) *Making Marketing Happen*, Elsevier, Oxford.

(10) Roberts, J. (2004) *The Modern Firm*, 1st ed., Oxford University Press, Oxford.

(11) Yankelovich, D. and Meer, D. (2006) Rediscovering Market Segmentation. *Harvard Business Review*, 84(2), 122–31.

(12) Jiang, P. (2000) Segment Based Mass Customisation. *Networking Applications and Policy*, 10(3), 215–26.

(13) Levitt, T. (1980) Marketing Success Through Differentiation – Of Anything. *Harvard Business Review*, January/February 1980, 83–91.

(14) Chandy, R.K., Prabhu, J.C. and Antia, K.D. (2003) What Will the Future Bring? Dominance, Technology Expectations and Radical Innovation. *Journal of Marketing*, 67(July 2003), 1–18.

(15) Johnson, G. and Scholes, K. (2001) *Exploring Corporate Strategy*, Prentice Hall, London.

(16) Hill, T. and Westbrook, R. (1997) SWOT Analysis: It's Time for a Product Recall. *Long Range Planning*, 30(1), 46–52.

(17) Eisenhardt, K.M. and Zbaracki, M.J. (1992) Strategic Decision Making. *Strategic Management Journal*, 13(Special Issue), 17–37.

(18) Mintzberg, H., Ahlstrand, B. and Lampel, J. (1998) *Strategy Safari*, 1st ed., The Free Press, New York.

(19) Smith, B.D. (2003) *The Effectiveness of Marketing Strategy Making Processes in Medical Markets*, Cranfield School of Management.

(20) Hambrick, D.C. and Mason, P.A. (1984) Upper Echelons: The Organisation as a Reflection of its Top Managers. *Academy of Management Review*, 9(2), 193–206.

(21) Hunt, S.D. (2002) *Foundations of Marketing Theory: Towards a General Theory of Marketing*, M E Sharpe, New York.

(22) Smith, B.D. (2004) *Getting Motivated*, Marketing Business.

(23) Porter, M.E. (1980) *Competitive Strategy*, 1st ed., Free Press.

(24) Leask, G. and Parker, D. (2004) An Application of Strategic Group Theory to the UK Pharmaceuticals Industry. *European Business Journal*, 16(1), 1–10.

(25) Economist, T. (2005) Prescription for Change. *The Economist*.

Chapter 2

(1) Mintzberg, H. (1990) The Manager's Job: Folklore and Fact. *Harvard Business Review*, March–April 1990, 163–76.

(2) Tengblad, S. (2006) Is There a New 'Managerial Work'? A Comparison of Henry Mintzberg's Classic Study 30 Years Later. *Journal of Management Studies*, 43(7), 1437–61.

(3) Schon, D.A. (1999) *The Reflective Practitioner: How Professionals Think in Action*, 1st ed. Perseus Books Group.

(4) Carr, D. (1981) Knowledge in Practice. *American Philosophical Quarterly*, 18, 53–61.

(5) Lewin, K. (1943) Defining the Field at a Given Time. *Psychological Review*, 50, 292–310.

(6) McDonald, M.H.B., Smith, B.D. and Ward, K.R. (2005) *Marketing Due Diligence: Reconnecting Strategy to Share Price*, Elsevier, Oxford.

(7) Doyle, P. (2000) *Value Based Marketing: Marketing Strategies for Corporate Growth and Shareholder Value*, 1st ed., Wiley, Chichester.

(8) Marshall, Hannah L. (1999) Trees and the Global Forest: Were 'Giant Redwoods' Any Different? in: *Learning by Doing in Markets, Firms and Countries* (eds N.R. Lamoreaux, D.M.G. Raff and P. Temin), National Bureau of Economic Research.

(9) Fligstein, N. (1990) *The Transformation of Corporate Control*, Harvard University Press.

(10) Omerod, P., Johns, H. and Smith, L. (2001) Marshall's Trees and the Global Forest: The Extinction Pattern of Capitalism's Global Firms. http://www.volterra.co.uk/ 2001Available from: URL: www.volterra.co.uk

(11) Omerod, P. (2005) *Why Most Things Fail and How to Avoid It*. Faber and Faber.

(12) IDC Reports. (2004) CRM Continues to Climb. *PM Network* 18(11), 14.

(13) Ewusi-Mensah, K. and Przasnyski, Z.H. (1995) Learning from Abandoned Information Systems Development Projects. *Journal of Information Technology*, 10(1), 3–15.

(14) Rigby, D.K. and Ledingham, D. (2004) CRM Done Right. *Harvard Business Review*, 82(11), 118–28.

(15) Zablah, A.R., Bellenger, D.N. and Johnston, W.J. (2004) An Evaluation of Divergent Perspectives on Customer Relationship Management: Towards a Common Understanding of an Emerging Phenomenon. *Industrial Marketing Management*, 33, 475–89.

(16) Smith, B.D., Wilson, H. and Clark, M. (2006) From Data to Dividends: Why are Some Firms Better than Others at Turning Information into Value? *Cranfield University Customer Management Research Forum.*

(17) Smith, B.D. (2006) The Marketer's Stone. *The Marketer,* 8, 32–33.

(18) Smith, B.D., Wilson, H.N. and Clark, M. (2006) Creating and Using Customer Insight: 12 Rules of Best Practice. *Journal of Medical Marketing,* 6(2), 135–9.

(19) Barney, J.B. (1991) Firm Resources and Sustained Competitive Advantage. *Journal of Management,* 17(1), 99–120.

(20) Barney, J.B. (2001) Resource-based Theories of Competitive Advantage: A Ten-year Retrospective on the Resource-based View. *Journal of Management,* 27, 643–50.

(21) Penrose, E. (1959) *The Theory of the Growth of the Firm,* 1st ed. Blackwell, Oxford.

Chapter 3

(1) Alchian, A.A. (1950) Uncertainty, Evolution and Economic Theory. *Journal of Political Economy,* 58, 211–22.

(2) Pfeffer, J. and Salancik, F. (1978) *The External Control of Organisations,* Harper and Row, New York.

(3) Bowman, C. and Ambrosini, V. (2007) Identifying Valuable Resources. *European Management Journal,* 25(4), 320–29.

(4) Nystrom, P.C. and Starbuck, W.H. (1984) To Avoid Organisational Crises – Unlearn. *Organizational Dynamics,* 4, 53–6.

(5) Raspin, P. (2003) Scanning Business Environments: An Investigation into Managerial Scanning Behaviour. PhD Thesis. Cranfield School of Management.

(6) Mintzberg, H. and Waters, J. (1985) Of Strategies, Deliberate and Emergent. *Strategic Management Journal,* 6, 257–72.

(7) Smith, B.D. (2005) *Making Marketing Happen,* Elsevier, Oxford.

(8) Mintzberg, H., Raisinghani, D. and Theoret, A. (1976) The Structure of Unstructured Decision Processes. *Administrative Science Quarterly,* 21, 246–75.

(9) Hambrick, D.C. (1982) Environmental Scanning and Organisational Strategy. *Strategic Management Journal,* 3, 159–74.

(10) Aguilar, F.J. (1967) *Scanning the Business Environment,* Macmillan, New York.

(11) Daft, R. and Weick, K. (1984) Toward a Model of Organizations as Interpretation Systems. *Academy of Management Review,* 9(2), 284–95.

(12) Mintzberg, H. (1973) The Nature of Managerial Work, Harper and Row, New York.

Chapter 5

(1) Kimberly, J.R. and Miles, R.H. (1980) *The Organizational Life Cycle,* Jossey-Bass, San Francisco.

(2) Milliken, F. (1990) Perceiving and Interpreting Environmental Change: An Examination of College Administrators' Interpretation of Changing Demographics. *Academy of Management Journal,* 33, 42–63.

(3) Daft, R.L., Sormunen, J. and Parks, D. (1988) Chief Executive Scanning, Environmental Characteristics, and Company Performance: An Empirical Study. *Strategic Management Journal,* 9, 123–39.

(4) Kefalas, A. and Schoderbek, P. (1973) Scanning the Business Environment – Some Empirical Results. *Decision Sciences,* 4, 63–74.

(5) Dess, G.G., Ireland, R.D. and Hitt, M.A. (1990) Industry Effects and Strategic Management Research. *Journal of Management*, 16, 5–25.

(6) Miller, D. (1991) Stale in the Saddle: CEO Tenure and the Match between Organization and Environment. *Management Science*, 37, 34–52.

(7) Aguilar, F.J. (1967) *Scanning the Business Environment*, Macmillan, New York.

(8) Bowman, C. and Daniels, K. (1995) The Influence of Functional Experience on Perceptions of Strategic Priorities. *British Journal of Management*, 6, 157–67.

(9) Keegan W. (1974) Multinational Scanning: A Study of the Information Sources Utilized by Headquarters Executives in Multinational Companies. *Administrative Science Quarterly*, Vol 19, 3, 411–421.

(10) Jennings, D.F. and Lumpkin, J.R. (1992) Insights between Environmental Scanning Activities and Porter's Generic Strategies: An Empirical Analysis. *Journal of Management*, 18, 791–803.

(11) Kimberly, J.R. and Miles, R.H. (1980) *The Organizational Life Cycle*, Jossey-Bass, San Francisco.

(12) Meyer, A. (1982) Adapting to Environmental Jolts. *Administrative Science Quarterly*, 27, 515–37.

(13) Tushman, M.L. and Romanelli, E. (1985) *Organizational Evolution: A Metamorphosis Model of Convergence and Reorientation*, JAI Press, Greenwich, 171–222.

(14) Mintzberg, H. (1973) *The Nature of Managerial Work*, Harper and Row, New York.

(15) Hambrick, D.C. (1982) Environmental Scanning and Organisational Strategy. *Strategic Management Journal*, 3, 159–74.

Chapter 8

(1) Toffler, A. (1973) *Future Shock*, Pan, New York.

(2) Vroom, V.H. (1964) *Work and Motivation*, 1st ed. John Wiley & Sons, Ltd, London.

(3) Hodgkinson, G.P. and Sparrow, P.R. (2002) *The Competent Organisation*, 1st ed. Open University Press.

(4) Argyris, C. and Schon, D.A. (1978) *Organisational Learning: A Theory in Action Perspective*, Addison-Wesley, Reading, MA.

(5) Smith, B.D. (2007) Strategy is Simple. *The Marketer*, March 2007, 10–13.

(6) Porter, M.E. (1980) *Competitive Strategy*, 1st ed. Free Press, New York.

(7) Treacy, M. and Wiersema, M. (1995) *The Discipline of the Market Leaders*, Harper Collins, London.

(8) Ansoff, H.I. (1957) *Strategies for Diversification*, Harvard Business Review, Spt/Oct 1957, 35(5), 113–24.

(9) Smith, B.D. (2005) *Making Marketing Happen*, Elsevier, Oxford.

Chapter 9

(1) Liyanage, U. (2005) A Customer Value Typology : Beyond the Functional – Emotional Dichotomy. *Sri Lankan Journal of Management*, 8, 147–71.

(2) Maslow, A.H. (1943) A Theory of Human Motivation. *Psychological Review*, 50, 370–96.

(3) McDonald, M.H.B., Smith, B.D. and Ward, K.R. (2005) *Marketing Due Diligence: Reconnecting Strategy to Share Price*, Elsevier, Oxford.

(4) Kaplan, R.S. and Norton, D.P. (2006) How to Implement a New Strategy Without Disrupting Your Organization. *Harvard Business Review*, 84(3), 100–9.

(5) Kaplan, R.S. and Norton, D.P. (2007) Using the Balanced Scorecard as a Strategic Management System. *Harvard Business Review*, 85(7/8), 150–61.

(6) Meyer, J.P., Becker, T.E. and Vandenberghe, C. (2004) Effects of Commitment on Organizational Behavior. *Journal of Applied Psychology*, 89(6), 991–1007.

(7) Smith, B.D. (2007) Untying the Gordian Knot: Getting to the Roots of Strategy Non-implementation. Unpublished Work.

(8) Shannon, C.E. and Weaver, W. (1949) *The Mathematical Theory of Communication*, 1st ed. University of Illinois Press, Chicago.

(9) Schein, E.H. (1991) What is Culture? in *Reframing Organizational Culture*, 1st edn (eds P.J. Frost, L.F. Moore, M.R. Louis and C.C. Lundberg), Sage, Newbury Park, California, 243–53.

(10) Vroom, V.H. (1964) *Work and Motivation*, 1st ed. Wiley, London.

Index of figures

Index of tables

Index

Index compiled by Annette Musker